With the Light Division

With the Light Division

The Experiences of an Officer of the
43rd Light Infantry in the Peninsula
and South of France During
the Napoleonic Wars

John H. Cooke

LEONAUR

*With the Light Division: the Experiences of an Officer of the
43rd Light Infantry in the Peninsula and South of France
During the Napoleonic Wars*
by John H. Cooke

Published by Leonaur Ltd in 2007

Originally published 1831-1835 across three volumes as follows::
Memoirs of the Late War Volume 1
Memoirs of the Late War Volume 2
*A Narrative of Events in the South of France and of the Attack on
New Orleans in 1814 and 1815*

ISBN: 978-1-84677-322-8 (hardcover)
ISBN: 978-1-84677-321-1 (softcover)

http://www.leonaur.com

Publisher's Notes

In the interests of authenticity, the spellings, grammar and place names
used have been retained from the original edition.

The opinions expressed in this book are those of the author
and are not necessarily those of the publisher.

Contents

Publisher's Note

The book you are holding, *With the Light Division*, is a unique and important record of one man's experiences during the Napoleonic Wars.

When John Henry Cooke joined the British Army in 1805 he was just thirteen years and eleven months old and less than five feet in height. Within a very short time he was commanding men on coastal defence duty in an isolated outpost on the banks of the Humber. He took part in the Walcheren expedition and then went on to witness and do battle in many of the iconic encounters of the Peninsular War—Ciudad Rodrigo, Badajos, Salamanca, Pampeluna, St. Sebastian among them.

It is surprising, therefore, that Cooke's military memoirs are so little known, but perhaps the patchy way in which they were first published has something to do with this. Originally published across three volumes—*Memoirs of the Late War Volume 1*, *Memoirs of the Late War Volume 2* and *A Narrative of Events in the South of France and of the Attack on New Orleans in 1814 and 1815*—between 1831 and 1835, Cooke's words have hardly had justice done to them.

As originally published *Memoirs of the Late War Volume 1* covered the author's career up to the latter stages of the war in the Peninsula. *Memoirs of the Late War Volume 2* is an oddity, approximately one third of the book continued Cooke's account of his experiences in the Peninsula and then into the south of France to the battle of Toulouse, the remainder of the volume was by other writers and was unrelated to Cooke's experiences. The third volume, *A Narrative of Events in the South of France and of the Attack on New Orleans in 1814 and 1815*, was at least solely by Cooke; it continued to relate his experiences in France and then, after his return to England and reasignment, recounted his adventures in the War of 1812.

For this Leonaur original, we have united Cooke's Napoleonic War memoirs into a one substantial volume; the relevant material from the three books discussed above is here presented as a single, continuous narrative that is logical from both the author's and readers' perspectives.

For the first time those interested in Napoleonic history have the chance to savour and delight in the well written and bloodily graphic accounts that Cooke gives us. The author had a fine eye for description and was obviously fascinated by the variety of military uniforms and local dress he came across; his words also allow us to experience life in camp and on campaign in much more detail than is usual in books such as this. In short, this is a rare and important book—and for those who want to know what happened to John Henry Cooke in North America, that tale is told in the Leonaur book *Light Infantry Officer!*

The Leonaur Editors

CHAPTER 1

My Early Days in the Army

On the 4th of January 1805, I made my *debut* on the parade as ensign in the first West York, powdered and equipped in full uniform, with an artificial tail of considerable length tied round my neck, a cocked hat square to the front and a sword five inches shorter than the regulation, made in proportion to my height, being only four feet eleven inches, and within one month of attaining my fourteenth year.

My diminutive figure soon attracted the attention of the leading company of the regiment, composed of gigantic Yorkshire grenadiers*, and excited so much merriment among them, and so increased my previous confusion, that my eyes became dim and my feet seemed scarcely to touch the ground. However, some kind expressions from the officers who came forward and surrounded me, and their gay appearance soon dispelled my inquietude.

A short time proved sufficient to instruct me in the duties required; and the varied amusements caused the early months of my career to glide rapidly on. Our uniform was plain, faced with green, but suddenly altered owing to an officer of expensive habits, who ordered a new coat to be made and covered with a profusion of gold lace, in which he appeared at the mess table, and so captivated his companions by his rich display, that a unanimous burst of admi-

---

* The grenadier company was composed of more than one hundred men, and only contained *eleven men* so *short* as five feet eleven inches.

9

ration broke forth. Although the lieutenant colonel was as much averse from any thing of the sort as it was possible for anyone to be, the new pattern was carried by acclamation, and a tacit consent wrung from the commanding officer, intermixed with his hearty execrations. Frequently, after the alteration, he used to wear his old coat at the mess table by way of a treat, when, to his extreme mortification, the very officer who caused the change would throw out hints about officers being unregimentally dressed.

Such was the ingenuity of this individual, that on being refused leave of absence, he waited personally on a general, and afterwards declared that he had represented the necessity of his appearance at home in such moving words, that he not only obtained double the time originally asked for, but also drew tears of sympathy from the general's eyes.

In the early part of the summer, General Sir John Moore inspected us on our parade ground, and was pleased to pass his high encomiums on the very fine appearance and steadiness of the men while under arms. Indeed the militia at large were equal to the line*, in the execution of their evolutions and discipline, and were well adapted for the defence of their native shores, at this epoch threatened with invasion by the French. Had their services been required to repel such an aggression—led on by experienced generals, without doubt they would have proved themselves equal to cope with any troops in the world; and those who had an opportunity of judging at that time, will, I am confident, fully coincide with me and join in just admiration at the high state of perfection that national force had been brought to.

During the summer the troops in the numerous towns and camps in Kent were reviewed. Our brigade left Ashford and joined two battalions of the rifle corps, 95th, at Brad-

---

1. Their code of military law, their pay, provisions, arms and accoutrements were the same as in the line; and they often marched three or four hundred miles at a sweep! In summer they went into, camp, or did garrison duty and each company possessed a *bat-horse* with a pack-saddle, to carry the *iron camp kettle*.

bourne Lees and manoeuvred before the Duke of York. The 43rd and 52nd light infantry regiments were organised under the immediate superintendence of Sir John Moore* (assisted by Major General McKenzie) at Hythe, and Shorncliff camp, in the most exemplary manner. Those corps were indeed the admiration of all, for their discipline, and the rapidity of their light movements, all of which being executed on the moveable pivot, by divisions, or sections, formed columns, squares, lines, and echelon, without a halt, by merely marking time.

The moveable pivot preserved a regular cadence, handsome to the sight, and of great utility. In course of time these useful evolutions extended throughout the army, and, for aught I know, are still called "Maw!" with perhaps a few alterations.

The officers of these regiments wore a neat soldier-like uniform of scarlet, facings white and buff, with a pair of small silver epaulettes; and such was the similarity of costume of the two corps, that, at a short distance, it was hardly possible to distinguish one from the other; and, when formed in a line on the green sod at Shorncliff, they presented a fine *coup d'œil*. The rifle corps wore dark green with black lace, helmets and long green feathers**.

It is a strange coincidence, that these corps should have been so near each other, (almost within sight of Napoleon's grand camp at Boulogne) for the purpose of joining their efforts to repel the threatened attack on the coast, and that, in after years, they should be united in a series of brilliant victories gained over the French legions, during a period of service, which, in future ages, will create wonder at the extraordinary rise and fall of Napoleon in the centre of civilised Europe;

* Sir John Moore offered commissions to Lieutenants Booth, Temple, and myself of the York. The two former joined the 52nd; but, as my brother fancied that I was too young and as I was not my own master, I was obliged to submit to his decision. Lieut. O'Reilly also entered the rifle-corps and was subsequently killed on the river Coa in Portugal; and Lieut. Booth was killed at the storming of Badajoz in Spain.
** The *pelisse* was subsequently introduced, and a soldier clad in (green tartan) the highland costume, carried a small standard. The three light regiments increased to seven battalions during the war; 43rd two; 52nd two and rifles three.

whose legions like an overwhelming lava spread death and destruction far and wide; drove all nature into mourning, and converted Europe into an hospital.

Napoleon at this period had formed at Boulogne and its vicinity a powerful army, Which he hoped to be enabled to throw across the channel by the end of August and effect a landing in England under the protection of the combined French and Spanish fleets, commanded by Admiral Ville-neuve, who was expected from the West Indies about that time to concentrate the different fleets in the French and Spanish ports, to be composed of sixty ships of war destined to cover the numerous flotilla which was also to be crowded with soldiers inured to war.

Every effort on the part of this country was made to frus-trate such a design. Martello towers had been erected along the coast of Kent at certain distances, and thousands of navi-gators and soldiers were hard at work cutting the military canal twenty yards wide across Romney Marsh. Beacons were placed on the tops of the highest hills, to light up, and alarm the country in case of a sudden descent of the enemy. Fortunately however the hostile movements of the Austrians obliged Napoleon to break up his camp at Boulogne, and march to oppose them. The latter part of this year produced extraordinary events; Napoleon was again overwhelming the continent by his military achievements, and Nelson in a like manner, by his naval exploits, was clearing all before him. These great commanders seemed striving to outvie each other on their peculiar elements, and each won a great battle*, and within a few months of each other.

During the autumn, the regiment to which I belonged marched to Chelmsford in Essex, and was stationed there a few weeks with other corps, previously to our proceeding to Norman Cross for the purpose of guarding some thousands of unhappy Frenchmen, cooped up at that place, and clothed

---

* Trafalgar and Austerlitz.

in yellow (the prison dress) to expiate their revolutionary sins by many years' captivity and exile in a loathsome prison, cut off from their relatives and friends.

Their necessities forced them to exert their ingenuity in making various curious toys, which they disposed of at a very low rate to enable them to procure a few comforts, to alleviate their extreme wretchedness, which was beyond description; for want of clothes many of them suffered every privation rather than be clad in a conspicuous and humiliating colour; others were in rags and almost in a state of nudity, having lost their all by gambling; and to so great an extent did the vice grow, that many would even stake their rations, and every trifle given to them by strangers, until, by their half famished looks, they bore a resemblance to skeletons.

The exterior of the prison was enclosed by strong wooden railings, as well as the four interior quadrangles, in the centre of which stood a circular block house bristled with three pounders on swivels, their muzzles peeping out of square apertures (similar to the ports of a ship) to play on the prisoners in case of their becoming refractory. Generals Boyer and Rochambeau were, for some reason or other, in close confinement; one of them played and sang most delightfully on the guitar.

The barracks stood about east and west, occupied by two regiments, with two field pieces always placed at the gates, in readiness to fire if necessary. The high north road ran within about two hundred yards of the west barrack. A troop of the 7th Light Dragoons* were quartered near at hand to pursue those Frenchmen who might attempt to effect their escape, which many accomplished by the utmost danger, and the most unaccountable perseverance; sometimes by working under ground for months, to excavate a way out of prison. One man, absolutely wrapped in straw bands, dropped himself into a night cart, (which he was aware would be drawn away that

---

* Now hussars.

night) and he was pitched out with the soil at the usual place on the slope of a hill; but, in his haste to extricate himself, he was discovered, and brought back half suffocated.

Many of the poor prisoners gave lessons in fencing; and while I was once displaying the proficiency I had made in that art to an amateur by placing him in a defensive position to ward off my rapid attack, he unfortunately guided the point of my cane up his own nostrils which caused him forthwith to ungrasp his sword, and apply both hands to the wounded part. Being much alarmed at the accident, I stood at a respectful distance from my friend, until the pain had subsided; fearing that, under such torment, he might take signal vengeance on my slender frame.

The winter passed heavily enough at this dull spot, and without doubt the best hour of the day was that when the drum struck up the *Roast Beef of old England*, the certain announcement of a well supplied board, covered with massive plate, and groaning under the weight of the choicest viands the season afforded.

Early in the spring the long wished for route arrived for Hull in Yorkshire. When we were on the march through Lincolnshire, a sudden thunder storm came on, accompanied by heavy rain, and we saw a poor girl at work in an adjoining field; but, before she was able to gain a place of shelter from the rain, a flash of lightning struck her on the forehead and killed her on the spot. Her lifeless body was conveyed to the nearest town, to her unhappy relatives. After the expiration of a few days we arrived at Barton, where we crossed the Humber (seven miles down the river) in the regular passage-boats to the place of our destination, having experienced the usual comforts of a march in England: such as good breakfasts, dinners, and a comfortable feather bed every night.

Soon after our arrival a detachment was ordered to take charge of some batteries on the right bank of the Humber in Lincolnshire, no great distance from Grimsby; and, for the good of my morals, I was selected for that duty, it being considered by excellent judges that so populous a town as Hull afforded too many temptations for one so young as myself. Every movement to me was a source of pleasure; already my new abode was anticipated, and some highly romantic spot pictured to my imagination. A fancied governor too, surrounded by the inhabitants of the adjacent country looking up with that respect so flattering to one placed in so responsible a situation!

The hour of my departure was hailed with joy, and I eagerly jumped on board a small packet procured for the transport of myself and party. The sails being spread out, I felt a secret wish that my brother and another officer had not been on board, so that I might have entered into my important avocations without further delay. We had glided a short way on our course, when the wind changed, and became adverse, and, after a few tacks, I lost my vivacity, my countenance turned pale, and my brother remarked that I was sea-sick.

"How can that be," faintly replied I, "when we are only in a river?"

Although it must be acknowledged that, owing to its proximity to the sea, the water was sufficiently agitated to cause some derangement in the stomach of a landsman.

At the expiration of a few hours' tossing, we anchored off a solitary habitation, three sides of which were encompassed by a dreary marsh of considerable extent, intersected with dykes. On landing, my companions surveyed the surrounding prospect, casting significant looks towards each other, and a half stifled laugh followed at my dejected amazement, as I contemplated the prospect before me, wondering how the coming six months were to be employed, or myself to be amused, in this swamp, whitened by innumerable flocks of sea gulls. On entering the boathouse I sat down with little appetite to partake of some eggs and bacon, that being the best fare to be procured. All my companions made a hearty meal, and, having swallowed a couple of tumblers of brandy and water, took their departure with a fair wind, leaving me to make the best of my way, over a pathless waste, in the direction of a small wooden building rearing its chimneys just above an earth entrenchment decorated by four heavy cannons mounted *en barbette* and a bare pole in the centre by way of a flag staff. The soldiers preceding me were a short way in front. In vain I strained my eyes in search of a second habitation, to cheer this monotonous scene; night was fast drawing to a close, and the disagreeable Humber and its muddy banks disappearing from my view, amidst a drizzling rain.

On entering the room allotted for my use, I seated myself on my baggage in no very cheerful mood, waiting the delivery of coals and candles, while my servant was busily employed mopping the floor. In the morning the men were placed at the guns, armed with rammers and handspikes, to learn to load, elevate, and traverse, so as to fire in case any French ships might enter the river, to disturb the whalers anchored off Hull.

A printed board of orders nailed to the wall at the extremity of my room showed me the necessity of visiting another battery under my charge (at stated periods) distant six miles up the river. I was also informed that I had a horse at my service; but, when the animal was brought forward, all hopes of a ride vanished, he proving lame of a leg, very old, and his coat sticking up like the bristles of a porcupine.

My instructions also specified that every Sunday the detachment was to attend divine service, at a church situated inland on a gentle rise, shrouded by trees, about two miles from the battery, which was to be left in charge of a corporal's guard.

The sixth day happened to be the Sabbath; the weather was propitious. I therefore decorated myself in hopes of getting a glimpse of some flowing drapery at the distant hamlet. On our arrival the bell was tolling, and a few infirm individuals were creeping into the old church. As the service had not begun, I squatted myself on a hay-cock—for the grass of this churchyard was turned to account, and, as far as I could judge, was as fine a crop as any around.

At length the bell ceased to reverberate, and I was about to enter the decayed doors of the church, when on raising my eyes I beheld a young lady of lovely face and form, stationary, with one foot placed on the top of the style (leading into the churchyard) and with her eyes apparently fixed in the direction of where I stood. She evinced an animation, which I shall long remember; for my heart began to beat with the most joyful anticipations. She passed close to me, while I remained fixed, and gazing on her with transported admiration. I soon followed, and was placed in a pew exactly opposite to her. Her raven tresses hung carelessly from under a little blue silk hat. Her checks vied with the roses, and the lustre of her sparkling black eyes pierced the inmost recesses of my beating heart. Before the service was concluded, we were both holding down our heads laughing; and the only excuse for such indecorous conduct, (if any can be offered), was our youth—for she was only sixteen, and I was half a year younger.

Two days after, I wandered towards the village, the peasants had gone forth to their daily labours. On looking about, I could see but one house likely to contain the object of my secret regard. It was a large old building encompassed by an extensive field in the shape of a park. However, I fancied this was not her dwelling, as she had entered the churchyard from quite a contrary direction. Having wandered some time without encountering a single person of whom I could make any inquiries, I at last felt convinced that the fair object of my search had come from a distant village, and that I should not again behold her fascinating smiles.

In retracing my steps from thence, the marsh became doubly odious to my sight; however, on the following Sunday, I placed myself on the same spot in the church yard, with my eyes steadfastly fixed on the style. The bell ceased to toll, the church doors closed, the service had begun, but my *belle* did not appear; and I now in real earnest began to consider myself a perfect exile, not having exchanged a syllable with anyone save my servant (or when giving some trifling orders) for thirteen days.

The next morning I started on foot to visit the other fort (mounting two guns, with a garrison of one Sergeant, a gunner, and fourteen men) to be assured that the lame horse had safely carried their provisions, and to see that the defences had not been washed away during the last spring tide. After a toilsome walk of no inconsiderable distance, along a dyke, overrun with long grass nearly up to my middle, I returned, well tired, and perfectly cooled in my governorship.

The next day I made towards the hamlet, being determined to summon up resolution, and make inquiries at some cottage, or to endeavour to find out from whence came the sole object of my thoughts. On my accosting an old woman, who very civilly answered all my inquiries, she communicated that the young lady was a gentleman farmer's daughter; expatiating upon her beauty and amiability, and concluded by remarking, that she supposed by this time she must have returned to school beyond Lincoln, as she had not seen her for some days. She then informed me that, when at home, the young lady resided in the large mansion already described.

Having now gained the long wished information, I wandered towards the spot, and espied a figure clad in white standing at the door of a cottage, at no great distance from the large house.

I instantly made my way across the field, full of doubts and fears, and when, within a short distance, I could distinguish the same figure, and the charming countenance I was in quest of—I hesitated, being fearful that the object of my search might vanish. At length with a palpitating heart, and extremely confused, I found myself opposite the *brunette*. I attempted to speak, but, alas! my words were unintelligible; she smiled, and I was rooted to the spot—she retreated backwards; her eyes, acting like load stars, drew me forward. I stumbled over the door-sill, and found myself in a small room in the interior of the cottage. At the extremity of it sat an ancient dame at her spinning wheel, who, looking through her spectacles at me, regarded so small a figure, in a rich scarlet uniform, with a degree of good-natured surprise. Some moments elapsed before anyone of this trio broke silence. My *incognita* blushed and cast the kindest regards towards her old nurse, who looked alternately towards us for some explanation; but, finding little chance of any from our confusion, she broke the awkward silence by requesting to know my pleasure?

In reply, I stammered out, that I had lost my way; she instantly arose, and offered the assistance of her son, to conduct me into the right road; but my *chère amie* now found her voice, and stopped her short, by offering her services to point out the way for me herself; and, almost in the same breath, asked me if I did not feel considerably fatigued after so long a walk? Then, entering into conversation the hours wore away imperceptibly, until the old dame reminded her of her unusually long absence from home, which might induce her mamma to send someone in search of her; we thereupon parted seemingly equally pleased with each other, and with an agreement to continue our acquaintance.

To my eyes the marsh now no longer presented a dreary waste; my heart was as light as a feather; I bounded over planks and ditches, for hedges there were none, Even the odious twenty-four pounders I could have turned to use, by loading them up to the muzzles with grape shot, against all pirates or rivals, and I do verily believe that had it not been for the presence of an old steady gunner, I should really have fired a salute on the occasion.

I ordered tea to be prepared and my fire made up. I then opened a box filled with books that day forwarded to me from Hull with a note from my brother, saying, that according to my wishes he had sent some novels, and also a few volumes of the *Roman History*, with his strict injunctions not to neglect the perusal of the latter in particular.

The first book I extracted was a deep romance; and the

pages were eagerly devoured with all those transports so natural to youthful minds. It was soon conveyed for the perusal of my *chère amie;* for in truth the *Roman History* had never entered my head.

A fresh supply being soon necessary, the box was returned, and the history kept as a reserve, and, like many other reserves, it was never brought into action.

After a short acquaintance, my little *belle* intimated to me, that I might expect an invitation when her papa (who abominated the red coats, great and small) should make his annual excursion. It struck me that a dark lantern might be of great utility during such parties as I might chance to attend. I therefore begged of my brother that one might be purchased for me, which was accordingly done, although such a request somewhat excited his surprise; however, on reflection, the extensive prospect he had previously surveyed the day he conducted me to my lonely abode, soon convinced him that a nightly tramp would be out of the question, and he set my request down to the effect of the romances I had recently perused.

At length the time of papa's departure was announced to me, with an invitation from mamma to take tea with her: and, on the appointed night, having secured my barrack room door, I walked a short distance, and turned my dark lantern, to enable me to explore my way over a path intersected by numerous ditches.

On my arrival near the gate at the end of an enclosure, leading to the house, the rays of my lantern fell on a figure all in white. I made a sudden stop, and opened my eyes to their full extent, to satisfy myself what so strange an appearance could be, so late, and at so lonely a spot; for various confused ideas crossed my mind, my fancy was worked up to the highest state of excitement, and a cold chill ran through my veins—when suddenly the ground gave way, and I was immersed above my middle in water in a ditch, the edge of which had given way. During my alarm, while I was endeavouring to extricate myself from my awkward situation, the figure moved towards me and I scrambled out of the ditch, covered with duck weed. As a last resort I summoned up my remaining courage, and demanded in a loud voice, or rather screech, "What are you?" when a plaintive voice answered, "It is I;" and the speaker instantly vanished.

After looking cautiously around, in apprehension of making another false step and getting a second ducking, I explored my way with considerable difficulty to the house, absolutely following the direction of the supposed phantom. There I found my new friend waiting for me at the door much alarmed, who informed me she had seen the light of my lantern gradually approaching, and had ventured to meet me, but the hearing the souse, and such a strange salute in total darkness, had so terrified her, that a hasty flight had been the consequence.

Her mamma had waited tea some time, and on entering the room I perceived that she was in full dress and highly rouged! I was introduced to her, wet through, and covered with a green weed, like some sea monster. She laughed immoderately. What was to be done? A change was necessary: the husband's clothes would not do. A huge country girl being called in, while divesting me of my coat, suggested that I should be attired in one of her young lady's dresses. This proposal afforded mamma much diversion, who agreed to the proposal, and I was led into the kitchen, to a rousing wood fire, blazing on the hearth, under a spacious chimney. Here I was unceremoniously stripped by the maid, who appropriated so much time to the adjustment of my female attire, that her *jeune maîtresse* demanded the reason of my person being kept so long in custody by this Amazonian wench. My *toilette* being arranged, tea and coffee were served up, and the time passed in the most agreeable conversation.

The night had far advanced, when an unexpected rapping was heard, with the butt end of a riding whip, heavily applied to the oaken doors, while a hoarse voice demanded admittance in the well known key of papa: but to my ears the notes were like the roaring of a lion. All lights were instantly extinguished, and the back door was thrown open, out of which I was led into a poultry yard, and from thence into a loft, where, seating myself on a truss of hay, I waited in much suspense, while the heavy bars were removed from the gate of the farmyard, to admit the squire and his horse. His gruff voice soon died away, the gates were again closed and all became quiet. Shortly afterwards a rustling noise and gentle footsteps struck on my ear, when my *belle* again made her appearance accompanied by the before mentioned Amazonian *fille de chambre* with my dried *paraphernalia* under her arm.

Meanwhile mamma was left to conduct her bloated spouse grunting to bed, quite overcome, after his devotions to Bacchus and the malt tub. Soon after I had assumed the attire of my own sex, the crowing of the feathered tribe announced the time for my departure, when, bidding tender *adieus*, I rapidly stole across the meadow, and just before the sun arose, I found myself once more within my camp bed—*minus* my dark lantern.

I often bended my steps during these May days towards the peaceful hamlet far removed from any neighbouring village, from whence a green sod, hedged on each side, was the sole outlet or vestige of a road winding into the interior, through a rich pasturage country; it was in these rural shades, and unbeaten tracks, that my blooming companion and I rambled at large, and, when fatigued, her old nurse would place before us her best China service, and seem to participate in our happiness.

The summer months flew away, and my indescribable departure was announced. I presented the hospitable old dame with a new pair of spectacles, and she wiped her eyes. The Yorkshire-men buckled on their knapsacks, the wind was fair, the bark cut through the water, the old church vanished from my sight, and I again landed at the busy and trafficking town of Hull.

Here the merchants entertained the military with turtle,

and such feasts as their rapidly accumulated wealth enabled them to spread out in gorgeous abundance. The card parties were crowded to excess, and very high stakes played for; more particularly as many of the officers were possessed of large landed property, and also displayed most splendid equipages.

The venerable Earl Fitzwilliam, who was the Colonel of the regiment, was there, and when I was introduced to him, he asked me whether I did not find the colours very heavy in my hands? My face instantly coloured up; the fact was, I had been blown down, colours and all, while at a field day at Ashford in Kent. The amiable nobleman, with his characteristic kindness, took care that I should see my name in the next gazette as a Lieutenant.

After a very short stay at Hull, we were ordered to Whitby, Burlington, and Scarboro', situated on the sea coast. I had the good fortune to march to the latter town, with which I was much struck on entering. It is compact, and situated in a valley, with the fine old castle rising abruptly and commanding a bird's eye view of the town, and the beautiful and extensive sands, which become so hard, that at low water horse racing used to take place, and with great safety, as there is hardly a pebble to be seen.

This was a grand place of resort, where the healthy dames and their daughters from the North, came to sip the spa, to flounder in the sea, to see and be seen, and to listen to the mild sayings of strangers from the south, while hurrying down fifty couple at Donna's rooms, with rosy cheeks, and hair somewhat out of curl. One whole year passed at this place in a continual round of amusements, such as balls, parties, picnic excursions, gay promenades, and horse-racing.

The band was magnificently attired in green and gold; in fact, Earl Fitzwilliam gave up the whole or the greater part of his pay for the benefit of the regiment. The volunteering into the line continued from time to time; the greater portion of the men, being of large stature, entered the foot guards, the artillery, and marines.

The route at length arrived; and on the morning of our departure the band struck up, the bass drum beating the marching time, a signal for windows to be hastily thrown open by many fair ladies *en déshabille,* waving their white handkerchiefs and delicate hands, until a wind of the road concealed them from our admiration. The sun shone brightly, and, as we cast a lingering look behind, the venerable white turrets of the castle and the sparkling blue sea foaming at its base receded from our view. We had proceeded about ten miles over the bare wold, when, our appetites becoming rather keen from the sea breezes, we began to cast our longing eyes towards a small sequestered village, surrounded by stone walls, and a few scattered trees, which proved a welcome sight.

On entering, we drew up opposite a small rustic inn, for the purpose of taking breakfast—the chubby cherry-cheeked maids flocked around us, and became so elated at the sounds of the music, and at the sight of the red coats, that in their hurry to lay before us such provisions as the pace afforded they pushed and jostled their rustic swains out of their way, who, while resting on their pitchforks looked uneasy, as if doubting for the first time in their lives the true constancy of their sweethearts.

After partaking of a most excellent breakfast, we resumed our road, and at the expiration of three days again entered Hull, when we soon received an order to proceed to Bristol; we passed through Beverley to Hull, then to Doncaster, Birmingham, Derby, Litchfield, Gloucester, and Worcester, besides many towns of smaller note interspersed through this highly cultivated country. Having accomplished a march of three hundred miles, we reached Bristol.

While passing through a town, an old woman perceived the officer of the light company with a knapsack on his back: she hobbled towards him, and addressed him by the familiar appellation of "Sergeant;" he answered with a smile, "My good old lady, Sergeants do not carry knapsacks in this regiment," at the same time casting a glance towards a few of that rank who had left theirs on the baggage wagons. The officer loaded himself in this way for the comfort of a speedy change, on the march during wet weather.

A number of French prisoners were confined at Stapleton prison, about five miles from Bristol This duty we found unpleasant, having to tramp over a dirty road in the winter, in white kerseymere breeches, for the purpose of mounting guard. A most fatal affray happened here betwixt four French prisoners, owing to a dispute which arose out of a trifling gambling transaction. The two principals first engaged, having split a scissors into two parts and tied the points to the end of canes, with which they fought, one was soon killed, the seconds then engaged, when another fell mortally wounded; in fact, both the friends on one side fell.

We frequently visited the village of Clifton within a mile of Bristol. It is beautifully situated, overlooking the river Avon, which romantically winds at the base of steep declivities, decorated with overhanging shrubs. The promenades and balls were very fashionably attended, and it was surprising to observe the superiority of manners, costume, and dancing, compared with those of the company attending the assemblies at Bristol.

Early in the summer of 1808, we again moved, and passed through the counties of Somerset and Devon to Plymouth, there to do duty over the arsenals and more French prisoners.

I had now reached my seventeenth year. One evening while rambling about, I accidentally met an officer, and entered into conversation with him, when I was not a little surprised at his making use of my elder brother's name, in no very complimentary strain, and, as I was aware that such sentiments could not be used unintentionally by a man of the world, I made a suitable retort, and left him. On reaching my brother's barrack room which was adjacent to mine, I found him poring over a volume of Shakespeare, with his usual *theatrical* delight, and, not wishing to disturb his transporting meditations, I bade him good night and retired to my bed, having given my servant directions to call me the next morning early, which being duly executed, I sent a friend with a message to the officer already alluded to, which he instantly accepted; but, as the regiment was under arms much earlier than usual, to fire ball cartridge at a target, it was agreed that we should manage to get leave with our seconds, and fall out one at a time, so as not to create any suspicion of our intentions.

Our uniforms having been thrown aside, four of us proceeded some distance before we could find a spot to suit our purpose. The usual distance being measured, we tossed up for sides. I lost, and stood with my face towards the sun, as no other level spot could be found at hand. Having taken our ground, the usual distance (by word), we both fired without effect: the pistols being re-loaded, a second discharge was about to take place, when my adversary addressed me by my Christian name, and said he wished the affair adjusted, so that all that had passed between us should be forgotten, and that we might be the same good friends as heretofore—the seconds then interfered, and all was amicably adjusted*.

A general order appeared about this period, exploding hair-powder and tails throughout the army. But, previously to its coming out, a most ludicrous occurrence happened. An officer who possessed a very good figure and a fine head of hair, had shown a great antipathy against wearing powder, so much so, that it was only by a repetition of orders, that he could he induced to use the puff, and even then it was so sparingly put on his crown, as to be scarcely visible. One morning as usual he appeared on the parade, with his bead unwhitened; the captain of his company not a little roused, at having so frequently reminded him of his neglect of duty, again remarked that he was without powder; when he care-

---

* My brother and the same officer had a dispute eight months after this affair. They met; and at the first fire my brother received his adversary's ball through the upper part of his thigh, but eventually recovered.

lessly answered, that he supposed a puff of wind must have blown it out; which so incensed the captain that he forthwith reported the circumstance.

The whole of the officers being assembled to the front, the culprit patiently heard the accusation against him, and as coolly received the slight reprimand from the commanding officer, who had no sooner finished what he had to say than the accused officer fixed his eyes steadily on his captain, and, without uttering a syllable lifted his cap slowly from his head at arm's length, showing a head as white as snow, while his accuser stood petrified and confounded, to the no small amusement of the surprised circle who burst into an unrestrained laugh, joined in by the senior officers. The fact was, that the rear of the company was close to the soldiers' barrack, and, while the captain was in the act of reporting his junior officer, the latter had run into one of the men's rooms, seized a flour tub (used by the soldiers) and, with its contents, had covered his head, leaving the side locks untouched as before.

About this time, the expedition to Portugal put into Plymouth, and as there appeared some probability of an opening for the British army on terra firma, I felt an anxiety to enter the line. A commission was promised me in a light infantry regiment, which I soon after obtained; at this time Plymouth was crowded by Portuguese officers, that had fled from their native country with the royal family of Portugal, who had departed for the New World. Portugal being cleared of the *French* and *Spanish invaders* the British entered Spain to threaten the right flank of the French army under Napoleon, in the depth of winter, which ended by Sir John Moore being killed, and the whole of the English army re-embarking at Corunna. The different regiments landed in England in the most deplorable condition, having been overtaken by a tempest, which had scattered them over the face of the waters.

The inhabitants of Plymouth received these troops with open arms, and threw wide their doors for the benefit of the suffering officers; they watched over their sick beds in the most assiduous manner, and supplied them *gratis* with every comfort, such as shirts and shoes, and crowned all this magnanimous hospitality, by advancing money to many of the convalescent officers to enable them to reach their far distant homes, in England, Ireland, and Scotland, But how different was the treatment of the army (who had freed Portugal) elsewhere! A young and handsome officer had landed at another port in a wretched state, bare-footed, his feet tormented with gravel, suffering from a fever, and supporting himself against a wall: then creeping along in an exhausted state, he was unnoticed by the passers-by, until a sailor said, "Why, soldier officer, you are aground, come, take hold of my arm, I will take care of you."

In march, 1809*, I obtained my ensigncy in the line, and journeyed to Colchester to join the second battalion 43rd light infantry. When an officer entered this corps it was an invariable custom to send him to drill with a squad, composed of peasants from the plough tail, or other raw recruits. First learning the facings, marching and companies' evolutions. That being completed, the officer put on cross-belts and pouch and learned the firelock exercise; then again he marched with the same: and when it was considered that the whole were perfect, with, and without arms, they began to skirmish in extended files, and last of all learned the duties of a sentry, and to fire ball cartridge at a target. The officer after all this was not considered clear of the adjutant, until he could put a company through the evolutions by word of command,

---

* In that month the first battalion marched from Colchester to Harwich to embark for Portugal with the 52nd and the Rifle corps, under Major General R. Craufurd, and joined the army in Spain the day after the battle of Talavera de la Reyna, having made a forced march in good order, in hopes of participating in that sanguinary battle, where they found the remnant of those men who had been left sick or wounded (in the battalion of detachments) in Portugal after Vimiera, and who had been engaged at the passage of the Duoro near Oporto, and at Talavera. The 43rd had upwards of one hundred men hilled in that battle; and of officers, brigade Major Gardner killed, and Lieutenant Brown wounded—the latter now commanding the second battalion Rifle brigade.

which he had already practised in the ranks. It generally took him six months in summer at four times a day (an hour at each period) to perfect him in all he had to learn. The drill was never kept more than an hour under arms, when, to a minute, the time beater rolled his drum, the only one, (light infantry regiments used bugles) in the corps; and the recruits were instantly dismissed.

The orderly officer of each company made out the daily morning state with his own hand. Subalterns inspected squads on parade: the company was then formed and given over to the captain, who, with the rest of the officers, never quitted their company to lounge about, so long as the soldiers continued under arms. The corps paraded twice a week in heavy marching order, and the mess was equally well conducted, in a system of style and economy happily blended.

Chapter 2

Walcheren

In June 1809 we left Colchester with other corps, for the purpose of embarkation; our route lay through Chelmsford, Gravesend, Maidstone, to Shorncliff barracks (in Kent) placed on the summit of a hill extending to the verge of the white cliffs overhanging the sea, and commanding a clear view of the straits of Dover, and the opposite coast of France.

On the 16th of July we marched through Dover to Deal, where innumerable boats lined the shore for the purpose of conveying troops to the various ships anchored in the Downs for their reception. Large bodies of soldiers were pouring into the town by all the roads to join the vast armament about to rendezvous at this point. Hurrying into the boats, the hardy sailors pulled away: the beach and the bay were covered with thousands of soldiers, intermixed with the fair daughters of Albion, who had come from afar to witness this brilliant spectacle.

The army was in a fine state of discipline, and filled with enthusiasm, while the ensigns of many naval victories floated in the breeze from the mast heads of those men of war, that had for years swept the ocean, opened the whole commerce of the world to this island, and filled the coffers of England with almost inexhaustible resources.

We had no sooner arrived on board the *York*, seventy four, commanded by Captain Barton, than the usual bustle prevailed on such occasions, which had in some measure subsided, when a large fat man in a small boat was seen making towards the ship, dressed in light fawn-coloured breeches, white cotton stockings and shoes, with a loose coat, evidently of provincial cut. Coming alongside, he eagerly demanded the number of the regiment on board, which proved to be the identical one he was in search of; he then mounted the side of the ship with breathless exertion, and attempted to bustle through the crowd of soldiers huddled together.

However, the butt ends of some firelocks falling heavily near his toes, formed a sufficient hint to arrest his progress, and he was much confounded at finding himself jostled amongst such a concourse of troops for the first time in his life. After waiting some time with intense anxiety, he at length succeeded in clearing the way, crying out in accents of one whose patience had been quite exhausted by hopelessness of redress:

"Will any man in this ship have the goodness to point out the Paymaster's berth? for really, gentlemen, I have striven in vain to obtain an answer of the many persons whom I have already addressed"

A voice from the crowd replied, "Why, there is no such thing,"—at which unwelcome intelligence the countenance of the applicant underwent a painful transition from hope to despair.

While at anchor in the Downs, the wind blew sufficiently strong to cause the unpleasant motion of the ship which produces sea sickness, and, being one of the junior officers, I was not so fortunate as the Paymaster, who had secured a berth, for I wandered for three days into different quarters of the ship, in a state unnecessary to describe to those who have experienced the heaving of a ship at anchor. A midshipman about my own age kindly offered to provide me with such accommodation as the cock-pit afforded, which offer I thankfully accepted, in hopes of at least getting into a quiet uninterrupted corner. I had scarcely entered the hammock hung for my reception, when I was assailed by quantities of cock chafers crawling over my face, and under the blankets, (the ship having just returned from a cruise from the West Indies.)

The prodigious armament consisted of thirty-five ships of the line; two of fifty guns, three of forty-four guns; and one hundred and ninety-seven sloops, bombs, and other armed small craft—with an army of thirty-nine thousand, two hundred and nineteen men, including officers, all assembled in the Downs on the 27th of July, 1809. The whole were under the command of Rear-Adm. Sir R. Strachan and Gen. the Earl of Chatham, in conjunction. These Commanders sailed in the *Venerable* at daylight, on the 28th of July, and arrived in the East Kapelle roads, off the island of Walcheren on that evening; but, owing to the boisterous state of the weather, and contrary winds, a landing could not be effected on the Domburg beach. The other two divisions of the fleet followed in succession from the Downs.

The object of the expedition was, to capture or destroy the enemy's ships, building at Antwerp and Flushing, or afloat in the Scheldt; also the destruction of the arsenals and dockyards at Antwerp, Ternuese, and Flushing; to reduce the island of Walcheren, and render, if possible, the Scheldt no longer navigable for ships of war; with directions to the commanders, should they not be able to effect all these objects, that after the reduction of Walcheren, (which was to be kept possession of, and a force left for its protection,) the remainder of the troops were to be re-embarked, and to return to England.

The island of Walcheren is thirty-four miles in circumference, including St. Jootsland, and is situated between the mouths of the East and West Scheldt, enclosed by Cadzand on the south, South Beveland and Wolfertsdyck on the east, and North Bevel on the north east.

Our division of the fleet sailed from the Downs at half-past ten o'clock a.m. on the 30th, and came to anchor the next afternoon, in the East Kapelle roads off Walcheren, when we observed the mortar and gun-vessels keeping up a heavy fire on the small town of Ter Veere, whilst a small body of English troops were lying behind the sand-hills, keeping watch on the road towards Middelburg, the capital of the island. Part of the fleet had already entered the Veere Gat, and had landed a large force, with three divisions of sailors (three hundred) the day before, at half-past four in the afternoon, on the Bree-sand, a little more than a mile west of Fort de Haak, the fire of which had been previously silenced by the gunboats and mortars. The peaceable inhabitants sent a deputation from Middelburg to the headquarters; the army advanced the next day, the 1st of August, and took possession of that place, drove the enemy into Flushing, and took from them some field-pieces.

Gen. Sir John Hope landed his divisions in South Beveland the same day, and took possession of Ter Goes, the capital of the island, which is thirty-five miles long. The French fleet had retired beyond the chain which was drawn across the Scheldt near Fort Lillo.

On the 3rd, a few vessels were observed leaving Flushing; some boats were sent in chase; the weather was fine, the wind S.S.W., and the flood tide nearly down, which gave every hope of their effecting a safe return. The *Raven* sloop of war went to their protection, when the enemy's vessels again retreated into Flushing. The wind suddenly flew west in a squall, first blowing hard and then baffling. The boats got safe off, but the fire continued on the sloop for four hours without intermission, round shot passing through her from the Breskens batteries, and grape dropping on board from the ramparts of Flushing. She suffered severely in the hull, masts, and rigging, and had two guns dismounted, the top-mast shot away above the lower caps, the main-mast, bowsprit, and main-boom, rendered unserviceable, the sails and rigging completely cut in pieces, and her Commander, Capt. Hanchett, and eight men, wounded. Night coming on, she grounded on the Ellboog; at daybreak two brigs were sent to her assistance, and at seven she floated.

The enemy were very apprehensive lest our army should make an attempt to pass the East Scheldt, near Zandvliet, opposite fort Bathz, which they attacked on the 5th with twenty-eight gunboats, but were driven off by the batteries. The weather continued so bad until the 7th, the wind blowing S.W. and S.S.W., that the sea blockade of Flushing could not be accomplished, and the enemy continued to convey their wounded soldiers to Cadzand, and also threw one thousand men across the Scheldt, one mile and three-quarters, to reinforce the town. At half-past five o'clock in the evening of the 7th the enemy made a sortie on the right of the line from Flushing, but were repulsed and pushed back at the point of the bayonet.

While all these things were going on, our regiment had been removed from the line-of-battle ship into small craft, and anchored in the Sloe passage, between Walcheren and South Beveland.

On the morning of the 9th, ours, the light brigade, composed of the second battalions of the 43rd, 52nd, and the Rifle corps, part of Earl Rosslyn's division (two thousand and twenty-two men) were under the command of Major Gen. Stewart. He considered, from the nature of the service we were likely to be employed on, and probably cut off from our baggage by dykes and rivers, that small black knapsacks, with brown straps, would prove of essential service to the officers: for these we had paid half-a-guinea each, previously to our leaving England. However, subsequently, as he expected us to carry them at brigade field-days, some little discussion arose on that head, behind a windmill.

A day's salt pork and biscuit being served out, and all the officers with their knapsacks strapped on their backs, we began our march; the day was extremely sultry, without a breath of air; the road was perfectly flat, as well as the whole face of the country, which was intersected with ditches, covered with a thick ooze or vegetable substance, and high dykes rising on each side of the way. The Paymaster had joined the column, as the place of the greatest security.

As guns from the gunboats were sounding at intervals, in front and rear, we persuaded him that it was probable we might become engaged without any previous warning, by a front, flank, or rear attack, which information, added to the heat of the atmosphere, put him into such a state of perspiration, that when we halted, a liquid stream of hot water poured from his forehead, such as I have never before, nor since beheld; added to which, his tailor had fitted his corpulent sides to a nicety, although equal praise could not be bestowed on his hatter, who had manufactured his cap so large, that it fell over his face like an extinguisher, and the worst of it was, both his hands were occupied; in his right he held his wig and drenched pocket-handkerchief, while his left was in momentary request to disentangle his sabre from betwixt his legs.

"Well," said he, with a good-tempered smile, "if ever I knew anything like this!" and, notwithstanding his uncomfortable plight, he cracked his jokes, and proved himself a man of more ready wit, and possessing a greater fund of anecdote and humorous stories, than anyone I ever met with, so that he became a general favourite throughout the regiment; but such a figure in a light infantry jacket! Such skirts, with pockets large enough to have stowed away half the striplings of the corps!

When the brigade was put in motion, he remained in the middle of the way, as they passed him right and left, and waited for the light wagons carrying our baggage; then stowing himself comfortably away in one of them, he was brought to our cantonments perfectly sick of campaigning.

As we passed along, we were much struck at the great cleanliness of the cottages, and at the contented air of the well-dressed peasantry. The females were decorated with silver or gold ornaments about their persons, and many of them wore a plate of the same metal across their foreheads. The little boys of five or six years old held pipes in their mouths, smoking with all the gravity of men, and wore their hair long behind, broad-brimmed hats, brown jackets, short breeches, shoes, and silver buckles, precisely similar to the elders.

We passed through Ter-Goes, a fine old brick town, surrounded by earth ramparts and a wet ditch; it opened its gates without making any resistance to Sir John Hope's corps. Continuing our march half a league farther on, we arrived at the clean village of Cloting, containing a good church, and a handsome house in the centre of it, which was the residence of the Burgomaster; we took up our quarters in the different houses, and the men in the spacious handsome barns, painted green, such as may be seen near gentlemen's houses in England. Five companies of our regiment were detached to another village. The humble dwellings of the peasantry bore an air of comfort, and the abundantly supplied dairies, paved with well washed tiles, presented a freshness seldom exhibited among the poorer classes of other countries.

A considerable flotilla proceeded to Bathz, where they arrived on the 11th; the enemy attacked the fort with two frigates, one bearing a Vice Admiral's flag, thirty brigs, eight luggers, one schooner, and fourteen gunboats; at the expiration of a smart firing, they were beaten off, leaving six gunboats aground, five being destroyed, and one brought in. In the afternoon of the same day, Capt. Lord W. Stuart, commanding the *Lavinia* and nine other frigates, availed himself of a light breeze from the westward, (notwithstanding the tide was against the proceeding,) sailed up the west Scheldt, and passed the batteries between Cadzand and Flushing; the ships were under the enemy's fire for nearly two hours, without any material accident, with the exception of a shell striking the *L'Aigle*, and falling through her decks into the bread-room, where it exploded: one man was killed and four wounded, and her stern frame much shattered. The *Amethyst* got aground after passing Flushing.

On the 13th, the batteries before Flushing being completed, and some frigates and bombs having taken their station, a fire was opened at half past one p.m. from upwards of fifty pieces of heavy ordnance, including mortars and howitzers, which was vigorously returned by the enemy; an additional battery was finished during the night, of six twenty-four-pounders, (worked by sailors,) and the whole continued to play on the town; until late on the following day.

At half-past ten on the morning of the 14th, the following line of battle ships (anchored in the Duerlo passage) got under weigh: the *St. Domingo, Blake, Repulse, Victorious, Denmark, Audacious,* and *Venerable*—and ranged along the seafront of the town, led in by Rear-Admiral Sir R. Strachan; but before they had opened their fire, the wind came more southerly, and the *St. Domingo* grounded inside the Dogland; an officer, not knowing her situation, passed inside of her, by which means the *Blake* also grounded; the other ships were ordered to haul off to anchor as at first intended. The *Domingo* was soon got off, and the *Blake* became again afloat, and came to anchor with the rest of the squadron; the ships continued to ply the enemy with a furious cannonade until four in the afternoon, when the town presented a vast conflagration, burning in all quarters.

The firing having nearly ceased from the ramparts, Gen. Monnet, the Governor was summoned to surrender, but he having given an evasive answer, hostilities recommenced and continued until two o'clock in the morning of the 15th, when the enemy demanded a suspension of arms, and within an hour the Governor surrendered the town, (when two detachments of the Royals and 71st regiments took possession of its gates,) and the whole of the garrison, prisoners of war, besides those already taken in the different forts and islands of Walcheren, South Beveland, Shouwen, Duivland, Brouwershaven, and Zierigkzee, with all the valuable stores therein.

The loss in killed, wounded, and missing of the British, during the siege, was about seven hundred and twenty, including officers.

From this moment offensive operations seemed at an end; we were surrounded with abundance, our days were occupied in the sports of the field, our evenings passed at each others' quarters in idle and pleasant conversation, pay was issued al-

37

most to the day that it was due. Provisions of all descriptions were offered for sale at a very low rate: tea, sugar, and coffee, were not half the price of the same in England; wines, brandy, Hollands, and liqueurs, might he purchased for a mere trifle, and fat fowls or ducks for tenpence the pair.

In this land of plenty we were lulled into a fatal security, for, about the 20th, the soldiers fell ill, staggered, and dropped in the ranks, seized by dreadful fevers*, and with such rapidity did this malady extend, that in fourteen days, twelve thousand and eighty six soldiers were in hospital on board ship, or sent to England; the deaths were numerous, and sometimes sudden; convalescence hardly ever secure; the disorders ultimately destroying the constitution, and causing eventually the destruction of thousands in far distant climes.

The natives now became ill, and informed us that one-third of them were confined to their beds every autumn until the frosty weather set in, which checked the exhalations from the earth, and gave new tone to their debilitated frames, and thereby stopped the progress of the complaint.

Independently of the records of the unhealthiness of these islands, where every object depicts it in the most forcible manner, the bottom of every canal that has communication with the sea is thickly covered with an ooze, which, when the tide is out, emits a most offensive effluvium; and every ditch that is filled with water, is loaded with animal and vegetable substances. If persons living in these islands from their infancy, who practise a cleanliness that cannot be excelled, and live in good houses, cannot prevent the effects of the climate, it may readily be supposed how much more a foreign army must suffer.

The inhabitants informed us, that in the preceding autumn, two hundred French troops were quartered in the village, out of whom one hundred and sixty had the fever, and seventy of them died.

---

* The sailors on board ship did not suffer much from the malady.

Our landing had excited a great sensation in the north of France; so much so, that numerous corps of the national guards marched to the succour of Antwerp, only garrisoned when we first made our descent on the coast with three thousand men, besides the eight thousand sailors on board the fleet, that had retired up the Scheldt. Many of the national guards suffered from the climate, and shortly returned to their families with ruined constitutions.

The town of Flushing, after the siege, presented a deplorable appearance, with many houses burnt down, and most of them unroofed, and scarcely supplying sufficient covering for the sick soldiers, who continued to increase so fast, that ten inhabitants to each regiment were requested to assist as attendants in the hospitals. The medical officers were extremely harassed, numbers of them became incapable of attending on their patients, being themselves seized by the same fatal malady, so that, as the fever gained ground, the doctors diminished in numbers. At one period, four hundred and ninety-eight soldiers died in a fortnight in Walcheren, which place the Austrians were very solicitous our troops should continue to occupy as long as any chance remained for them against Napoleon, who was at this time in the very heart of their empire.

Early in September, while at dinner, a sudden order reached us to move towards the coast, when we instantly packed up and reached the beach in two hours, where the troops began their embarkation. The captain of the company, with agitated looks, ran towards me, and told me that, in the hurry of moving off, he had left the whole of his company's books in the corner of the room we had occupied, and that the commanding officer had most positively refused him permission to fetch them. Under these circumstances, and at his urgent entreaties, and promises to have a boat in waiting on my return, I undertook the unpleasant excursion, and, rapidly retracing my steps, I re-entered the village at a quick pace, in little more than an hour; it appeared quite tranquil, as if no foreigners had ever been amongst them.

One or two natives only were looking from their windows. A sudden thought now struck me that I might be seized and made prisoner, which caused me much uneasiness; but yet to decamp without accomplishing my object, was sorely against grain with me. While assailed by such conjectures I entered the door of the house that we had previously occupied, which I found open, and saw the contented inmates enjoying a comfortable meal, nor did they evince the least surprise at my reappearance. Without uttering a word, and passing into the inner apartment, I seized the books, (the dinner was still untouched on the table exactly as we had left it,) and with hasty strides re-passed the room where the family were seated, making a alight inclination of the head: they half rose at seeing me loaded; but not a syllable was exchanged between us.

Some of the inhabitants had now come out of their houses, and regarded me with suspicious looks: I feigned indifference; but no sooner cleared the village, than I started almost at speed, and had made great progress, when I espied at a distance the light wagons and fat hollow-backed horses, with flowing manes and tails, returning from the beach at a trot; and, being aware that the soldiers were not very ceremonious on these occasions, I was apprehensive the drivers of these vehicles might be disposed to treat me in the same manner, or probably take me back as a hostage, I therefore concealed myself behind a bank until they should have passed by.

Night soon came on, but I could descry the lights in the ships' tops, and, in my hurry to follow their direction, I took the wrong road, which led me into a field where it ended. However, with the hope that a short way farther would enable me to reach the beach, I darted onwards, and found a broad ditch impeding my farther progress. It was in vain I ran up and down in search of a narrow part; in almost a fit of desperation, I hurled the books across, one after the other, tried my footing, retired some paces, and, at a run, sprang across it with the greatest exertion, while a momentary joy gleamed over my countenance, on mounting a bank, to find myself at the water's edge.

The lights were still stationary, but not a boat to be seen. Owing to my great exertions and haste in. passing, over fourteen miles of ground, I was in a profuse perspiration, which was soon succeeded by a cold shivering, such as I imagined was the disorder incidental to this swampy country. I feared that I should be left to perish before I could reach the ship; a heavy dew fell, and I was almost perishing with cold, having no other covering than my light infantry jacket, sash, and pantaloons, without drawers or a waistcoat of any sort. Frequently I was forced to run up and down, to keep my blood in circulation, and my teeth from chattering. In this manner, alternately sitting, running, or casting my eye towards the lights, which, at times, and in the exuberance of my fancy, I thought were receding, I passed the dreary hours of the night.

At daybreak, some sailors pulling in shore, discovered my flying pocket handkerchief, and came to my relief, and, after a considerable pull, we found the regiment on board the *Ganges*. Then, giving my last dollar to the sailors for grog, I mounted the side of the ship, and descended into the ward-room, where I found the officers scattered about, and lying on a main-sail, that had been spread out for their accommodation.

Delivering the books to the owner, I was fully determined never again to volunteer such a Quixotic excursion. The officer assured me that all his endeavours to procure a boat had been unavailing.

The next day two hundred sick soldiers and officers were removed on board small craft to proceed to England, and, as I happened to be one of those for detachment, we left the line-of-battle ship, went on board a transport, and steered our course for the Downs, where we arrived in two days, and cast anchor for forty-eight hours, then again got under weigh, and buffeted about for four days more, between the Downs and Harwich, where we landed our sick soldiers and officers.

When we were stepping on shore, a countryman, looking towards us, exclaimed, "There goes the King's hard bargains."

The evening we landed, a fine healthy-looking young sergeant brought me the orderly-book—and, on visiting the hospital at ten o'clock the next morning, I heard he had been dead one hour. So much for the Walcheren malady! In fact, the most fatal battle could hardly have made such havoc in our ranks. Thus, in the short space of seven months, the English coast had been inundated with sick soldiers and scattered regiments from the Land's-end to Yarmouth.

Walcheren was finally evacuated in the end of December.

Napoleon had humbled his rivals, had ridden out the storm raised against him, and repulsed all his enemies. Pope Pius the Vllth had indeed thundered forth a spiritual excommunication against him and his followers at the beginning of the Austrian campaign; but he had unluckily fallen into the power of his temporal master, who, seated in the saloon of the Palace of the Tuileries, was meditating new conquests, and weaving silken cords for the Emperor of Austria's daughter.

CHAPTER 3

To the Peninsula

The regiment soon re-landed in England, and marched to Colchester, where a vast number of the men died, of ours as well as all the other corps, thereby keeping the clergy in constant requisition to repeat the funeral service over the rudely-shaped coffins of the dead soldiers. Nearly the whole of the corps to which I belonged were laid up with ague and fever, to such a degree, that those able to walk and the few fit for duty were removed to Sudbury, for the benefit of change of air. This proved very beneficial and restored the strength of those who had not been very badly affected with the malady.

At the expiration of two months we were able to muster again about two hundred, out of six, fit for duty. Those officers whose health was sufficiently re-established frequented the balls at Bury St, Edmunds, which were extremely well attended by the neighbouring families; added to these, occasional jaunts and a few private parties made the time pass pleasantly enough until we were ordered to Weeley Barracks, where we spent a sombre winter, (with two other regiments) which passed without any occurrence worth mentioning, except that of the garrison being called out to fire a *feu dé joie* in celebration of George the Third's having reigned over this country for fifty years.

In the spring we shifted our quarters to Colchester, being perfectly sickened of our rustic amusements of shooting larks, skating, or pacing up and down a solitary barrack-square of great extent, and surrounded by a rich grass country, without any thing worthy the appellation of a village for a considerable distance. Soon afterwards myself and another officer went to Portsmouth to receive volunteers. The officers of a regiment invited us to dine with them at Gosport, and so plied us with peppered turkeys' legs, devilled biscuits and port wine, that we were unable to beat a retreat until two o'clock in the morning.

On reaching the ferry, there was not a boat to be seen; wherefore, from necessity, we were reduced to content ourselves with a seat on some stone steps, and there to await the rising sun, whose beams no sooner crimsoned the western hemisphere, than we hailed the first morning ferry boat, and reached our lodging, right glad to quaff a smoking cup of coffee in order to settle our stomachs from the last night's debauch.

In a few days we left the rustic vicinity of Portsmouth, and reached the red-bricked town of Colchester, where our time passed in such amusements as are usually practised at a provincial quarter and are so well known to most of the British army, who have had the honour of promenading up and down its *pavé*.

One day a Water party was talked of, and no sooner proposed than put into execution. A boat was procured and rowers selected—the rest of the party being armed with fowling pieces for the destruction of gulls and carrion crows, or such other birds as might chance to cross us during our aquatic excursion on the river Colne. The boat being put in motion, after an hour's hard pull, the river became considerably wider, the tide was on the ebb, the weather propitious, and so much way made that we resolved to obtain a glimpse of the sea, which soon being accomplished, we pulled inshore, made good our landing and selected the most rural spot to partake of those viands prepared for the occasion, which, being spread out on nature's green carpet, were speedily devoured by eight hungry young officers, and every bottle of wine and brown stout ' emptied to the very dregs.

The party, full of hilarity, then returned to their slender bark; but great was our surprise to find it high and dry, the tide nearly out, and only a narrow stream remaining of the spacious Colne water we bad quitted a few hours before. A launch being necessary, our jackets and caps were hurled into the boat, and, by the most strenuous exertions, it was shoved through the mud, and again afloat; then rapidly plying our oars, we made some progress, notwithstanding that the tide was still running out; when at length the water entirely failed, leaving us aground, amid channel, with extensive banks of mud rising to a considerable height on each side of us—the sight of which afforded much mirth at the idea of our having rowed during high tide over hill and dale; so much for our geographical knowledge and nautical skill!

While in this plight, one of the party was in the act of .divesting himself of superfluous dress, and tying the articles into a bundle, pleading in excuse that an appointment with a *fair damsel* obliged him to land. A noisy debate ensued amongst us; by way of intimidating him at the same time, a threat was added, that should he attempt to desert, some small shot should be discharged at him. While we were loading the guns, he sprang from the bark and scrambled some yards, assailed by the vociferations of the party, but, before he had reached the prescribed distance, twenty yards, his situation became most alarming: every succeeding step, he sank deeper into the mire; and he was now up to his middle, calling out for help, forty yards from us, and one hundred from the shore. To return was impossible—the fowling pieces dropped from our hands, as we watched his motions in fearful anxiety, every instant expecting to see him disappear.

Despair gave him strength and perseverance: but he became a mass of mud, and his features were no longer distinguishable. I can truly assert, that at no period of my life did I ever feel stronger feelings of commiseration; a hundred weight seemed at my chest. In this way he continued his exertions, and, from time to time, while resting, it could scarcely be ascertained whether he was not gone altogether, so identified was he with the mud, Again he moved, and at the expiration of half an hour's toil, he emerged from his miry bed, presenting the appearance of an alligator, after a wallowing immersion, more than any thing else! As he reached the shore, the most unbounded expressions of joy on our part hailed his deliverance from his perilous situation. Then, spreading out his bundle of garments in a very dirty state he put them on, waved his hand, and speedily vanished from our view—whilst we, less adventurous, or not being so particularly engaged on that evening, were left shivering and lightly clothed, until some time after dark, when we had sufficient depth of water to enable us to steer our course.

When at length in motion, the wind being astern, the only cloak amongst us was hoisted by way of a sail, but it was long after midnight before we reached the place from whence we had started.

About this time (June 1, 1811), three hundred and twenty men of the second battalion, with a proportionate number of officers, were ordered to proceed to Portsmouth for embarkation to join the first battalion in Portugal. On the morning of their departure the bugles sounded the march. My mortification was extreme, for positively the last officer was selected to accompany them, and two of my seniors stood by my side, who of course had a prior claim to mine, and who could not succeed in obtaining permission to go; so that all hope for me seemed now entirely to vanish, and we were obliged to content ourselves by accompanying them a short way on the road, until their first halt—the merry notes of the horns striking up "over the hills and far away," the signal for wives to be torn from their husbands, children from their fathers, friends from their companions—many bidding a long and last farewell.

The detachment followed the broad path of their profession, while we, through dire necessity, took that which led to peace and pasturage amongst the Essex graziers; but no sooner had we reached our quiet quarters, than another consultation took place, between Lieutenants the Honourable Charles Gore, Wilkinson, and myself, wherein we pledged ourselves, that the trio should not be separated for individual interest, (and, as I was the junior officer, that point was of consequence to me), then hastening to the house of the senior officer, we assailed him *ensemble* by entreaties and arguments, until, finding we were bent on carrying our point, he consented to forward a memorial to the Duke of York, penned by us, which he signed.

That done, we ran down to the post office, popped it into the box, and by return of post a favourable answer was given. What a moment! Gore and myself rubbed our hands and the little corporal Wilky (for that rank he had borne at the Military College at Marlow, and still continued the title), fell on his knees and returned thanks to Heaven, for his good fortune. Our heavy baggage was crammed into the store, and ourselves, with light hearts, that evening proceeded to London.

Notwithstanding the usual hurry and preparation when going on foreign service, I managed to find my way to Wimbledon Common, where, I heard, a grand review was to take place on the 10th of June of the household cavalry, a brigade of hussars, commanded by Lord Paget, (now Marquis of Anglesea), a brigade of the foot guards, a battalion of foot artillery, wearing cross belts and white pouches, armed with muskets and a multitude of volunteers, besides a proportional train of artillery. When the Prince Regent rode down the line, I was much struck at the Duke of York's preceding him, dismounting in front of the two regiments of foot guards, and standing with his sword across his body, while his royal brother passed. This was an excellent example of discipline, so like the prince, the soldier, and the gentleman.

The next day, leaving the metropolis, we arrived at the place of embarkation, and so managed as to meet the detachment about the same distance from Portsmouth, that we had left them on the road from Colchester; being not a little anxious to observe the astonishment that our unexpected reappearance would create amongst them.

My friend instantly ran towards me and expressed the happiness he felt at meeting me in such a way; and, almost in the same breath, said, "Oh! We have had such fun this morning!"

On leaving Chichester at the break of day, the head of the column had been thrown into the greatest confusion by the assistant surgeon; "Halt! halt!" cried he, "stop, pray stop; you are trampling on my teeth," at the same moment throwing himself on the ground, and groping in the dust for four artificial teeth that had dropped from his mouth. The officers and soldiers were confounded at his exclamations, while the wondering circle encompassed him in mute expectation. At length, having put several questions, to which they only obtained confused and unintelligible answers, an officer ordered the men to proceed; and several voices, joining in chorus, exclaimed: "Why, he's mad; the doctor's intellects are impaired;"—for they did not fully comprehend his real loss, owing to his wild incoherent and extraordinary gesticulations—nor did he overtake the party or make his reappearance until they had halted at the halfway house, where he found them seated round a smoking tea urn, hot muffins, toast, chickens, ham, and all those little delicacies so tempting after an early walk to those possessing youth) health, and *good grinders.*

The woebegone countenance of the doctor, on his entering the room, caused a momentary commiseration; but no sooner did he open his mouth, and display the scant orifice, which no longer left any doubt of the-nature of the loss he had sustained, than bursts of merriment, and noisy pity, were the only consolation the unlucky and crestfallen *medico* received—who merely vented his wrath in broken monosyllables, no longer daring to trust his mouth with a laugh.

The *Monarch* transport of three masts, and of considerable tonnage, was lying at anchor at Spithead for our reception.

Nearly the whole of us being embarked, and the Blue Peter flying at the mast head on the 18th, there was a sufficient warning to the few left on shore to hasten on board. The sails being hoisted, and spreading their white bosoms to the gale, we cut through the water, with a spanking breeze, cleared the Needles, and, steering a prosperous course, in three days were brought into the Bay of Biscay. The wind howled, the vessel heaved and cracked, one instant on high, and the next moment hurried downwards as if about to be engulfed and buried in the mighty waters; the huge waves lashed and beat against her sides with foaming violence, whilst every loose article rattled about the cabin; the strife of pots and kettles being only interrupted by the smashing of cups and saucers, and other brittle utensils.

During this combination of sounds I lay in my berth, with a wash-hand basin betwixt my legs, ready at a moment's warning, and with my eyes, half-closed, fixed on a solitary candle, sliding to and fro on the table, and threatening to extinguish itself into one of the lower berths. Thus stretched out, and sinking into a disturbed and feverish slumber, I soon again awoke with my tongue parched, a horrible taste in my mouth, and my lips glued together, counting the tedious hours of the coming morn, till I should be enabled to procure a refreshing glass of water.

At last the happy moment arrived, my trembling hand was put forth to grasp the liquid stream—my mouth opened— but my nose gave warning of that which smelt and tasted like the Harrogate Spa, and was anything but *aqua pura*. The next evening I made an effort to gain my sea legs, crept out of the cabin, mounted on the deck, and slipped and staggered towards a poultry-coop, on which I sank in a reclining position, to inhale the freshness of the air. The dark and broad clouds flitted past, and at intervals veiled the moon, which seemed flying away in the opposite direction, and smiling in derision at our clumsy progress, (with double reefed topsails,) over the troubled waves. Perpetual motion seemed at last accomplished, as the bows and stern of the vessels rose alternately, and in rapid succession.

In the morning a thick haze hung over the atmosphere, through which we could discern the outlines of the ponderous mountains of Spain, rising one above the other, until their gloomy shadows were lost to view in the interior.

Chapter 4

We Arrive in Portugal

On the tenth morning, with a gentle breeze, and spotless sky, we glided along the rugged coast of, Portugal, and observed a number of barks making towards us, decorated with white flapping sails, and filled with swarthy ragamuffin pilots, who were hallooing, pulling, and hauling at each other in a confused way, which gave the frail bark the appearance of being about to overturn keel uppermost, and leave its brown visaged, cocked-hatted navigators floundering and splashing for their existence in the briny waves of the dark blue ocean.

Shortly afterwards we entered the sparkling waters of the Tagus, skirted by purple-capped mountains, curling vines, fragrant orange groves, and a white city, reflected in its glassy waters, canopied by an azure sky, a golden sun, and a genial atmosphere. We dropped our anchor within a short distance of Lisbon. The following day, the 28th, we landed, and the soldiers took up their quarters at the Convento di Carmo.

The interior of the city by no means corresponds with the exterior viewed at a distance, owing to the general narrowness of the streets that are choked up in some places with heaps of filth, continually stirred up, and eagerly devoured by packs of prowling and half-famished dogs.

Towards evening a small piece of paper was handed to myself and friend, with the name of a Portuguese inserted, at whose house we were to be quartered. Having made the necessary inquiries of a bragging native, he pointed out to us the direction we ought to take, and also made motions, by way of intimating to us our good fortune in having so spacious an abode for our accommodation. Having traversed over a great portion of the town, in search of our billet, we at length came to a large, gloomy looking mansion, the door of which we found open, and ascended a dirty stone staircase, where at each landing-place we found ponderous doors: but it was in vain we kicked, thumped, and called; the echo of our own voices was the only answer returned.

Night coming on, we again sallied forth into the streets, and, while passing near a church, we met a procession following a deceased nobleman for interment. Large wax tapers being offered to us, about four feet long, and thick in proportion, we each grasped one, and entered the church with others. The lid of the coffin being removed, we beheld the pale corpse attired in a magnificent satin dress, and mantle superbly embroidered with gold; the pantaloons were of white silk, and full satin rosettes were attached to the velvet shoes. A full-dress court sword lay by his side, and a black hat of velvet, with a nodding plume of ostrich feathers, looped up with a brilliant stone, rested at the head of the coffin. His costume, in short, was similar to that worn by Don Juan on our own stage. The ceremony being concluded, a man stepped forward with a basket filled with quick lime, which he threw on the dead body in the presence of the spectators: that done, all the bystanders instantly retired, and gave up their tapers to persons waiting to receive them at the church door.

Much fatigued, we returned, and reached the cloisters of the convent, in search of our servants and baggage. While we were debating on the best method of securing a place of rest for the night, an athletic figure came stalking towards us, enveloped in the garments of a friar, having a fine dark countenance, and jet black hair cut short and shaved on the crown of his head, about two inches in diameter. He demanded how it was that we seemed wandering about at so late an hour of the night.

We briefly informed him of our situation, when he most courteously invited us to follow him and led us through several passages and up many flights of stairs to a couple of small bedrooms at the very top of the convent; then retired for a short time, and reappeared, loaded with wine and sweetmeats. My friend had previously been in the country, and therefore could make himself understood; and, as he was acting quarter-master at eighteen for the detachment, he was glad of this opportunity which now offered to be near the men, to enable him to superintend the serving out of rations early on the following morning. Our host proved to be the abbot, and after a short conversation he wished us a sound repose to follow our sea voyage, and retired.

During our stay at Lisbon, we made a point of seeing the handsome churches, the opera, the grand aqueduct and other curiosities. The night previously to our quitting this place, the Consul gave a ball, to which we were invited; and I was surprised to observe the Portuguese gentlemen in coloured clothes, with pink and various-coloured silk stockings. The costume of the ladies was gaudy, but their dresses were ill made and worse put on. We only danced one set, and, some hours having elapsed without any appearance of supper, which was of serious consideration to us, as we were ordered to be on the banks of the Tagus the next morning at daylight for the purpose of embarking in boats for Villada, some distance up the river, I explored a suite of rooms at the extremity of which I espied on a sideboard a huge dish filled with wafer cakes: but, not wishing to attack such a prize without an ally, I hastened to my companion to communicate my good luck, who, without further ado, assisted at their demolition. Although they were the largest of the kind I had ever before seen, our young teeth cracked them with an extraordinary rapidity; *smash! smash!* they went, and two layers had now disappeared, when a Portuguese attendant out of livery, observing such dreadful havoc, advanced to their rescue, assuring us with solemn physiognomy that they were reserved for the ladies. Hostilities ceased on their protector's consenting to procure us a bottle of wine, two goblets of which we hastily swallowed, and instantly sallied out into the odoriferous streets.

"*Agua fresca, agua fresca*" resounded from all quarters, while buckets of the most nauseous contents fell with a splash from the upper stories of houses into the space below—like the bursting of water spouts.

"Conceal yourself," cried my friend, "or you will be scented and sprinkled all over."

In this manner, running the gauntlet at every turning, we proceeded until we reached the dark and narrow flight of stairs leading to our heavenly apartments, where we had no sooner entered than I put my foot on the body of a man, who lay stretched at full length across the doorway. I hung back, and we re-groping our way down into the court yard, and alarming the guard, lights were procured: the rays of the lamp fell on the face of my drunken snoring servant, encircled with bottles—having emptied the contents into his own stomach. From the effects of this he had scarcely recovered at the hour of our departure, leaving me the agreeable task of packing up, and seeing my mule safe off, as the baggage and animals were to cross the grand lines of Torres Vedras, and meet us at the place of disembarkation.

Passing through the principal streets, we entered the boats for our conveyance (after a stay of eleven days at Lisbon) and landed in the evening at Villada.

CHAPTER 5

Enter the Light Division

Our animals and baggage having joined us the next day, we took the road towards Santarem, and about dusk reached the causeway leading up a steep hill into the town, where the French, previously to their retreat under Marshal the Prince of Essling, had thrown the dead from their hospitals into the wells—the idea of which caused such horrible thoughts, that we could scarcely summon up sufficient resolution to drink while at that place.

The excessive heat of the following day having somewhat subsided, towards the cool of the evening we began our march, but, by some unaccountable accident, took the wrong road for upwards of a league before the mistake was found out. Retreading our steps, we at length regained the identical spot from whence we had previously started nearly three hours before; glancing my eye towards the battlements of the town, a smile prophetic passed my countenance, that I should not again behold its turrets. Turning our backs, and pursuing the right road, we gaily tramped along toward Golegam; and, as the morning dawned I was loudly knocking for admittance at the door of a small house, on the confines of the churchyard, that was strewed with skulls which had been torn from the sepulchres and graves, in search of gold, by the French soldiery.

After the usual halt we pursued our march through Punhete to Abrantes, where two of us were nearly carried away amongst the quicksands, while bathing in the river Tagus, and only reached the shore by making the greatest efforts. Various individuals had been drowned at this place by the current.

Having halted here one whole day, we crossed over the bridge of boats to the southern province of the Alentejo, and entered Gaviao, where I was billeted in a very poor house. At night I entered a recess, much fatigued, and, upon quitting the mattress in the morning, the bugs had made such a feast on my right leg from the hip to the very sole of my foot, so that I could scarcely walk, and was in a most dreadful state of irritation.

Passing onwards in our march, on the ninth day, we ascended a high hill on the summit of which stood Aronches, commanding an extensive prospect over a diversified sandy country, intersected with forests, vineyards, rocks, and small fields of Indian corn, and encompassed by dilapidated walls formed of loose stones carelessly heaped one on another without mortar. The streets of the town were narrow, and almost deserted, with huge shapeless rocks at every few yards, rearing their heads, and blocking up the way, whilst a solitary Portuguese was seen striking an old battered guitar with all his fingers (as on a tambourine) and hallooing forth some ditty loud enough to be heard in the distant valleys. The heat of the day was quite overpowering, the firmament was of heavenly blue, while the sun shone forth in full splendour, forcing us to retire to some shady spot from its scorching rays, and to take some repose after the fatigues of the march.

Towards the close of the evening we again stood on the ramparts to inhale the cool and delicious air. The shades of night had scarcely hidden the face of the country from our view, when the moon, rising in all her grandeur, threw a pale light around, and tipped with silver the battlements of those venerable towers built by the Moors, which for centuries had endured, and had frowned defiance on the flitting shadows of many generations, gliding by their grey walls unheeded and forgotten.

As we gazed in sweet contemplation on the surrounding scenery, all nature seemed hushed, and the universe sunk into slumber, when suddenly the bell of a monastery close at hand tolled loudly, and in the gentle breeze, at intervals, we heard the solemn dirge of a religious procession, which, by degrees, arose on the ear, and gradually increasing became louder, and swelled in to such an awful bass strain, as one might conceive to inspire reflection in the firm, horrors in the nervous, and all the terrors of purgatory in the dying. The long procession of monks passed us, wrapped in their sombre drapery, as if they had emerged from the very bowels of the earth. The scene was impressive.

After we had retired, my slumbers were disturbed by the horrors of the nightmare; and, when the merry rays of the sun sparkled in at the windows the next morning, I felt as if delivered out of some dungeon, longed for the camp, and hoped that, should fate cut short my career, the sun and moon might alternately throw their rays over my expiring body, rather than that I should die a lingering death, surrounded by wax tapers and priest-craft, and then buried in satin and gold, and finally extinguished by a basket of quick lime.

On the 20th of July we descended into the valley, and, at the edge of a wood, awaited the coming of the division, from an advanced camp on their way to Castello de Vida; Every eye was on the stretch, and in the distance we descried a cloud of dust rolling towards us, the bright sparkling rays of the sunbeams playing on the soldiers' breast plates, when suddenly the leading regiment of the Light Division burst forth; their bronzed countenances and light knapsacks, and their order of march, all united to inspire a conviction that their early discipline had not only been maintained amidst privations, battles and camps, but had become matured by experience.

They had reversed mountains, and forded rivers; the grim and icy hand of death had grasped many in the unhealthy marshes of the Alentejo, and with sure effect had scattered balls amidst their ranks without distinction: yet the remainder of these veterans were still bent onwards, to gather fresh laurels in the rugged and uncertain paths of fortune. Seven regiments of light infantry and riflemen defiled before us with their threadbare jackets, their brawny necks loosened from their stocks, their wide and patched trousers of various colours, and brown-barrelled arms slung over their shoulders, or carelessly held in their hands, whilst a joyous buzz ran through the cross-belted ranks, as their soldier-like faces glanced towards us to greet many of their old comrades now about to join in their arduous toils after a long separation. A cloud of dust alone marked their further progress as they receded from our view.

Following in succession, we brought up the rear. At the expiration of an hour's march, we entered a wood, formed column, called the roll, and the whole division was then dismissed. The assembled multitude of voices, the tearing and cutting down of branches of trees, crackling of fires, rattling of canteens, shooting of bullocks through the head, and the hurrying of parties of soldiers for rum and biscuit for rations, the neighing of horses, braying asses and rampant mules, all resounded throughout the forest, giving new life and merry echoes to its most intimate recesses. Groups of officers stood in circles; every countenance seemed decked in smiles, and a hearty welcome greeted us from all hands.

Under the wide-spreading branches of a venerable cork-tree, decorated with pack-saddles, accoutrements, and other military trappings, dinner was served up and laid out on a pair of hampers, which served us instead of a table. Beef, biscuit, tea, rum, and wine, composed our fare, it being a usual custom to join breakfast and dinner, so as to make one meal serve for the twenty-four hours, the troops merely halting to cook and refresh themselves during the heat of the day. A more happy meal, I can safely say, I never partook of; and with infinite admiration did I regard the purple jackets and battered epaulettes of my companions.

Our small keg of wine being emptied, the word passed to pack up and accoutre; and, in an incredibly short space of time, the column re-formed.

The "assembly" sounded (the signal of march) threes, from the right of companies, the bands struck up, and at the end of two hours' march, and towards nightfall, we entered another wood. The same ceremony gone through as already described, the blankets were spread out, the earth our bed, knapsacks our pillows, and the overhanging trees our canopy, the busy hum of life no longer vibrated through the bivouac, and thousands of soldiers slumbered and reposed their weary limbs, lying scattered throughout the forest, or around the dying embers of expiring fires.

My companions insisted on stretching themselves on each side of me, protesting that they ought to do thus, as a protection against cold for the first two or three nights, since a very heavy dew fell, so as almost to wet through the blankets, notwithstanding the great heat of the weather by day. For some time I was unable to close my eyes, owing to some insects flocking up my legs in swarms, and creating much irritation.

Let us, for a moment, withdraw the veil of futurity, and make a few anticipations. On my right tranquilly slumbers a youthful warrior of sixteen years old, and on my left unconsciously sleeps the other, one year older. Lieutenant E. Freer is doomed to undergo two more years of the toils of war, to suffer sickness and privation, and, at the sanguinary assault of Badajoz, to receive a severe wound in the upper part of the thigh; and lastly, at the age of nineteen, while in the Pyrenees, a ball passes through his right arm, and enters his side: he staggers, utters three words, and falls a lifeless corpse amid those dreary regions!

Lieutenant J. Considine, at the assault of Badajoz, receives a ball through his body, and, stretched on the damp sod, enveloped in darkness, bleeds inwardly. A light is held over his pale face, and discovers the blood flowing from his mouth. Borne, however, to a place of security, he recovers. The next year he is tormented by a malignant fever, and afterwards, on the highest pinnacle of the Pyrenees, a ball strikes him; his thigh-bone is broken near the hip, he cries for help. I look down; he lies prostrate between my legs. The balls carry death and destruction around; we are under the walls storming a fort, and fighting hand to hand. Four soldiers attempt to carry him off, and, not being aware of the place of his wound, hoist him up, and turn his left foot outwards over his shoulder; by which means the thigh-bone is completely broken asunder. His screams are dreadful, and two of the soldiers fall dead, pierced with balls. The battle ended, he is carried to a place of security, where he eventually recovers!—and he now commands the 53rd regiment.

Early the next morning we were again on the road. The martial music struck up, and continued to play for a short distance; the word passed to march at ease: conversation then commenced. The soldiers lighted their pipes and, before the sun had reached its meridian, we filed into Portalegre. The streets were marked off, in the first instance, for different corps; then the houses, again, subdivided amongst officers and soldiers; the latter portioned off according to the size of the different dwellings; the butt ends of the soldiers' firelocks serving as knockers, to rouse the sulky inmates, who would fain plead ignorance of the arrival of so many guests.

It was by no means an uncommon occurrence for owners of houses to try all kinds of expedients, by absence, paltry excuses, or otherwise, to drive away the tired officers in disgust, who presented billets of lodgement. One day, an officer on the staff had patiently waited some time at a door without being able to gain admittance, until at length the *patron* walked up from the street and feigned civility, making a low bow, and saying to the officer, "Señor, I have no key;" when the officer returned his salute, coolly lifted up his long leg, and applied it to the door with such force that it flew open at the first blow—then turning to the astonished Portuguese, said, "*Señor, tiengo bon chave,*"* and, at a slow march, and with clanking sabre, took possession of the house. From that day he was known by the appellation of *Bon chave* throughout the army.

Another division entered the town the same day. The army was composed of eight divisions of infantry, besides cavalry and artillery; the former force was known throughout the army by the following familiar appellations: "the gentlemen's sons," "the surprisers," "the fighting division," "the supporters," "the invisibles," "the never heard of," "the all-sorts," and "the division:" but, before the end of this most sanguinary war, they all fought again and again, covering themselves with fame and lasting glory.

The following day we proceeded to Castello de. Vida, an ancient fortified place within a league of Marvao. The first brigade entered the town, and the second bivouacked in a grove without its walls. The adjacent country presented a wild Appearance; but more particularly the latter town, which was perched on a rugged and stupendous mountain, inaccessible on every side, save only one approach, and even that impracticable for carriages, the road winding under the overhanging shelving of rocks, others of which reared their rugged points in the very middle of this (hardly to be so termed) pathway. A party of us with difficulty ascended to this strange place, at a season of the year when every particle of vegetation is parched and dried up. The adjacent grey precipices presented a frightful wilderness—the hiding-place of innumerable wolves.

The mind of the beholder on surveying such a prospect became perplexed how so barren a spot, even at the remotest period of antiquity, should have been fixed on for any

---

* A jargon mixture of the Portuguese, Spanish, and French languages was frequently resorted to in our anxiety to make ourselves understood by the natives, and when one word failed another was substituted. An officer who had just entered the country was most anxious to procure an egg, and having failed to make himself understood, as a last resource, he cut a piece of *pipe clay* into the shape of an egg, and was instantly supplied.

human habitation, far more for a fortification. Some cannon of ancient construction were still on the ramparts, but few mounted, and even the carriages of those mouldering to decay. Here and there a few miserable Portuguese were observed basking in a sunny corner, grouped and huddled together, and consisting of young and old women with dark countenances, and still darker tresses, enveloped in shabby blue cloth cloaks, and extracting *piochos* from each other's heads; that occupation being the greatest source of delight and amusement amongst them. Their general food consisted of roasted chestnuts, washed down with cold spring water—which caused their teeth to decay at a very early age; and when they could procure a little dried fish, or *sardines* with black sour bread, they would consider it a point of luxury.

The extreme heat of the weather, and the exertions that we had used to reach this spot, created excessive thirst; looking round, therefore, in search of a house of entertainment, we espied a leafless branch of a tree suspended over a doorway, which bespoke the object of our search. On our entering and demanding wine, the corner of a pig-skin was untied, out of which spouted the wine into a filthy measure. It was strongly impregnated with the taste of the skin, about milk warm, and exceedingly thick, owing to its having been recently removed from a mule's back. These animals are usually loaded with two dried pig-skins, sewed up and slung across a pack saddle for the conveyance of wine from one place to the other—the muleteer being astride in the middle, and, above all, singing a wild air, and beating time with his heel a against the bags.

Quitting this isolated place, and returning to our quarters, we remained there two or three days, and then resumed our march towards the northern frontier. The first night we halted in a wood near Niza. The next morning, an hour before daylight, we started, and, while passing over the summit of a high hill, as the morning dawned, we observed a thick mist overspreading an extensive valley. As the sun rose, its refulgent light pierced through the white fog, which resembled a beautiful floating sea, out of which peeped forth the tops of hills covered with investing shrubs. As the rolling mist passed away, so these apparent islands enlarged, until nothing of this enchanting illusion remained, except a bare country covered with *gum cistus,* (a small tree,) producing a most sickly smell, and the more particularly to those with empty stomachs.

After a fatiguing weary march, half suffocated by heat, added to which our eyes, nose, and mouth, were filled with sand, we descended the pass of Villa Velha, where we observed a number of vultures perched on the pinnacles of inaccessible rocks, as if watching our motion, or waiting in anticipation of more devoted victims.

Crossing the Tagus by the bridge of boats, we bivouacked under the agreeable shade of an olive grove. The surrounding scenery presented everywhere a beautiful, romantic, and grand spectacle; the river foamed over the rocks that had fallen into its dark stream from the overhanging crags. The narrow road running at the base of the adjacent mountains was filled with loose stones; woe, therefore, to the sore-footed soldier who happened to stumble amongst them! Woe to the sick or wounded to whose lot it fell to be placed in those Portuguese cars, rudely constructed, with small solid wooden wheels, revolving *on* an unoiled axletree, and causing an indescribable creaking noise to be heard at a very considerable distance, sounds so horrible, that the bigoted peasantry declare they frighten away the *evil* spirit of Old Nick himself!

The jolting of these vehicles frequently tore off the plasters, and ripped open anew the wounds of the suffering soldiers; nor was it at all unusual to behold the sick, wounded and dying, with pallid countenances expressive of unheard-of agonies, while these engines of torture, drawn by a pair of bullocks, with their heads thrust under a shapeless piece of wood, (for the purpose of yoking them together,) rolled on their heavy way. The conductor guided them with a long pole, with a piece of pointed iron at the end of it, which he poked into the beasts' necks, and directed them by such sort of "sharp practice".

CHAPTER 6

We Enter Spain

Continuing our route through the town of Castello Branco and several villages, we obtained to the left a view of the tremendous ridge of snow-capped mountains of the Sierra d'Estrella. The barrier of bare and rugged rocks towards the Spanish side, when gilded by the departing glare of the setting sun, assumes the grandest appearance, and, in the revellings of imagination, a thousand palaces of burnished gold may be fancied amid these adamantine rocks, vying with each other in height and endless variety of form. Afar off, an old monastery might be descried, perched on the summit of bare and wild precipices; its spiral turrets shooting on high, and encompassed by the immensity of space; the frowning battlements overhanging the valley below, and threatening to overwhelm the passing traveller with loose stones and crumbling ruins—while the deep tones of the monastic bell chimed the vesper hour.

On a solitary eminence a lonely shepherd stood, tending his flock, with a carbine slung across his shoulder, and a couple of wolf-dogs crouching at his feet, their necks encircled by strong iron collars bristling with long spikes, to protect them against the grip of the voracious wolves. All around seemed of other times in this precipitous part of the country, composed principally of solid rock. The rude hand of time had identified towns and villages with their primitive stones; houses had fallen to decay, but nothing new had arisen on the ruins;

streets branched out, but it was no wise uncommon to find huge rocks, of many tons weight, sticking up in the middle of them, never having been removed, and leaving the traveller the option of a choice of one of the two narrow roads round these natural obstacles.

As the division threaded its march over winding and difficult roads, its horse-artillery might be heard rumbling in the rear, while the winding notes of the bugle horns echoed in the distant valleys.

Major-General R. Craufurd commanded the Light Division. His arrangements and regulations of march stood unrivalled; at the expiration of every hour, the division formed close columns of regiments, and halted for about ten minutes; the leading corps were generally again marching off by the time the rear came up. When any obstacles came across the line of route, each officer, commanding a company, saw that they were closed up before he put them into the regular marching pace, and that even if a break in the column happened of fifty yards between each company. I have frequently witnessed the whole division marching in this manner through a difficult country, by which means they were always in hand, ready to engage by companies.

If a man found himself exhausted between the halts, the senior officer of the company ordered him to have a ticket, which he was obliged to hand over on his arrival in camp, or to show to anyone who questioned him on the road as to his authority for being absent from his corps. The code of discipline was very strict, but everyone knew exactly that which was required of him, and, in the event of any irregularity even on the line of route, amidst wilds and mountains, no matter where, the column was closed up *instanter,* and a summary punishment inflicted on the spot. This was far from harsh treatment: it was lenity in the end; it preserved the health of the soldiers, by keeping them in their ranks; it maintained discipline and concentration, the great requisites in war; it prevented marauding on the inhabitants, soldiers were debarred from coming to unpleasant collisions and assassin-like encounters; and thus peace and harmony were established among those whom we were bound to defend.

The followers of the division (and of the army) were composed of lank Barbary bulls and bullocks; mules loaded with bags of biscuit, kegs of rum, kegs of ball cartridge, reserve ammunition; a few hardy women (mistresses, or wives of soldiers) mounted on strong and weak asses; Portuguese boys, drivers, officers, milch goats, purveyors and medicine chests; and sometimes a few suttlers, headed by a man better known by the name of *Tick*, owing to his giving credit to officers in precarious times. This person, by the bye, as a natural consequence, would lay on an enormous percentage for small articles of luxury; disposing of bread itself at nine shillings a four-pound loaf. Tea, sugar, and brandy in a proportionate ratio.

On the 9th of August we emerged from Portugal, and passed Albergeria, a village on the Spanish frontier. My astonishment and curiosity were highly excited on observing the extraordinary difference between the natives of Spain and Portugal, and that it could be possible, for people living so near one another, to be so dissimilar, in complexion, costume, and manners—even when inhabiting respectively the banks of a narrow stream, which holds its course near the frontier of the two kingdoms, being scarcely two yards wide, and only ankle deep.

The merry Spanish peasant girls came forward with bold smiles and strutting steps, greeting us in familiar terms, such as *Vivan los Ingleses; vivat los Coluros, y Milaños a ustedes;* then pulling out their *castanets,* jumping and saying, *den nosotros la música: vivan los Ingleses.* Others came running, forward with pitchers, and, against all rules, broke the ranks, insisting on supplying the soldiers with water. Some of them were extremely pretty, their lively manner and becoming costume made them appear to great advantage. Their complexions generally are of a fine healthy brown, they have sparkling black eyes, and dark hair combed back and tied in a knot with a bunch of black ribbons, hanging down their backs; their jackets of brown or blue cloth are laced up the front, and slit open at the sleeves, so as to display a white chemise. Their petticoats are of various bright colours, reaching just below the knee; and their stockings are red, blue, and white, most fancifully worked up the middle of the calf of the leg. Their feet are remarkably small, with silver buckles in their shoes, besides gold or silver ornaments in their ears and round their necks. When going to church or visiting each other, they wear a black cloth *mantilla* over the head, and held across the breast with both hands. On entering a place of worship, they cross themselves quickly and drop down on the pavement on both knees, looking very devout, unless some object of attraction happens to catch their attention.

The male peasantry are hardy and well-made, but by far the shortest race of men I ever saw in any other country, although their picturesque dress gives them the deceptive appearance of a height which they really do not possess. Their principal amusement out of doors is the game of hand ball, or throwing an iron bar with the right hand a considerable distance, and also pitching it betwixt their legs in various other ways which may suit their fancy. On Sundays and fete days they dance *boleros* with their village maids, who beat time with their *castanets* and sing when music cannot be procured. That favourite dance is formed by four or eight couples standing opposite one another, not unlike the formation of a quadrille party. The male attire in the province of Leon is a large *sombrero*, or broad-brimmed hat, with a wide black ribbon tied round it, a brown jacket slit open at the sleeves, a blue or green velveteen waistcoat decorated with two rows of long-shanked silver buttons, and cut out at the breast, showing a white shirt, handsomely plaited or worked, with a collar about half an inch wide, fastened with a clasp. The belt round their waists is of durable leather, about five inches broad. Their breeches are dark brown, stockings of similar colour, with shoes and silver buckles. When they go out, or during holidays, they envelope themselves in large brown cloaks, which they throw gracefully over the shoulder, and conduct themselves with a manner and deportment very far beyond the peasantry of other countries.

Their villages are built in a cluster round good churches, the body of those edifices towering high above the small houses of one story high that encircle them. The floor is usually composed of earth beat down to a hard substance. There is no glass in the windows, which .are merely small square apertures, one foot by six inches, divided by an iron bar, with a little shutter on hinges, which is closed at night. Their usual furniture consists of a bedstead, wool or straw mattress, covered by very coarse sheets and blankets, a table, two or three forms with backs to them, a large chest with a partition for the double purpose for stowing away flour and holiday apparel. Sometimes in winter a brass pan with handles is used under the table, which they fill with hot embers to keep their lower extremities warm. The only chimney in the house is in the kitchen, where they use a small iron lamp filled with *aziete,* or oil, and burn wood from their neighbouring forests, and when afar removed from woods, and that article becomes scarce, charcoal is substituted for cooking. Their usual food is sausages, garlic, and chocolate, the latter made into cakes ready sweetened, but only used as a luxury, and mixed so thick, that a tea spoon will stand upright in it. The bread is extremely white, and compressed, without yeast, made in the shape of a pancake, being ten inches in diameter, and about two inches and a half thick, and weighing four pounds.

The women wash by the side of streams, and continue to dip the articles in the water, and then strike them on a large round stone, on which they kneel, and, finally, lay them on the ground to dry, by which means they bleach their linen very white.

It is curious to observe a mother dressing a young child:

after putting on its petticoat, she rolls several yards of coarse cloth so tight round the body of the infant, that a stranger would conceive it would be unable to respire, as its little arms stick out horizontally.

We continued our march over the plain of Fuente de Guinaldo, and within half a league of that place took up our ground in a wood, where we encamped, that is to say, cut down branches of trees, and constructed huts; and although the canopy of heaven, or a rudely formed hut, for months in succession, was the only shelter for the troops, the bivouac resounded with merriment, and afforded frequent good cheer.

For my own part, I felt perfectly happy; my eyes and inclinations were directed towards the front; I felt myself securely lodged on *terra firma,* and no longer a sort of amphibious animal. I had escaped the dreadful fever and mortality of Walcheren, nor could I well call to mind the having ever experienced a day's serious illness. This was about the period of the year when the sickly season commenced; but I flattered myself that any impression on my unimpaired constitution was quite out of the question; in fact, I never troubled myself with gloomy thoughts. A wide field was now open, to which I looked forward with great anticipation, little dreaming of the example that was about to be visited, in the space of a short week, on my active limbs.

What situation is superior to the camp? And what period of a soldier's life is called to mind in such glowing colours as the days of youth, when he was reclining under the shady branches of a forest oak, surrounded by young companions in arms, with light pockets and still lighter hearts, cheerfully talking to each other of glittering and moving armies, and all the imposing grandeur and pomp of war?—Or fancy him nourishing the fonder feelings, and expatiating on the beauty of some foreign damsel, by whose wit and graces all hearts are captivated; while many another, more constant, indulges the fond hope of once more clasping the native mistress of all his thoughts to his arms, on his return to his own shores.

Spain, of all countries, tends to produce in the mind the most romantic thoughts, from the salubrity of its climate, its diversified scenery, clear sky, and bright sun—a sun which shines throughout the summer from morning till night, so that to those who sleep under the canopy of heaven all days seem the same, and when summer closes and clouds darken the atmosphere, the preceding season appears to the imagination as one continued day. These and many other feelings are indelibly fixed on the mind of a soldier, who closes his eyes on the highest mountains, in the deepest valleys, in woods, in morasses, in dusty, parched, and arid plains, or amid orange groves, luxuriant gardens, and beneath the marble fountain; or amidst frost and snow—the inmate alike of the palace, or of the peasant's menial hut—one night reposing on a bed of down, enveloped by satin drapery, the next stretching his tired limbs on the ground, or on a miserable bed filled with vermin—one hour gazing on the sumptuous, light, flowing drapery and satin slipper of the graceful *señora,* the next on the ruddy healthy cheek of the more, humble *muchacha.* All these opposite changes attend the soldiers' career in rapid succession.

But lo! dinner is served up and announced. A truce to reflections! While we were employed handling our knives and forks, displaying a hungry dexterity, and bolting morsels of unchewable ration beef, a smoke was observed issuing from a valley, in the direction of our outposts, a mile to the front, which continued to increase, and then burst into a flame. A gentle wind blew towards our bivouac. The blaze increasing, and extending with great velocity, the cry of "fire," resounded from all quarters—"The camp's on fire."

All was confusion; officers and soldiers seizing their baggage, ammunition, and horses. In the meantime, some tore large branches from the trees, and advanced to check the devouring element, the dried corn burning and whizzing towards us with the noise of a whirlwind; the heat was excessive; opposition was useless; the trees of the, forest blazing away like a wisp of straw, and the whole brigade were *en déroute*, flying to save their lives, by reaching the road, where the second brigade had hastily formed, with boughs in their hands, as a last effort to endeavour to repel this vast conflagration. Fortunately the wood here ended, and the grass burnt itself out to the edge of the sandy road, which was one of great width, such as are frequently met with in the open parts of Spain. Had I not been an eye-witness to so quick and extensive a devastation made in a short time, I could hardly have pictured to my mind such a grand and awful spectacle.

Taking up fresh ground for the night, we descended in the morning the precipitous banks of the river Agueda, leading to the remote village of Martiago, nearly at the base of the Sierra de Gata. On the night we entered it, a pack of famished wolves devoured a donkey, and tore the hind quarters of a horse away. The poor animal was found in the morning, having crawled from his ferocious pursuers into the middle of the village for refuge, in that miserable condition.

Ciudad Rodrigo was to be reconnoitred. As convoys of stores and provisions were expected from Salamanca, through the great forest, of four days' march, between those places; and as Don Julien Sanches, with his guerrillas, hovered about ready to cut off all small parties, the French were under the necessity, with incalculable inconvenience, to assemble their army, stretched over a great extent of country, to keep the inhabitants under control, to protect their hospitals, levy contributions, and to make perpetual counter-marches in order, to keep open their line of communication.

On the 11th of August, before daylight, our division was bending its course over ravines, and almost impassable pathways, to show front during a reconnaissance made by Lord Wellington, who usually wore in the field, at this period, a small low-crowned cocked hat, a blue *pelisse* coat, and a hussar sash.

The sun blazed forth as usual, (for not a drop of rain had fallen since I had put my foot into the country), and biscuit and rum were served out to refresh the exhausted soldiers; a humble refection which no one would think of grudging to those who had been under arms for ten hours, under a burning sun, and crowning the highest hills without a bush to shelter them, or a drop of water to refresh their parched lips.

With my rum in one hand, making a shallow appearance at the bottom of a soldier's tin, and my mouldy biscuit in the other, I beheld an officer approach me, in the act of drawing from his bosom an old, ragged, black silk neck-handkerchief worn out in the service, and now converted into a pocket-handkerchief. He fumbled it over for a whole corner to apply his nose to; and during this operation, his eyes were fixed on my tin. After a variety of *hems*, *coughings*, and such like indications, he took courage to beg that I would permit him to dip his dry biscuit into my shallow allowance of rum, to moisten his lips: his request being granted, and thanks returned for the given relief, he told me that, in the hurry to grasp his share, he had unfortunately upset it on the ground, and had the additional mortification to see it dry up in an instant.

We were spread out rank entire within sight of the garrison, for the governor to suppose our force stronger than it really was, so that he might inform the Duke of Ragusa, and oblige him to bring up and deploy his whole army, for the protection of his intended convoy.

Late in the evening we reached our cantonments in good spirits, though well tired, but not so much so as to prevent my making a good meal. Turning into a small recess, and getting into bed for the first time for weeks, after some hours I awoke rather feverish, went to the door in my shirt to cool myself, and found the air so refreshing that I continued stationary for a considerable time, certainly much longer than my prudence ought to have dictated; however, I did not feel any ill effects from it at the time.

On the day following, our paymaster was encircled by a group of officers, who were listening to his odd remarks, relative to warfare. He declared that he hated *bullets* and *swords,* but with fists he flattered himself he was able to cope with, and would not turn his back on any man.

"Oh!" said he, "how I should like to see a fine boiled leg of pork, and a pease pudding, smoking before me; why the very thought makes me ravenous, and I could eat anything, from a gnat to an elephant; yes sir, I could eat an elephant stuffed with militiamen!" Then with both hands, pulling his cheeks, his breeches and his waistcoat, for in quarters he actually wore the identical dress he had joined the regiment in; "Look at these," said he, "why they fitted me as tight as a drum before I came to this cursed country; and look at them now! Well, only let me get my wife on my knee by my comfortable fireside once more, and, if ever I leave old England again, may I be————! and as my poor brother *did die,* I wish he had taken his departure before he ever persuaded me to enter the army!"

CHAPTER 7

I am Attacked by Illness

Three days after our long reconnaissance I became blind with *ophthalmia*, was seized with violent rheumatic pains in the soles of my feet, and took to my bed. My legs and knees swelled to an enormous size, first turning red, then blue, and I was no longer able to move.

Many other officers became sick, and were ordered to the rear. I for one, mattress and all, was shoved into a Spanish car. Our feelings during the passage of the Agueda were indescribable.— Ye invalids, stretched on your beds of down! Comfort yourselves; submit to your pains with Christian philosophy, and bless your lucky stars that you did not belong to the army of Portugal. Rejoice that your very lives are not shaken out of you by such ups and downs; first over one rock, then over another, and dragged along by bullocks sometimes forced into a run, owing to the steepness of the adamantine roads. I could no longer bear the terrible pain. In my shirt, with my legs enveloped in bandages of the car, I begged and entreated to be lifted out, being quite helpless and blind.

To get on a mule's back was quite out of the question, my legs and knees were so inflamed. At length some sick soldiers offered to try and carry or rather drag me from rock to rock. First I got a jolt on one side, then an unintentional bump on the other; the men were exhausted; and I entreated them to hold up my feet, (while my head lay in the road), for I could not bear them on the ground.

At the end of the second day's tormenting journey, we entered Castel Nero. The cars were drawn round a stone fountain, and while waiting for our billets from the *Juez de Fora,* the howling of wolves was distinctly heard in all directions, amid the surrounding woods and rocks.

For five burning days we travelled from morning until nightfall at the rate of a mile an hour. Each night I was dragged out of the car, mattress and all, shoved into some horrible recess that was almost alive with vermin, and replaced in my uneasy vehicle in the morning for the continuation of the journey. On the fifth day, when within two leagues of Celorico (the place of our destination), we drew up, as Major Ellers of our regiment requested that he might rest for a short time, since he could no longer bear the jolting of his vehicle. In a few minutes however he expired, and his body was carried forward and interred.

The heat of the weather was almost past endurance. On our arrival at Celorico, with an empty room for my quarter and the floor for my resting place, I remained sixty days nearly immoveable, my only covering a filthy blanket, which had been stained all over from my mule's sore back. On the journey it had been placed under the animal's pack saddle to save its back, by day, while in turn I had the benefit of it as a covering by night. In this miserable plight, what with bleeding and blistering, and long confinement, I had become a perfect skeleton, and reduced to the most wretched condition.

Five medical officers came to hold a consultation at the foot of my mattress, and, having examined my now lank legs, and big feet, they assured me, that they could not hold out any hope of a speedy recovery, and even doubted whether I should ever again be enabled to straighten my right leg, the knee of which had become contracted during the pains of my rough journey.

The staff doctors held out every inducement to persuade me to go to England, by first offering a spring wagon to convey me to Lisbon. My suffering had been great, my arms hung nearly useless by my side, my legs refused their office: yet I still cherished the hope, that they would again carry me forward. Doctor MacLean most kindly pressed me to acquiesce in their advice, but without effect (poor gentleman—I understood he died a few days subsequently of a fever!)—how could I leave the army, whom I found amongst mountains feeding on hard biscuit and drinking rum impregnated with the mosquitoes? A pretty warlike story to recount at home! The very thought was frightful!

More bleeding and blistering were therefore resorted to, by which means, added to a good constitution, at the expiration of another month I was enabled with the assistance of crutches to reach my window, the trellis work of which being thrown open offered me ineffable delight at once more enjoying the sight of a few living objects in the street. The rain now fell in torrents for days together, and thousands of British and Portuguese soldiers (now crowding the churches which had been converted into hospitals) were dying by hundreds; of fever produced by the sickly season. The excruciating torments, suffering and privations of the common soldiers were such, that an adequate description is impossible—many of them lingering in raging fevers, stretched out on the pavement, the straw that had been placed for their comfort, having worked from under them during their agonies, while hundreds of flies settled on and blackened their dying faces: and so stationary did these tormentors become, that those who still maintained sufficient power were obliged to tear them from off their faces, and squeeze them to death in their hands.

Cars piled up, and loaded with the remains of these unfortunate victims to disease, daily passed through the streets for the purpose of pitching their bodies into some hole by way of interment. The medical officers were overpowered by the numbers of sick, and also fell ill themselves, so that it was a total impossibility, notwithstanding their strenuous efforts, to surmount all difficulties, and to pay that attention to all that could have been wished. The very hospital orderlies were exhausted by attending, burying, and clearing away the dead. These scenes of misery cannot be fancied: the sick pouring into the town, lining the streets, and filling every house, set at nought all theoretical conception. Our paymaster entered the town with a raging fever. His hopes were not realized: he never again beheld his wife or his comfortable fireside. At the end of a few days' anguish he expired, and was buried with the rest.

Captain Poppleton was the commandant at this station. Officers of other corps held similar commands (with certain privileges) at *Belem, Santarem, Niza*, and other towns for the purpose of regulating quarters for the sick and stragglers of the army.

At the expiration of four unhappy months I became so far convalescent, as to be enabled to proceed to join my corps. I counted every step forward which carried me further from the hated and detestable *dépôt*, where every surrounding object depicted misery, and where, when the *lively* army happened to be in motion, such gloomy reports were, spread, as to intimidate the sick and frighten the convalescents out of the country. Having passed through Guarda, Sabugal, and several miserable Portuguese villages, at the expiration of five days I reached Fuente de Guinaldo, the headquarters of the division.

It is unnecessary to say that a hearty welcome hailed my arrival, and various interesting incidents, which had occurred since I left, were related by my companions, but none were more agreeable to my sanguine mind, than to hear that the division had not fired a shot during the time of my absence; so far dame Fortune had befriended me.

The enemy, under the Duke of Ragusa had advanced on the 25th of September to throw provisions into Rodrigo, and had attacked the fourth division at Adea de Ponte, and part of the third division, who had distinguished themselves against the French cavalry on the heights near El Bodon, they having made several vain efforts to break their little squares for two leagues over firm charging ground; little, I repeat, because the regiments composing the brigade were very weak in point of numbers.

The Light Division was stationed on the right bank of the Agueda, hovering on the enemy's left flank; but, owing to the central attack, it was obliged to march a *détour*, so as to accomplish a concentration with the third division at Fuente de Guinaldo. This was done with the loss of one man, and that was the *parson* attached to the division, who had entered a house and turned snugly into bed, while the soldiers were shivering on the ploughed ground with keen appetites.

During the night, the troops retrograded a short distance, suffering all the while from cold. The march was much impeded owing to a trifling stream in the road, and other obstacles, which the soldiers could not at first surmount, for the extreme darkness. By some accident the parson was not aware of this movement. Towards morning, while wrapped in the arms of Morpheus, he felt a gentle tap, and on opening his leaden eyelids, he saw four French heavy dragoons wrapped in white cloaks, with weather-beaten visages and huge mustachios, crowned by brazen helmets, surmounted with tiger skins, hanging over him in deep consultation on the best way of disposing of his person. The debate closed by their allowing him to put on his sable garments, to be conveyed a prisoner to the governor of Ciudad Rodrigo, who, on being informed of his harmless pursuits, gave directions for his liberation, so that he might go in search of the English army. On his being conducted to the gate of the town, the French soldiers rudely divested him of his coat and waistcoat, using their feet besides, in a most unceremonious manner, and left him to pursue his journey in his shirt sleeves.

Although the house occupied by the officers of the company was small, they declared that I should not seek a bed elsewhere, and one of my friends assured me that he would soon supply me with that article. Without further ado he hastily retired, and in a few minutes we heard a great uproar in the street, and, making for the door, we found my friend running towards the house loaded with a mattress on his back, and pursued by a woman out of whose house he had taken it.

Rushing into the room breathless and convulsed with laughter, he threw it on the floor, which he had no sooner done than the furious owner burst in, and, laying violent hands on it, began to tug away, showering forth a string of Spanish imprecations, too numerous to mention, but easily to be guessed at by those who have heard such refined salutations from an enraged Spanish *mugger*. It was not until her strength had entirely failed her that she would admit of an explanation; but, on money being offered her, she turned away indignantly; and as she had not shown any relaxation of the muscles of her brown visage, and her large black eyes continued to express unutterable things, the officer thought it better to reload himself and return that which, in a frolicsome moment, he had earned off with so much dexterity; but the woman pulled it from off his shoulder, and, with all the natural generosity of the sex, gave him the use of it, (as it was for a convalescent comrade,) as long as it might be required.

A dance was to take place that evening. The officers, therefore put on their best uniforms, and decorated themselves with all the precision and care used when about to attend a ball of a more enlightened circle.

On entering the room we observed the females decorated in their best attire and trinkets. The band struck up a *bolero;* that being concluded the male peasantry retired, leaving their mistresses to hop down our country dances, and to instruct us in those figures we had attempted to teach them. Generals, and all ranks, mixed in these rustic dances, where a variety of little coquetries were practised on the half-enamoured swains. The smell of garlic was scarce tolerable; but these were no times for niceties.

Every effort was exerted to do ample justice to Christmas. The different officers' messes dined alternately with each other, to partake of lean roast beef and plum pudding. Poultry was procured, in fact, no expense was spared. A four pound loaf cost a dollar, moist sugar three *pecetas* a pound, and every other commodity equally expensive; still the festive board was well supplied, and the evenings most joyfully spent.

One of the suttlers who had taken post with our division, to amass a fortune, was a German of ordinary appearance with a pretty wife. Here it so happened that our sergeant-major, a man of portly figure, was possessed of more small talk than usually falls to the lot of men in his' station of life; and, being remarkably fond of good living, and other amusements, proved a very losing customer at the above worthy suttler's shop, who could not help seeing the decline of that stock which he had brought from Lisbon at so much expense; besides other annoyances which he *could not see*. He, therefore, in a fit of extreme irritation, without his hat, made for the commanding officer's quarters, where he entered unceremoniously, and then laid bare all his wrongs. *"Sare,"* said he," *your sergeant-major is a very bad man. He drinky my wine. He eaty my sugar. He drinky my tea and my coffee. He kissy my vife, and he kick ★★ ★★★★. Sare, your sergeant-major is a very bad man."*

Every morning the officers were engaged rehearsing their different parts, or superintending the making of theatrical dresses, (as the tragedy of Henry IV was to be performed by various officers,) and scene painting. The latter was principally executed by Bell, (the assistant quarter-master general of the division,) in an old chapel, within one hundred yards of the village, which had been gutted of its ornaments by the French or the priests.

The compact and small village of Fuente de Guinaldo stands on an eminence in an open plain, encircled at a certain distance by a number of stone crosses, said to have been placed there by the peasantry to frighten away evil spirits. There are no enclosures, no out-barns, or farm houses, in this part of Spain, which gives the plain during winter a very lonely aspect, skirted as it is by a distant wood, and a ridge of wild mountains on the summit of which is a monastery, which is only to be seen on a clear day; for if the weather is at all hazy, it is enveloped by clouds. The communication from one village to another, is a sort of track beaten into the shape of a road by the footsteps and small traffic of many generations.

The natives of this part of the country form a little colony, unmixed by a second order of society, as there is no resident beyond the rank of a peasant, the principal holding the authority of *Alcalde,* and completely governing the village in all judicial affairs. He exercises his power with mildness, which is perceptible in the independent manners of the people.

The girls sing very pretty airs in praise of some renowned chieftain, or of her who happens to be the acknowledged beauty, Maria Josepha, of Fuentes de Onor, was the happy *Moza* whose charms were extolled at this period: but what most struck my attention was a song about Marlborough's knowing how to make war, and sung to the same tune as in England. The mothers lull their children to sleep by it; and when bodies of troops enter towns, or the girls dance *boleros,* this is a general tune. I inquired of a *muchacha* where she learnt it; she opened her eyes with a ludicrous surprise, and made answer, in the quick witty manner usual amongst the Mozas, "Why, of my grandmother— *Que edad tiene V. M?" (How old are you?)*—by way of giving me a hint not to consider myself the instructor.

The long expected night of performance having arrived, written bills of the play having been distributed throughout the village (which was filled like a beehive with officers who had come a considerable distance from other divisions of the army, with flowing *camlet* cloaks, and mounted on *bóricos,* mules, and ragged-maned stallions;) and tickets being issued for pit and boxes, we moved in Bacchanalian groups towards *el Teatro* (or chapel). It was crammed to excess, as we had not forgotten to reserve some room for *los soldados.* The curtain no sooner drew up, than the wonder of the *muchachas* knew no bounds, and they became so loquacious in admiration of the scenery and dresses, and in disputing among themselves which was *el Principe,* and which the various characters the officers were to personify, that it was a considerable time before they could be so far tranquillized as to permit the performance to proceed, which, however, went off with great *eclat.* "Poins, and be hanged." Alas! no; Poor Poins was badly wounded, and blown up a few days after!

CHAPTER 8

The Siege of Ciudad Rodrigo

At the expiration of some months' travail by the engineer department, in procuring stores from various places, active operations were commenced to collect them near at hand—such as the battering train, cannon balls, ammunition, gabions, fascines, scaling-ladders, sand bags, shovels, spades, pick-axes, &c—for the purpose of laying siege to Ciudad Rodrigo, (in the province of Leon,) which stands on an eminence on the right bank of the river Agueda, surrounded by an open country, and was garrisoned by two thousand French soldiers. The walls of the fortress are rather more than a mile and a quarter in circumference, enclosing monasteries, convents, and churches—which gives the city at a distance the appearance of an immense gothic castle.

A few days previously to the siege, Lord Wellington reviewed the Light Division on the plains of Guinaldo. He was dressed in full uniform, and merely rode down the line, looking at the troops in a cheerful manner. Just as his Lordship was leaving the ground, which was covered with snow, General Craufurd appeared, and soon after the troops returned to their quarters. The second brigade came from Martiago, and returned that night—an immense march. A few days subsequently to this review, the whole division was concentrated, the first brigade moving to La Encina, the second to El Bodon. During this march a tremendous storm of sleet and snow took place; the snow froze and adhered to the horses hoofs, forming balls which raised them several inches from the ground. Fortunately, the march was short, as fatigue-parties of soldiers were obliged to return to prop up the weak and staggering baggage-animals, that had suffered previously from bad provender.

On the 8th of January, 1812, the Light Division crossed the Agueda, *sans culotte, (a cooler!)* at a ford about four miles above Ciudad Rodrigo. The day was fine, and, indeed, during the operations of the siege, the atmosphere was mild for the season of the year, although sometimes frosty of a morning.

The division bivouacked for some hours two miles from the town. When the darkness had set in, three hundred soldiers drawn from the 43rd, 52nd, and the rifle corps, moved under the command of Colonel Colborne, to assault the fort of Francisco. The enemy fired about two rounds; our good troops did not allow more time, and the fort was taken.

It was situated on a rising ground, six hundred yards from the town, was of a square form, with two small howitzers, *en barbette,* and had a garrison of two officers and forty soldiers, who were made prisoners. Six or eight others either were killed or escaped into the town, where the drums began to beat to arms, and a furious fire of shot and shell opened on us, while digging a parallel close to the captured fort; the earth being thrown up on the town side. The land is arable, and bestrewn with loose stones, which were flying on all sides from the impulse given by the cannon balls, and the bursting of shells, which were exploding on every side, killing and maiming many soldiers.

The great convent of Saint Francisco, in the suburb, was carried a few days before the storming of the town, and also the ruined convent of Santa Cruz. On the morning of the 14th, about five hundred French soldiers made a sortie from the city, and before they retired were very nearly succeeding in entering the batteries, where the battering cannon had been placed the night before. The twenty-four pounders were of iron, mounted like field guns, on handsome carriages, painted lead colour.

An hour before dark on this day, the batteries opened within six hundred yards of the ramparts for the purpose of battering in breach. The first, third, fourth, and light divisions, employed in the siege moved by turns from their cantonments, each taking a twenty-four hours' spell.*

On the 19th of January, the Light Division was ordered to the assault out of its turn. During the greater part of the day we remained cooking behind the convent of the Norbortins, a most splendid ruin, with very extensive cloisters, situated close on the right bank of the Agueda, three miles S. E. of the town. Soon after three o'clock we moved towards the ground occupied by the foot guards, who were halted one mile and a half from the suburbs of Ciudad Rodrigo. These troops came forward to wish us success, and our band struck up the *Fall of Paris*. The third division occupied the trenches, and the garrison must have observed the march of the Light Division from the ramparts—extra troops! The governor should have pondered on it! If he had kept a sharp look-out, he must have been expecting the assault.

There were two breaches effected in the walls of this town. By the small breach the large one was taken in reverse.

At half-past six o'clock the Light Division was formed behind the convent of Saint Francisco, near the suburb, and almost exactly opposite to the small breach, and about four hundred yards from it. The third division, under General Sir Thomas Picton, was also formed behind the ruins of Santa Cruz, and in the trenches opposite the large breach. All was silent, four or five shells excepted, which were thrown by the enemy into our left battery, and fell not a great distance from

---

* During the siege, the enemy threw a vast quantity of shells. One night two mortars kept up an incessant discharge; and the soldiers called out "Here comes a shell from *big Tom;* and here comes another from *little Tom."* All the cannon shot that flew over our trenches lodged on a hill one mile north of the town, at the base of which was a *spring,* where I saw a soldier killed while stooping down to fill his canteen with water. This hill, owing to its being so ploughed up with balls, was familiarly named by the soldiers *plum-pudding hill.*

our column. Now, if the governor thought that the assault was preparing, he ought not to have fired at all from the ramparts, as it prevented the approach of the troops from being discovered by the ear.

I heard the town-clock strike seven, and at the same time saw a match lighted in one of the embrasures—(very awful!) at that moment the "forlorn hope," headed by Lieut. Gurwood, of the 52nd, and the storming party (composed of three hundred soldiers, with a proportion of officers) moved on, carrying a number of bags, filled with dried grass, to lessen the depth of the *fausse braie* and the ditch. In a few minutes they were on the brink of the ditch, and the fire of the town opened briskly on them. There was a sort of check, but no longer than might be expected, as they had to scramble in and out of the *fausse braie,* and then to jump into the dry ditch; but having gone too far to the left, the advance got on the wrong side of the tower, which was not breached, and the soldiers, for a few seconds, were knocking with the butt-ends of their fire locks against the wall, crying out "Where's the breach?" For although the enemy were firing- rapidly from the top of the wall, still the troops, on first descending to the bottom of the ditch, were in total darkness.

This state of suspense lasted, however, a very short time, for two soldiers, stumbling on the loose rubbish, called out "Here's the breach," and Lieut. Gurwood, who took the governor of the fortress prisoner, led up it; but the French swore they should not enter, and fought most desperately on the crest of the breach, throwing down large stones and missiles, and keeping up a most deadly fire. Here many brave officers and soldiers fell. General Craufurd received a mortal wound, and fell into his aide-de-camp's arms, on the glacis, while cheering on the main body of the division. Major-General Vandeleur and Colonel Colborne were wounded.

How the troops contrived to force the breach I know not: I can only say that it was well done. The breach was exceedingly steep: about five yards wide at the top, having a cannon, of heavy calibre, placed sideways, to block up the passage; however, there was a clear yard from the muzzle of the gun to the wall, a sufficient space for one or two soldiers to enter at a time, besides those who could pass underneath the muzzle of the gun, or over the wheels of the carriage.

The moment the division entered, a number of soldiers rushed to the right, along the ramparts, to the large breach *(one hundred and fifty yards)*, and then engaging those of the French who were still firing on the third division, absolutely drove them over the breast-work, on to the large breach. At this time a wooden spare magazine, placed on the rampart, exploded, and blew up some French grenadiers, and many of the Light Division. Lieutenant Patterson, of the 43rd, and Lieut. Uniacke, of the rifle corps, were of the number. This occurred just behind the traverse, which, on the enemy's right, confined and guarded the great breach.

On ascending the small breach, directly after it was carried, I found myself with the crowd. Lieut.-Colonel M'Leod managed to collect, with the assistance of some other officers, on the rampart about two hundred soldiers of our regiment, and was exhorting them to keep together. At this time there was not any firing on us, with the exception of a few stray shots from the opposite buildings; but there was sharp musketry still at the great breach.

I ran towards the large breach, and met an officer slowly walking between two soldiers of the rifle corps. I asked who it was, when he faintly replied, "Uniacke," and walked on. One of his eyes was blown out, and the flesh was torn off his arms and legs. He had taken chocolate, with our mess, an hour and a half before! He died in excruciating agony!

The regiment was now formed, and Colonel M'Leod immediately detached officers with guards, to take possession of all the stores they could find, and to preserve order. These parties ultimately dissolved themselves. If they had not done so, they would have been engaged in the streets with our own troops.

Colonel M'Leod caused Lieutenant Madden, of the 43rd, to descend the small breach with twenty-five men, ordering him to continue at the foot of it during the night, and to prevent soldiers leaving the town with plunder.

At eleven o'clock I went to see him; he had no sinecure, and had very judiciously made a large fire, which, of course, showed the delinquents to perfection, who were attempting to quit the town with plunder, in the garb of friars, nuns, or enveloped in silk counterpanes, or loaded with silver forks, spoons, and church plate, all of which was of course taken from them, and was piled up, to hand over to the proper authorities on the following day. He told me that no masquerade could, in point of costume and grotesque figures, rival the characters he stripped that night.

The fire was large, and surrounded by the dead bodies of those who fell in the first onset at the foot of the breach. The troops must have rushed up and taken the latter without hesitation: had the governor of the town only placed a few obstacles on the crest of the-breach, he must have stopped the entrance of the Light Division altogether. He had time, as the firing from our batteries ceased two hours before the assault, and then from the rampart there was a gentle slope into the town, leading into a narrow lane, which was blocked in with a cart only, leaving a sufficient space for one person to pass at a time. The Governor was most culpable! There was no musketry from any part of the ramparts until the head of the Light Division column was close to the small breach.

Amongst others lay Captain Dobbs, of the 52nd, on his back, at the foot of the breach, and stripped of his uniform. An officer at first thought he was a Frenchman, who had tumbled headlong during the strife from the top of the breach; but, while he was holding a piece of lighted wood, to contemplate, with admiration, his extremely placid and handsome countenance, even in death, a captain of the 52nd knew it to be the body of poor Dobbs. On lifting him up, the blood flowed copiously from his back, a musket ball having entered at the breast, and passed through his body. A soldier of the third division came up to me and said, "Captain Hardyman, of the 45th, is killed!" for although three generals and seventy other officers had fallen, yet the soldiers fresh from the strife talked of him; and if a soldier's praise can add to a man's fame, certainly no one had a greater share than Hardyman; he was the real type of a soldier, and kind to everyone.

When the troops had sipped the wine and the Cognac brandy in the stores, the extreme disorders commenced. To restore order was impossible; a whole division could not have done it. Three or four large houses were on fire, two of them were in the market-place, and the town was illuminated by the flames. The soldiers were drunk, and many of them for amusement were firing from the windows into the streets.

I was talking to the regimental barber, private Evans, in the square, when a ball passed through his head. This was at one o'clock in the morning. He fell at my feet dead, and his brains lay on the pavement. I then sought shelter, and found Colonel M'Leod with a few officers in a large house, where we remained until daylight. I did not enter any other house in Ciudad Rodrigo, and if I had not seen, I never could have supposed that British soldiers would become so wild and furious. It was quite alarming to meet groups of them in the streets, flushed as they were with drink, and desperate in mischief.

On the morning of the 20th the scene was dreary; the fires just going out; and about the streets were lying the corpses of many men who had met their death hours after the town had been taken.

At eleven o'clock, I went to look at the great breach. The ascent was not so steep as that of the small one, but there was a traverse thrown up at each side of it on the rampart; hence there was no way into the town, as the wall was quite perpendicular behind the breach. When the third division had gained the top of the rampart, they were in a manner enclosed and hemmed in, and had no where to go, while the enemy continued to fire upon them from some old ruined houses, only twenty yards distant.

I counted more than sixty-three soldiers of the third division lying dead on the *terre-plein* of the rampart exactly between the traverses I have already described. I did not see one dead soldier of that division on the French side of those traverses; but I saw some of the Light Division.

I saw General M'Kinnon lying dead on his back, just under the rampart, on the inside, that is, the town side. He was stripped of everything except his shirt and blue pantaloons; even his boots were taken off. He was a tall thin man. There were no others dead near him, and he was not on the French side of the traverse either, nor was there any possibility of getting at the General without a ladder, or traversing a considerable distance along the ramparts to descend into the town, and then passing through several narrow lanes, ruined houses, and over broken stone walls being a distance of at least a quarter of a mile, and what no human being could have accomplished during the night. It is said that he was blown up. I should say not. There was no appearance indicating that such had been his fate. Neither the state of his skin nor the posture in which he was lying, led me to think it. When a man is blown up, his hands and face, I should think, could not escape. I never saw any whose face was not scorched. M'Kinnon's was pale, and free from the marks of fire. How strange, that with the exception of the General, I did not see a soldier of the third division who had been stripped! Neither was there any officer among the dead, or else they had been carried away. I should not wonder, (if it is not uncharitable,) that the General had been killed with all the others between the traverses, and that some *tender-hearted* follower of the army had taken his clothes off, and then just given him a hand over the wall, and so placed him in the position described.

The two divisions attacked without knapsacks. The greater portion of the Light Division lay at the foot of the *small breach* in the ditch; hence it was that they fought on the slope, and rolled down in succession as they were killed; but, on gaining the ramparts (there being no interior defences) they followed the French right and left, who retreated, panic-struck, into the interior of the city, keeping up, however, a running fire from the different streets, or the massive stone buildings.

The third division, at the first onset, were fired on from the parapets of the rampart, and assailed by missiles and live shells, which were rolled from the summit of the wall: but the enemy did not stand on the crest of the great breach to oppose their ascent for, if they had, it would have been impossible to escape behind their traverses. The enemy had left a space for one man to pass at a time, on the left of the right traverse, but expecting the attack, they had previously blocked it up with barrels filled with earth, having placed others behind to stand on for the purpose of firing over them. Before the morning, all these barrels, except one, were thrown down the scarped wall.

The fact is, that the third division mounted to the *terre-plein* with facility; but when on the rampart, they were fired on in front and both flanks, as before described, and in this small space, they suffered a tremendous loss of nearly five hundred heroic officers and soldiers. During the fighting, their dead and wounded were piled one on the top of the other, crying out in agony as they were trampled upon, and impeding the progress of others, who exerted themselves in vain amongst such havoc to carry the traverses.

The moment the wooden magazine blew up, all firing nearly ceased, for the enemy literally jumped over the right entrenchment on to the *terre-plein* of the great breach, to save themselves from the bayonets of the Light Division, A young Italian officer there seized Captain Hopkins, of the 43rd, round the neck, and implored his life.

At about eleven o'clock in the morning (of the 20th) the great explosion took place a few yards to the right of the *small breach*, blowing up the *terre-plein* of the rampart, four yards in breadth and ten in length. This fatal explosion (which was accidental, owing to some sparks of fire igniting some barrels of gunpowder in a casement,) happened while the French garrison were marching out of the city by the *small breach,* which had become so hard, owing to such numbers of soldiers walking up and down it, as to make the ascent nearly impracticable.

The French, as well as the British soldiers, were carried up into the air, or jammed amongst the rubbish, some with heads, arms, or legs sticking out of the earth. I saw one of the unfortunate soldiers in a blanket, with his *face, head,* and *body,* as black as a coal, and cased in a black substance like a shell; his features were no longer distinguishable, and all the hair was singed from off his head, but still the unfortunate man was alive. How long he lived in this horrible situation I cannot say.

A tall athletic soldier of the 52nd lay amongst the dead at the foot of the breach, on his back; his arms and legs being at their full extent. The top of his head, from the forehead to the back part of his skull, was split in twain, and the cavity of the head entirely emptied of the brains, as if a hand-grenade had exploded within, and expanded the skull, till it had forced it into a separation with the parts ragged like a saw, leaving a gaping aperture nine inches in length, and four in breadth. For a considerable time I looked on this horrible fracture, to define, if possible, by what missile or instrument so wonderful a wound could have been inflicted, but without being able to come to any conclusion as to the probable cause.

From this place I walked to the convent of Saint Francisco to see a wounded friend. The interior was crowded with wounded soldiers lying on the hard pavement. A soldier of the third division was sitting against a pillar, his head bent forward, and his chin resting on his breast, his eyes open, and an agreeable smile on his countenance. For half a minute I stopped with surprise to observe him sitting in so contented a posture, surrounded by the groans of his companions. At length, I addressed him, but, no answer being returned, I called a doctor, under the impression that the man was delirious. On the contrary, we found he was quite dead.

In the afternoon we returned to our quarters by regiments across the stone bridge, having been relieved by the fifth division, which came from the rear, and took charge of the city.

A few days after the assault, most of the officers of the Light Division attended General Craufurd's funeral. He was buried under the wall near the small breach.

In a few days we moved from La Encina to El Bodon, where our principal amusement consisted in playing at rackets, with wooden bats, against the side of the church, or riding about the country.

One day we visited the heights about half a league from this place, where, on the previous September, a brigade of the third division had been engaged. Many skeletons of the French horses lay in deep ravines, or on the shelvings of rocks, to the very summit of the ridge, on the crest of which some of the Portuguese gunners were cut down; and where for a short time the cannon remained in the hands of the enemy. It must have been at this moment that the second battalion of the fifth regiment retook them by charging in line, before the enemy's cavalry had time to form. I rode up the ragged ground myself with the utmost difficulty; the ground near the summit was so steep that the Portuguese, while throwing balls into the valley, could not see the advance of the French cavalry until quite upon them. Not that I wish to detract from the deserts of the Portuguese; but, as it has been stated that they stood to their guns, to the last, I only wish to demonstrate how it happened. The very print of the wheels of the cannon were still indented in the ground, and showed, to an inch, where they had stood.

The whole of the dead French soldiers lying in the valley were stripped, and in a perfect state of preservation, blanched like parchment by the alternate rain and sunshine; and their skins had become so hard, that the bodies on being touched sounded like a drum. The vultures had picked the bones of the horses perfectly clean, but had left the soldiers untouched; and, although *four months* had elapsed since they had fallen, their features were as perfect as on the day they were killed. Some of these soldiers were gracefully proportioned, and extended in every possible attitude.

The rubbish of the breaches at Ciudad Rodrigo having been cleared away, the parapets built up with gabions and fascines, all the trenches filled up, and a garrison of Spanish soldiers left for its defence—at the latter end of February we marched towards Badajos, for the purpose of laying siege to that fortress, a distance of one hundred and sixty miles, the road more than half way lying through the rocky provinces of Portugal, where the villages are generally built on the tops of the highest mountains, with the remains of Moorish castles, or towers, studding the wildest rocks and the most tremendous precipices.

We remained a week at Castello de Vida, then resumed our march, and, on the 16th of March, entered Elvas, the principal fortress on the frontier of the Alentejo, three leagues distant from Badajos. It is situated on a hill, flanked on the right by a fort or citadel, half a mile without its walls, and on the left by the fort La Lippe, which stands on a scarped hill, a mile from the town.

While quartering off the soldiers, I observed a very pretty young lady looking out of a casement, which occasioned her house to be selected for our quarter. In the evening, myself and messmate were invited to take chocolate and sweetmeats with the family; and, before retiring, the good old *Senhora* remarked our youthful appearance, and begged that, should either of us be wounded, we would come to her house. My companion was subsequently shot through the body, and, being conveyed back to Elvas, the mother and daughter kindly watched over him until he was perfectly recovered.

CHAPTER 9

Badajos

On the morning of the 17th of March we formed contiguous columns, outside the walls of Elvas, and entering a spacious plain, passed the river Guadiana by a pontoon bridge, a few miles below Badajos, which Was garrisoned by nearly five thousand French soldiers. It is situated on the margin of the left bank of the Guadiana, in the province of Estremadura, in Spain, and encompassed by an open country, without a tree, a shrub, or even a hut to be seen without its walls. The ramparts are about two miles in circumference, and were protected by the forts San Cristoval, Napoleon, and the *Tete de Pont* at the head of the fine stone bridge, which communicates with the right bank of the Guadiana.

The fort Picurina, the outworks of Pardalaras, and the *lunette* of Saint Roque, constituted the general outworks of the city, on the left bank of the river.

As we drew near the ramparts of the fortress, we saw the flag of *three colours* majestically waving on the top of the great lofty square tower, in the centre of the old castle, which stands on the summit of a hill, whose frowning battlements overhang the town, and overlook the adjacent plains for a considerable distance.

The third, fourth, and light divisions invested the city on the left bank of the Guadiana. Some Portuguese troops watched the right bank of the river on the side of Portugal, but, during the latter end of the siege, part of the fifth division under General Leith took that duty.

Our division bivouacked within one mile and a half S. S. W. of the town, our position communicating in a manner with the bridge of boats. The day was fine; but at six o'clock in the evening the rain began to fall in torrents, and continued the whole night, which prevented the enemy hearing the troops when they commenced the first parallel, and the latter continued to work all night without being molested.

Before daylight on the 18th, the parties fell in to relieve those of our division who had first broke ground, a thousand yards S. E. of the town; we had to make a quarter circle, which rendered the march nearly three miles to the mouth of the trench, where we arrived at daybreak, and I saw the first shot; it was fired from the Fort Picurina, and killed two poor fellows in the covering party of the fourth division, which was formed under the slope of a hill. In a few minutes the round shot came up the road quite often enough to put our blood into circulation; and we immediately took our station under a small natural rise of ground, where we remained covering the workmen for twelve hours. The cannonade was pretty regular during the day, both from the town and from Fort Picurina.

We returned to camp an hour after dark, and I was surprised to find the division had been supplied with Portuguese tents. I found my friend waiting in one for me, and the canteens laid out with all the affection of a youthful soldier. I had been exposed in the rain for twenty-five hours, and this was one of the happiest moments of my life.

On the 19th, at mid-day, the firing from the town was very heavy; everyone in the best position for security, which it was not difficult to obtain, as the trenches were well advanced, but everybody cried "Keep down," for which truly there was no occasion.

Notwithstanding this cry, Israel Wild, (I have often been told, from undoubted authority, that this soldier was one of the first who entered the small breach at Rodrigo, and whose Stentorian voice rose above the din of arms,) and another man of our regiment, who was afterwards killed, (a splendid soldier,) got on the top of the trench. I caught hold of Israel's jacket, to pull him down, but he turned round, and said, in a most furious manner, "We know what we are about;" then looking forward for a moment, shouted, with an oath, that the French were coming on, and instantly sprung out of the trench like a tiger, following his Comrade, just such another fine fellow.

Two or three French dragoons at that instant fired their pistols into the trenches, having approached within a few yards without being perceived. We had just entered the mouth of the first parallel, and all joined in a simultaneous attack on the enemy's infantry, without regard to trenches or anything else. The French being beaten out of the advanced lines, retired and formed line under the castle, having two field-pieces on their left flank. I cannot say how they entered the town, there was so much smoke covering them, when near the walls. *General Philippon knew his business well.* Fourteen hundred men came out—two battalions.

We had quite abandoned the trenches, and approached near to the castle. I perceived two soldiers of another division, who were stretched close to where I stood: one was quite dead, a round shot having passed through his body; the other had lost a leg, his eyelids were closed, and lie was apparently dead. An adventurous Portuguese began to disencumber him of his clothes. The poor soldier opened his eyes and looked in the most imploring manner, while the villain had him by the belts, lifting him up. I gave the humane Portuguese a blow with the back of my sabre, that laid him prostrate for a time, by the side of the soldier he was stripping.

I know not what became of the wounded man, as my attention was attracted by an extraordinary circumstance. I saw a heavy shot hopping along, till it struck a soldier on the hip; down he went, motionless. I felt confident that the wounded man was not dead, and begged that some of his comrades would carry him off to the rear, (we were now retiring under a heavy cannonade); my words were at first unheeded, but two soldiers, at the risk of their lives, rushed back, and brought him in, or he, with many others, would have been starved to death, between our lines and the ramparts of the town. His hip was only grazed, and his clothes untorn; but, of course, he was unable to walk, and seemed to feel much pain, for he groaned heavily.

The sortie took place about a quarter after twelve; *(military time, quite correct;)* we were filing into the trenches. The day was fine, and the time well selected by the governor, as he concluded that the front parallel would be vacant while the relief was coming in; but there was an order against that.

The trenches were very extensive. The weather again became bad, and our right battery was silenced; but when the great breaching battery was completed, it fired salvos, which the enemy returned in a similar manner from a battery just under the castle gate, on a commanding situation. One morning, at daylight, the enemy brought a light gun out of the town to enfilade the right of the front parallel; but as the relief came in at the time, I do not know the sequel of it.

The left of our lines, previously to the escalade of Picurina, ran within about a hundred yards parallel to it. One hundred of our regiment were employed one night on the delightful job of carrying the trenches across the Seville road. We commenced at the distance of one hundred and fifty yards from the fort. The instant the enemy heard the pickaxes striking on the hard road, they opened, when, strange to relate, eleven rounds of grape were poured on us, and yet only one officer was hit. The gunners could not depress their artillery so as to cover the spot we were on.

I was surprised that they used no musketry; hut I Imagine they had orders not to do so at night, unless an attempt was made to escalade the fort.

Picurina was situated on a rising ground, without the least appearance of strength. Three hundred of the enemy formed the garrison, and latterly they were obliged to block up their embrasures with sandbags, to screen themselves from the musketry of our lines; now and then they cleared away to fire grape shot.

Towards the end of the siege the weather became beautiful. One day in particular, the enemy scarcely fired a shot, all our troubles were forgotten, and two or three of us amused ourselves by reading a novel in the trenches.

Lieutenant Wilkinson, was among the wounded on that day. There was a path across a field, which communicated with our grand battery, and an order forbade any person to cross it in the daytime, as the French were continually firing small arms whenever any lazy-fellow took that road. Poor little Wilky's curiosity was excited; he made a start out of fun, was just entering the battery, when alas! he fell, shot through the thigh.

On the night of the 25th, a part of the third division, and also one hundred of the Light Division, carrying ladders, assailed Picurina, directed by General Sir James Kempt, and for a long time without success: no wonder! The ditch was terrifically deep, and narrow at the bottom. The soldiers walked round the fort, prying into all corners, and got upon the gate, which they broke down, and then entered, bayonets in advance. The French grenadiers would not give in—a desperate bayoneting took place, and much blood was spilt; already five hundred French soldiers from the town were at hand. The struggle continued with hard fighting, inside and outside of the fort. The enemy wished to vie with their comrades who had defended Fort St. Christoval at the former siege. Victory was some minutes doubtful; at length the fort was taken, and the reinforcements were beaten back into the town, I was sitting at the door of my tent, and witnessed all the firing.

The garrison of Badajos fired every morning, for a few days previously to the grand assault, a certain number of rounds, as if for practice, and to measure the ground.

The first order for storming the breaches fixed it to take place on the 5th of April. I was informed that my turn for trench duty fell on that evening, because the officer just preceding me was out of the way. I resolved to play a like trick, and for a like reason, namely, not to miss the assault. I therefore got a friend to persuade the Adjutant to allow that the men should march off without me, promising to follow. This anecdote I relate, because of the curious circumstance that it led to.

When I was quite certain that the assault was not to take place that night, I mounted my horse, and, riding to the entrance of the first parallel, I gave the animal to my batman, and proceeded on foot. I had just crossed the trench, and got into a field, taking a short cut, when I observed two figures making towards me. There was not any firing; a solemn silence reigned around. Coming up at a half run, I put my hand to my sword, for the night was clear, and I saw they were not soldiers; they soon closed on me, demanding boldly, and in Spanish, the way out of the trenches. I pointed out the road to them, but, an instant after, suspected they were not *Spaniards,* but spies, I noticed they kept their hands behind them, and I thought it also very *civil* of them not to fire, for I am confident they were well armed, *"Buenos noches, Señor."* said they, and hastily retired. When I reached the great battery, and found everybody in it asleep, I thought the place bewitched. This was my last trip to the trenches. Thirteen times I visited them during the siege.

A long order was issued relative to the positions the troops were to occupy. On the 6th of April, the day was fine, and all the soldiers in good spirits, cleaning themselves as if for a review. About two o'clock I saw Lieutenant Harvest of our regiment; he was sucking an orange, and walking on a rising ground, alone, and very thoughtful. It gave me pain, as I knew he was to lead the "forlorn hope". He observed, "My mind is made up; I am sure to be killed." He was killed!

At half-past eight o'clock that night the ranks were formed and the roll called in an under-tone. Lieutenant-Colonel M'Leod spoke long and earnestly to the regiment before it joined the division, expressing the utmost confidence in the success of the attack, and finished by repeating, that he left it to the honour of all persons to preserve discipline, and not to commit any cruelty on the defenceless inhabitants of the town.

The division drew up in the most profound silence behind the large quarry, three hundred yards from the *three* breaches, made in the bastions of La Trinidad, and Santa Maria. A small stream separated us from the fourth division. Suddenly, a voice was heard from that direction, giving orders about ladders, so loud, that it might be heard by the enemy on the ramparts. It was the only voice that broke on the stillness of the moment; everybody was indignant, and Colonel M'Leod sent an officer to say that he would report the circumstance to the General-in-Chief. I looked up the side of the quarry, fully expecting to see the enemy come forth, and derange the plan of attack. It was at half-past nine this happened, but, at a quarter before ten, the ill-timed noise ceased, and nothing could be heard but the loud croaking of the frogs.

At ten a carcass was thrown from the town; this was a most beautiful firework, and illuminated the ground for many hundred yards; two or three fireballs followed, and, falling in different directions, showed a bright light, and remained burning. The stillness that followed was the prelude to one of the strangest scenes that the imagination of man can conceive.

Soon after ten o'clock, a little whispering announced that "the forlorn hope" were stealing forward, followed by the storming parties, composed of three hundred men, (one hundred from each British regiment of our division;) in two minutes the division followed. This was with the exception of the two regiments of Portuguese Caçadores, who were left in reserve in the quarries; but many of them afterwards came towards, the breaches.

One musket shot, *no more,* was fired near the breaches by a French soldier, who was on the look out. We gained ground leisurely—but silently; there were no obstacles. The 52nd, 43rd, and part of the rifle corps, closed gradually up to column of quarter distance, left in front; all was hushed, and the town lay buried in gloom; the ladders were placed on the edge of the ditch, when suddenly an explosion took place at the foot of the breaches, and a burst of light disclosed the whole scene—the earth seemed to rock under us—what a sight! The ramparts crowded with the enemy—the French soldiers standing on the parapets—the fourth division advancing rapidly in column of companies on a quarter circle to our right, while the short-lived glare from the barrels of powder and combustibles flying into the air, gave to friends and foes a look as if both bodies of troops were laughing at each other.

A tremendous firing now opened on us, and for an instant we were stationary; but the troops were *no ways daunted*. The only three ladders were placed down the scarp to descend into the ditch, and were found exactly opposite the centre breach, and the whole division rushed to the assault with amazing resolution. There was no check. The soldiers flew down the ladders, and the cheering from both sides was loud and full of confidence.

While descending the ladders into the ditch, furious blows were exchanged amongst the troops in their eagerness to get forward; at the same time grape-shot and musketry tore open their ranks. The first officer I happened to see down was Captain Fergusson, who had led on our storming-party here, and at Rodrigo; he was lying to the right of the ladders, with a wound on the head, and holding a bloody handkerchief in his grasp; he had also two unhealed body wounds open, which he had received at Rodrigo, and one in the trenches at Badajos a few days before. I snatched it out of his hand, and tied it round his head.

The French were then handing over the fireballs, which produced a sort of revolving light. The ditch was very wide, and when I arrived at the foot of the centre breach, eighty or ninety men were formed. One cried out, "Who will lead?" This was the work of a moment. Death, and the most dreadful sounds and cries encompassed us. It was a volcano! Up we went; some killed, and others impaled on the bayonets of their own comrades, or hurled headlong amongst the outrageous crowd.

The *chevaux-de-frise* looked like innumerable bayonets. When within a yard of the top, I fell from a blow that deprived me of sensation. I only recollect feeling a soldier pulling me out of the water, where so many men were drowned. I lost my cap, but still held my sword. On recovering, I looked towards the breach. It was shining and empty! Fireballs were in plenty, and the French troops standing upon the walls, taunting, and inviting our men to come up and try it again.

Colonel M'Leod was killed while trying to force the left corner of the large breach (The right corner looking from the ramparts; but, as we attacked, it was on the left.) He received his mortal wound within three yards of the enemy, just at the bottom of some nine-feet planks, studded with nails, and hanging down the breach from under the *chevaux-de-frise.*

At half-past eleven the firing slackened, and the French detached soldiers from the breaches to repulse the other attacks, and to endeavour to retake the castle. I heard the enemy calling out on the ramparts in German, "All is well in Badajos!"

The British soldiers did as much as *men could do.* The wood-work of the *chevaux-de-frise* was ponderous, bristling with short, stout sword-blades fastened in it, and chained together. It was an obstacle not to be removed, and the French soldiers stood close to it, killing deliberately every man who approached it. The large breach was at one time crowded with our brave troops; I mean the fourth division, the heroes of many hard-fought victories and bloody fields. The Light Division had recently been crowned with victory; but to remove such obstacles was impracticable by living bodies, pushing against them up a steep breach, and sinking to the knees every step in rubbish, while a fearless enemy stood behind pushing down fragments of masonry and live shells, and firing bullets, fixed on the top of pieces of wood, the sides of which were indented with seven or eight *buck* shot.

Generals Picton, Colville, Kempt, Bowes, Hervey, Walker, Champlemond, and almost every officer commanding regiments, besides more than three hundred officers, and between four and five thousand gallant veteran soldiers, fell around these walls.

The left breach had not been attempted at all (there was a trench three feet wide and four deep, cut between the centre and left breach, which was choked up with the dead and wounded,) until a quarter before twelve o'clock, when Captain Shaw of our regiment, collecting about seventy men of different regiments, and with great difficulty, after such slaughter for two hours, made a desperate effort to gain the top; but when halfway up, as if by enchantment, he stood alone. Two rounds of grape and the musketry prevented any more trouble, for almost the whole of the party lay stretched in various attitudes!

Captain Nichols, of the Engineers, was of the number (the engineer officers suffered terribly in killed and wounded during the siege, as they joined in all the desperate attacks); he now showed great courage; and when asked by Shaw, if he would try the left breach, answered he would do anything to succeed. A grape-shot went through his lungs, and he died three days after.

This attack was very daring. It was a forlorn hope, under accumulated dangers; almost all the troops had retired, (the fourth and light divisions retired at midnight from the breaches; but many of the soldiers did not leave the ditch, being unable to ascend the ladders owing to the heaps of dead and wounded; the fourth division descended opposite the large breach by only two ladders,) and, a few moments before, a great alarm was excited by a cry from the heaps of wounded, that the French were descending, into the ditch.

To exaggerate the picture of this sanguinary strife is impossible—the small groups of soldiers seeking shelter from the cart-wheels, pieces of timber, fireballs, and other missiles hurled down upon them; the wounded crawling past the fireballs, many of them scorched and perfectly black, and covered with mud, from having fallen into the *lunette,* where three hundred soldiers were suffocated or drowned; and all this time the French on the top of the parapets, jeering and cracking their jokes, and deliberately picking off whom they chose. The troops lining the glacis could not fire sufficiently, as they were terribly exposed, and could scarcely live from the cross fire of grape-shot.

Colonel Barnard did all in his power to concentrate the different attacks. It was in vain; the difficulties were too great. But Badajos was not the grave of the Light Division's valour, nor of the fourth division's either.

Philippon, the governor, a *Frenchman,* and our enemy, gave the full particulars of this affair to a friend of mine, while travelling in England; he paid that he thought the great explosion would have finished the business, but he was astonished at the resolution of the British troops, who, he said, were fine fellows, and deserved a better fate.

The single musket-shot, fired just as the "forlorn hope" descended the ditch, was a signal of their approach, which, shows how determined the French were to have a good blow-up, for not a ball was fired before the explosion. The efforts of the garrison to preserve the place did them much honour. Philippon was determined not to do as the governor of Ciudad Rodrigo had done. Had not the Earl of Wellington planned the two extreme attacks by escalade, on the castle, by the third division, and on the south side of the town by part of the fifth division, and on the Fort Pardalaras by the Portuguese, the result might have been very serious.

The Duke of Dalmatia was within a few leagues, and opposite Generals Hill and Graham. The Duke of Ragusa had pushed his advanced dragoons as far as the Bridge of Boats at Villa Velha, and at length got entangled in the labyrinths of Portugal. I have heard and read of sitting down before a town, *opening trenches, blowing up the counterscarp, and all according to rule; but this was a crisis,* time was precious, added to which the Guadiana ran in our rear, and the pontoon bridge had been carried away once during the siege, by the swelling of the river.

When the French soldiers found that the town was falling by escalade on the south side, and that the castle was lost to them, they made an attempt to retake the latter by an old gate, leading towards the town; that gate was pierced by their musketry in numberless places. I never saw a target better covered with holes. The third division had in return twice discharged a gun through it, which made two large holes. An old handspike was placed under its breech to depress it, and remained precisely in the same way three days afterwards. The scaling-ladders were well placed, *five* quite close together, against an old round tower. Many slain soldiers had evidently been pushed from off the parapet, and rolled nearly fifty yards down the hill; some lay with heads battered to pieces, whilst others were doubled up, looking scarcely human, and their broken limbs twisted in all directions.

The third division had been obliged to cross the broken bridge over the small river Revellas, rank entire, (amidst a shower of grape-shot, bullets, and bursting of shells,) and during the work of death to drag the unwieldy ladders up a rugged hill, to plant them against the walls: their first effort failed; many of the enemy then, contrary to General Philippon's orders, evacuated the Castle, and went to assist at the breaches. At this moment, Lieutenant-Colonel Ridge of the fifth regiment called on an officer of his corps, "There, you mount one ladder, and I will lead up the other. Come on Fifth, I am sure that you will follow your commanding officer." *He was killed; but the place was carried!*

Let us pause and reflect that this act of heroism was executed after a long and fearful struggle, high walls and defeat staring them in the face.

The third division then filled the castle, and there remained until daylight. On the south side of the town, General Walker's brigade of the fifth division, hearing the rolling fire at the breaches, became impatient, and, with a simultaneous rush, gained (by escalade) the top of the walls, and even formed on the ramparts. On seeing a light, the cry of a *mine* was set up, and a short panic ensuing, the enemy at the same time charging forward at a run with fixed bayonets and shouting loudly, these troops were forced to give ground.

An officer informed me, that he had thrown himself over the ramparts to save the colours of his corps, while nearly surrounded by French grenadiers. This bold fellow had the choice of either being pinned to the wall, or the risk of breaking his neck: he chose the latter.

The rear regiment, however, fortunately stood firm. Many of the enemy then precipitately abandoned the town, accompanied by the Governor, crossed the bridge, and shut themselves up in Fort St. Christoval, on the other side of the Guadiana; and the next morning surrendered themselves prisoners of war. This brigade continued to be *hotly* engaged in the streets during the *whole night*. Some even asserted, that many of the Spaniards fired from their windows on our troops, and *held out lights* to guide the French; knowing that their property would fall a sacrifice, should the town be taken.

The place was eventually completely sacked by our troops; every atom of furniture broken; mattresses ripped open in search of treasure; and one street literally strewed with articles, knee-deep. A convent was in flames, and the poor nuns in *dishabille*, striving to burrow themselves into some place of security; however, that was impossible; the town was alive, and every house filled with mad soldiers, from the cellar to the once solitary garret.

When I examined the three breaches by day, and witnessed the defences the enemy had made for their protection, I was fully satisfied that they were impregnable to men; and I do declare, most positively, that I could not have surmounted the *chevaux-de-frise, even unopposed,* in the day-time.

Some *talk* that grappling-irons would have moved them. Who would, who could have done it? thousands of warlike

French soldiers standing firmly up to the points, not giving an inch, and ready for the fight. They fought in the streets to the last, and tried to retake the castle—*Que voulez-vous?*

The *chevau-de-frise* were fixed after dark. Round-shot alone could have destroyed these defences, which were all chained together, and not made in a temporary. manner, as most military men imagine, but strong and well finished; and the enemy, behind all, had made a deep cut, over which they had thrown planks, communicating with the town, besides three field-pieces to enfilade the centre breach, if the *chevaux-de-frise* should be seriously shaken. Had it not been for this, the divisions would have entered like a swarm of bees.

One man only was at the top of the-left breach (the heaps of dead had, as a matter of course, rolled to the bottom), and that was one of the rifle corps who had succeeded in getting under the *chevaux-de-frise.* His head was battered to pieces, and his arms and shoulders torn asunder with bayonet wounds.

Our batteries did not play on the ramparts that night after dark; but when the explosion took place, the whole of them opened with *blank cartridge* in our rear—probably to frighten the enemy, or to make them keep down; but they were old soldiers, and not to be so done.

Poor M'Leod, in his 27th year, was buried half a mile from the town, on the south side, nearly opposite our camp, on the slope of a hill. We did not like to take him to the miserable breach, where, from the warmth of the weather, the dead soldiers had begun to turn, and their blackened bodies had swollen enormously; we, therefore, laid him amongst some young springing corn; and, with sorrowful hearts, six of us (all that remained of the officers able to stand) saw him covered in the earth. His cap, all muddy, was handed to me, I being without one, with merely a handkerchief round my bruised head, one eye closed, and also a slight wound in my leg.

The country was open. The dead, the dying, and the wounded were scattered abroad; some in tents, others exposed to the sun by day, and the heavy dew at night. With considerable difficulty, I found at length my friend, Lieutenant Madden, lying in a tent with his trousers on and his shirt off, covered with blood, bandaged across the body to support his broken shoulder, laid on his back, and unable to move. He asked for his brother—"Why does he not come to see me?" I turned my head away; for his gallant young brother (a captain of the 52nd) was amongst the slain!

Captain Merry, of the 52nd, was sitting on the ground sucking an orange. He said, "How are you?—You see that *I* am dying; a mortification has ensued."

A grape-shot had shattered his knee, and he had told the doctor that he preferred death rather than to permit such *a good leg* to be amputated. Another officer had just breathed his last between these two sufferers.

The camp became a wilderness, some of the tents being thrown down, others vacant, and flapping in the wind, while the musketry still rattled in the town, announcing the wild rejoicing of our troops.

Chapter 10

The Battle of Salamanca

The Duke of Dalmatia, on hearing of the fall of Badajos, retraced his steps towards Seville, followed by the British cavalry under General Sir S. Cotton.

On the 11th of April, the light and third divisions crossed the fine stone bridge to the right bank of the Guadiana, and entered Campo-Mayor. The march of the troops presented the most warlike appearance. Many of the soldiers' blood-stained and torn uniforms were discoloured from explosions, numbers of the soldiers held their arms in slings, and carried their firelocks and caps slung on their knapsacks; whilst others were seen with bandaged heads, or lame from contusions through wounds inflicted by the iron-crows' feet with which the enemy had strewed the ditch of Badajos.

In this manner did all those gallant soldiers, who were able to join their ranks, trudge along for ten days, for the purpose of chasing out of the province of Beira the Duke of Ragusa, who now blockaded and threatened the fortresses of Almeida and Ciudad Rodrigo.

Every morning before daylight we were creeping over the rough, flinty, and winding roads along the *Cordon* of Portugal, until we reached the neighbourhood of Ciudad Rodrigo, from which place the enemy had retired on our approach.

On the 19th of May, General Sir R. Hill, with the second division, attacked, and carried by escalade, and destroyed the forts Napoleon, Ragusa, and the *Tête de Pont,* which guarded the bridge of boats thrown across the Tagua near Almaraz in Spanish Estremadura. As the summer came on, officers and soldiers rejoined us with wounds scarcely healed; others arrived from England to fill up the vacant ranks, A fresh campaign was in contemplation, and the officers from various divisions of the army flocked merrily into Ciudad Rodrigo.

On the 12th of June, the army crossed the river Agueda, the Light Division leading the centre column. The march of the Light Division was worthy of notice. The men were not tormented by unnecessary parades—the march was their parade; that over, the soldiers (except those on duty) made themselves happy, while those with sore feet, by such a system, had rest, which enabled them to be with their comrades, when, by a mistaken notion of discipline, it would have been otherwise: their equipment was regularly examined, nor were the men on any pretence permitted to overload themselves—one of the most serious afflictions to an army.

A general may be endowed with transcendent abilities, and by a forced march place himself in a situation to overthrow his enemies; he may possess the number of divisions, and the number of regiments, but through internal bad management, half his army may be straggling in the rear. Again, nothing is so pernicious as keeping the soldiers under arms, while the officers are rambling about: it destroys all *esprit,* causing the officers to forget the sufferings of the men after a weary march, and creating feelings of dislike towards them in the breasts of the soldiers. Such a system did not exist in the Light Division; and when a young officer fell in action, the old soldiers proffered their services with parental care.

The baggage followed the line of march in succession. The mules of each company were tied together, and conducted by two batmen in rotation, right or left in front, according to the order of march. Each regiment found an officer, and each brigade a captain to superintend. The alarm-post for them in camp was on the reverse flank of respective regiments. When the enemy were at hand, the baggage was ordered to the rear—the distance according to circumstances.

The army was four days clearing the forest, which was clothed with verdure, and supplied the most delightful bivouacs. The Sierra de Gata lay on the right hand, covered with snow, while a cloudless sky formed our canopy, and the sunshine of hope and happiness was beaming on every countenance, not excepting those of the growling surly batmen, who were seen to smile at finding forage at hand for their animals.

On the fourth day the division encamped within two leagues of Salamanca, and quite clear of the wood. The German hussars had an affair on that day with the enemy's cavalry. The officers of hussars described it to us, and related the conversation that took place between them and the French dragoons stationed on picquet in front of Salamanca. The enemy requested the Germans not to charge; the hussars replied, while advancing, that if the French fired, they would. The enemy then fired their carbines to stop their progress. The hussars charged, and cut most of them down.

The next morning we advanced, and pushed a body of the rifle corps to feel their way through a village, near Salamanca, which they found to be unoccupied by the enemy. The division then brought up their left shoulders, and passed in open column of companies within cannon range of the forts, situated on the right bank of the Tormes, and within a short distance of the north side of the town. The enemy stood on the ramparts to see us pass; the whole plain was covered by our cavalry and infantry, crowding towards the ford of Santa Martha, where we all forded the river,, and bivouacked a short distance from the town. The French army had retired, leaving eight hundred men to garrison the three forts of St. Vincente, Gayetano, and Merced, that were constructed with the masonry extracted from the different handsome convents, monasteries and colleges, which had been pulled down to be converted into bastions.

The sixth division took possession of Salamanca, and invested the forts. Soon after we had taken up our ground, most of the officers hurried into the town; the inhabitants appeared much rejoiced to see us, and, as I entered, two ladies ran towards me, each seizing a hand. My Rozinante dropped her head in search of food, as I believe she had not enjoyed a feed that day, while I looked right and left, and thought such congratulations very romantic. The *Señoras*, in black silk, put numerous questions, few of which I could understand, nor am I confident whether they were civil or military, although, from the expression of their eyes, I concluded that they were on a *civil* subject. I much admired the female peasantry; they were healthy, well-made, with black eyes, red lips, little feet, and wore red, yellow, and blue petticoats.

Soon after, I ascended to the top of the cathedral, to reconnoitre the forts, when I had a full view into the interior of them, and saw that musketry might have been applied with effect from this point. I then descended, and entered into the festivities and pleasures of the place.

In the evening the town was illuminated, and resounded with music, while the merry Spanish *muchachas* were dancing boleros, and striking their *castanets* in the streets. The glare of light was reflected from the bright *arras* piled in the great square, surrounded by soldiers of the sixth division, many of whom were destined soon to fall within a few hundred yards of the fascinating scene.

Our division advanced the next day, and took up its ground a league and a half in front of Salamanca. On the 20th a staff officer rode up to a group of us, and said, "The enemy are advancing." I rode up the side of the position of St. Christoval, and descried them afar off in the vast plain. The division then fell in, and were ordered to. crown the heights, which they did; and at the same time some Spanish regiments came in our rear, with two pieces of cannon: the mules became restive; some went one way, and some another—every way but the right: they became entangled in their harness; some kicking, and others feeding on the uncut corn, and, finally, during this mutiny of the mules a gun was upset, and, rolling over the bank into the road, quite deranged the dignity of the Spanish march.

The different divisions of the army were now ascending the heights of St. Christoval at many points. The French army continued to advance, and soon after began to debouche from the different roads in order of battle. The view was not obstructed; the country was level, covered with a sheet of corn, as far as the eye could reach. To those fond of military evolutions, the scene was bold; to those of more tranquil habits, time was given to pray for the good of their own souls, and, if charitably inclined, for the rest of the army.

At first our division deployed on the left of the front line; then again moved, and took post in the centre of the second line; the whole army were deployed in two lines, to oppose the enemy, the cavalry to the right, and also some detached on the left, to scour the plain between us and Salamanca, where part of the sixth division remained to cover the forts of that place. The whole army present consisted of seven divisions, besides cavalry, artillery, the before-mentioned Spaniards, and some Portuguese infantry.

At five o'clock in the afternoon the French cavalry approached by the valley to the left of our position, where our light dragoons began to skirmish with them, and showed some disinclination to give ground; the enemy brought up six guns, and opened on our squadrons in reserve, when the dispute ended.

Towards evening the French made an attack on part of the seventh division, occupying a village at the base, and on the right of our position; after some sharp work, it was, carried by the enemy. A brisk cannonade then took place to our right between the two armies. Night put an end to the firing. The whole army slept on their arms in order of battle, and after dark the picquets were placed at the foot of our position.

An hour before daybreak, the troops stood to their arms,

fully expecting to be attacked. The dark shades dispersed; the sun rose; both armies tranquil, notwithstanding their proximity; the enemy were full in view, without a bush, or any obstacle to prevent close quarters. Their right was thrown back in *echelon* of divisions. I suppose our General-in-Chief wished them to come a little nearer, but the Duke of Ragusa was now cautious, for his army was inferior in numbers.

Our position was covered with uncut corn, which served the cavalry for forage, and the infantry for beds. The contending armies caused great devastation, and trampled down the ripe wheat for miles around. The river Tormes ran about two miles in our rear, with two fords. Our division was now withdrawn from the line, and placed as a column of reserve in rear and centre of the army, it protected the fords in our rear, and might be used as a moveable mass either to resist cavalry, or assist where required.

The Earl of Wellington was stationary from morning till night, watching the enemy, generally lone and on foot, at the crest of the hill, and in the centre of the position. His staff approached him one at a time to receive orders. At night the Earl slept on the ground, wrapped in his cloak.

The troops were much inconvenienced for want of water, as the river was at some distance, and only a few men could be spared, since it was impossible to know at what moment the enemy might not attack. Some Spanish ladies came from Salamanca, and walked through our lines. On the third night the French retired; our division took ground to the right, and were posted on the bare and conical hill of Cabrerizos. It appeared necessary that the forts and the command of the bridge at Salamanca should be secured before we made any forward movement. The Duke of Ragusa evidently wished to gain time, and to continue in the vicinity to succour the forts, also to infuse courage into the little garrisons, until his reinforcements should arrive.

The Earl of Wellington remained on the hill of Cabrerizos the whole day. The sun shone with great brilliancy, and it was burning hot. One of the soldiers of the 43rd put up a blanket to keep the rays of the sun from his lordship. Our bivouac presented a droll appearance, as the whole division had hoisted blankets in a similar manner. A Spanish *muchacha*, with sandy hair, named Agueda, from the *pueblo* of Fuente de Guinaldo, who preferred the sound of the bugle-horn to her domestic occupations, was the sole female to be seen amid the sunburnt soldiers, and the brilliant masses, that now covered hill and dale, ready at a moment to deploy in battle array.

The breaches at the forts were now considered practicable. At about nine o'clock at night the attack commenced; but after some time the firing became slack, and I saw three rockets thrown up from the forts; they were immediately answered by several rounds of artillery from the French army, on a rising ground two leagues to our right, which instantly satisfied me that the assault had not succeeded, and that it was done as a signal that they were still at hand.

On the morning of the 25th, at daylight, we heard some firing on the other side of the Tormes during a dense fog, which at first prevented the force of the enemy from being ascertained. The Earl of Wellington would not move. The soldiers laughed, and said, "Oh, they are only shaking their blankets on the other side of the water;" for in heavy weather musketry produced sounds such as I have described. As the fog cleared away, a few rounds of artillery took place; and the General-in-Chief sent a sufficient body of troops by the ford in rear of St. Christoval to meet the enemy. When the atmosphere cleared, we saw about a division of the French moving towards Salamanca. They were opposed by our heavy cavalry, which had been placed there to secure the flank and rear of our army.

At seven that evening, the French re-crossed, unmolested, to the right bank of the Tormes, by a ford a league to our right. I did not consider the movement a serious one, but merely as intended to encourage the soldiers in the forts to hold out.

On the 27th, St. Vincente being in flames, the enemy permitted our troops to ascend the breaches without opposition. It was a sort of half assault and half surrender. The troops in the other forts also laid down their arms, having suffered severely; and only marched out three hundred out of eight, their original force, and many of those scorched by the flames, or otherwise hurt.

The army now moved forward. Our division supported the cavalry, and advanced towards Ruêda. On the 2nd of July, Captain Bull's horse artillery and the cavalry overtook the enemy's rear guard near that place. Although the country appeared open, it was unfit for cavalry, as it was intersected with small vines, the size of gooseberry-bushes. On entering the town, I observed five of the French killed from the fire of the six-pounders.

The division bivouacked round the town; and the next morning we moved about two leagues in advance, and rather to the left, where an interchange of shots took place between the left of our army and the enemy, near Pollos, who had no idea of permitting us to cross the Douro at that time, as the French Marshal wished to maintain his line on that river for the base of his future operations.

We then returned and took up our quarters in Ruêda. Pay was issued, all of which we spent in gaieties and *iced wines*. The inhabitants had all returned to their dwellings. The mayor was informed that the officers would give a ball; when he procured *Señoritas*, according to custom. It was extremely pleasant, with waltzing, and all the fascinating mazes of the Spanish country-dance in perfection. The Marquis of Worcester, and others of the Earl of Wellington's staff attended.

On the evening of the 16th July our division was ordered to quit Ruêda, and marched the whole night over a dusty and arid country; and towards morning we took up our ground near Castréjon.

During this day the Valencians (commonly called the lemonade-men) came into our bivouac, the sure harbingers of the approach of the enemy. These men wear a spiral cap, of felt or leather, and have jet black ringlets hanging down each side of their dark olive faces; and their fierce black eyes give them a noble expression of countenance. A white linen jacket is thrown over the shoulder, and a red sash encircles their loins; they also wear a white linen kilt, like our Highland soldiers, reaching to the cap of the knee; the white half stockings are gartered under the knee, which is bare; and hempen sandals are tied round the feet. They carry a long tin can, strapped on their backs, cased in the bark of the cork-tree, which keeps cool the lemonade with which they are filled. These men generally marched with the French columns, and acted as spies to both parties.

Just before nightfall the company was ordered a quarter of a league to the front on picquet; the country was open, and, as the cavalry passed I heard a staff-officer giving orders, which led me to suspect that the enemy were at hand.

At break of day on the 18th, a few shots were exchanged to our right; the firing increased, and the cheering might be distinctly heard at intervals as the sun rose above the horizon.

Our dragoons became visible while retiring before the enemy's horse and light artillery, which at intervals were blazing away. The scene was sublime and beautiful. An officer said to me, "There will be a row this day; however, we had better get our breakfast, as God knows *when* we shall have any thing to eat, unless we take advantage of the present moment." The tea service being laid out, and a stubble fire kindled, to warm the bottom of the kettle, we suddenly espied some squadrons of French heavy dragoons in a valley to our right, pushing for the main road at full trot.

An absurd and ludicrous scene now took place. The crockery was thrown into the hampers; also the kettle, half filled with hot water; another officer, who had come to *déjeune* with us, from the rear, all the while vociferating, "God bless me! you will not desert my mule and hampers; they are worth four hundred dollars." In fact, to get off seemed impossible;

the company, however, formed column of sections, and fixed bayonets, fully determined to cover the old mule, who went off with a rare clatter, and we after him, in double quick time.

The enemy were now within two hundred yards of us, brandishing their swords, and calling out, when they suddenly drew up on seeing some of our cavalry hovering on their right flank. A rivulet, with steep banks, ran parallel with the road; but we soon found a ford, where we drew up, intending to dispute the passage. The right brigade of our division had moved forward, and had deployed to the succour of our dragoons first engaged, about half a mile to our right. Soon after this, two squadrons of our light dragoons formed on a rising ground, two hundred yards from us, with two pieces of horse artillery on their right, when about an equal number of French heavy cavalry, handsomely dressed, with large fur caps, made rapidly towards them, our guns throwing round shot at them during their advance. When they had arrived within one hundred yards of our squadrons, they drew up to get wind, our dragoons remaining stationary*.

A French officer, the *chef d'escadron*, advanced and invited our people to charge, to beguile a few moments, while his squadrons obtained a little breathing time. He then held his sword on high, crying aloud, *"Vive l'Empereur! en avant, Français!"* and rushed on single-handed, followed by his men, and overthrowing our light dragoons.

The guns had fortunately limbered up, and the horse-artillery fought round them with great spirit, the enemy trying to cut the traces, while the poor drivers held down their heads, sticking their spurs into the horses' sides with all their might, and passed the ford under cover of our picquet. The Earl of

---

* The company was formed up, and fronting the right flank of our dragoons. We, therefore, had an admirable view of the space between the combatants. The soldiers of the company had made ready, holding their firelocks horizontally, or rather at the charging position, but to have fired would have been rather unchivalric, and would probably have destroyed the valiant French officer, who, though our enemy, was an honour to his country.

Wellington was in the thick of it, and only escaped with difficulty. He also crossed the ford, with his straight sword drawn, at full speed, and smiling. I did not see his lordship when the charge first took place, but he had a most narrow escape, and, when he passed us, he had not any of his staff near him, and was quite alone, with a ravine in his rear.

A few stragglers of each party still continued engaged, and this part of the affray took place within twenty yards of us. One of our dragoons came to the water with a frightful wound; his jaw was entirely separated from the upper part of his face, and hung on his breast; the poor fellow made an effort to drink in that wretched condition.

The round shot now flew in various directions, one spun through a cottage behind us, and the shepherd ran out in great terror. The Light Division now commenced its retreat from the vicinity of Castrejon. The French had crossed the river Douro with reinforcements, and had made au amazing march to take us in flank. We had only retrograded a short way, when we obtained a view of the bulk of the French army, pushing forward on a ridge of hills to our left. The first false attack had been made at daylight on our right and in front, merely to draw all our force to that point, while the Duke of Ragusa executed this movement.

The fourth division were retiring in mass, within range of the enemy's fire, being critically situated in the valley, while the French cannon rolled on the crest of the hills above, and poured in their shot with effect on their right flank. Our division was obliquely to the rear, in column of quarter distance, with fixed bayonets, ready to form square, surrounded by large bodies of our cavalry. To avoid an action seemed impossible. The enemy's infantry were almost on the run, and we were marching away from them as hard as we could. While the round shot from a flank fire flew over us, a French division came running to engage and detain us until others came up, and obliged us to abandon the road, and trample down a tract of wheat.

The heavy German cavalry drew close round us. The country was open, and a vast sheet of corn enveloped us for many miles. The men became much distressed, owing to the rapidity of the movements and heat of the day. We were again enabled to regain the road (owing to our numerical superiority of cavalry), which made a curve down a gentle descent; and the men descried, at a short distance, a dirty meandering stream, called the Guarena, near Castrillo. A buzz ran through the ranks that water was at hand, and the soldiers were impelled forward, with their eyes staring and mouths open; and when within fifty yards of the stream, a general rush was made, I never saw the troops during my service so thirsty. The discipline of the division was such, that I have seen them pass clear water, unbroken, in the hottest weather, suffering under fatigue known only to those under the weight of a knapsack and accoutrements.

All this took place under a cannonade, which had continued, at intervals, for more than ten miles. This was following up with a vengeance.

We had no sooner crossed the river than some squadrons of the enemy's cavalry galloped up a hill immediately overlooking us. The division now moved more leisurely; and everyone was aware that had our cavalry given way, the division must have halted to repulse charges, which would have given time for the French infantry to come up; and had that been the case, the struggle must have been very sanguinary.

Our reserves now being at hand, we soon halted on a round hill, and showed front. The fourth division did the same; when a brigade of the enemy, covered with dust, came in contact with an equal number of the fourth division; who, firing a volley, charged with the bayonet, and overthrew the French in good style, taking many prisoners.

The French army had done their best to overtake us, but became glad of a halt as well as ourselves, and the firing ceased. We remained stationary during the day, when I fell asleep; and after some time, I suddenly awoke, with my lips glued together, and my person almost roasted by the scorching rays of the sun; and actually crawled some distance before I knew where I was. Dry biscuit was served out; but we could not get any water until eleven at night, when I obtained a draught of dirty water out of my batman's canteen; however, it cooled my inside; and I believe that many hundreds dreamed that night of limpid streams.

On the 19th the troops stood to their arms an hour before daybreak, but the enemy continued stationary, and well they might, as they had made the previous night and day an enormous march to cut us off in detail, according to the Duke of Ragusa's favourite expression; however, at four o'clock in the afternoon the Earl of Wellington rode up to Lieutenant Wilkinson of the 43rd, who was on picquet, and said, "What are the enemy doing?"

Wilkinson replied, "The French are in motion."

The dust was flying upwards from behind the ridge of hills in our front. The General-in-Chief said, " Yes—to the right now," and ordered the first brigade of our division to make a corresponding movement, by crossing a valley, to prolong our right. We ascended a high hill, and formed on our original front, when the French army issued from behind the hills, presenting a martial appearance, and a grand display of moving squadrons, with brazen helmets, and a great body of infantry flanked by their cannon.

The river Guarena was nearly dried up, and was the only obstacle between the contending armies, as the face of the country still continued bare and hilly, without even a tree to be seen. The Duke of Ragusa entered the valley to reconnoitre, surrounded by a numerous staff, when two guns of our horse-artillery opened, and a ball struck on the ground, and knocked up the dust in the very centre of the group, without killing anyone: they took the hint, and shifted their ground.

Eight of the enemy's guns instantly began a heavy firing on our brigade: the first shot struck an officer of the horse-artillery on the side of his helmet, and displaced him from his horse, after a short time the brigade went to the right about, to get out of range. At that moment the few Spaniards attached to us simultaneously started from the left of each regiment, and I do not recollect ever seeing them afterwards: it was most ludicrous to witness the flight of these patriots, in disorder, while our troops retired sloping their arms with the utmost *sang-froid*.

We soon halted, and faced about; the enemy's guns ceased to play, and a large force of our light dragoons mounted the, hill in our rear, with sloped swords. Night coming on, we formed columns in case of accidents. An officer and myself then stole down the hill on horseback, in search of water for ourselves and animals: having passed our advanced posts, some distance, and hearing strange voices, we looked at each other, and whispered that to go further would be indiscreet, wherefore rejoining the column, we wrapped ourselves in our cloaks, and fell into a profound slumber, out of which we were awakened by a great bustle and the trampling of horses. Word passed to stand to our arms, and the Portuguese Caça-dores fired some shots, but I was so overcome by drowsiness, that I continued in a squatting position, rubbing my eyes, too lazy to move. The confusion was caused by two or three; mules breaking their ropes, and becoming lively, not unusual amongst such animals.

On the 30th our division concentrated soon after daylight, and descended into the plain of Velesa, where we observed our whole army formed in a dense phalanx, ready to deploy in order of battle. The French army were not in sight) how-ever, it was evident they intended to avail themselves of the high ground; a brigade of our cavalry had pushed half way up the ridge, to entice them to show front, and to develop their movements, as it appeared during the night they had moved on a quarter circle, round our extreme right flank, and were now pushing on, and trying to cut off our com-munications. The Duke of Ragusa would not accept battle as long as he could gain ground without it, unless we attacked at a disadvantage, as he seemed to be a perfect master of the localities of the country.

Our army, under all these circumstances, broke up, and began to retreat, the different divisions arranged in such a manner, that, should it become necessary, by wheeling to the left, they could show front, and be ready to engage, the more particularly as both armies were again moving parallel to each other; and in this order they continued some leagues, and bivouacked. It became necessary for the troops to cook with fires of stubble, as there was not any wood in the neighbourhood.

A brigade of Portuguese cavalry happened to be left at some distance in the rear, and, as it slowly retired in line, presented such an imposing *front to their own rear,* that, by mistake, an artillery officer ordered them to be saluted by a couple of shot, which unfortunately did some execution.

On the 21st, two hours before daylight, we began our march, branching off towards Salamanca, and took up our ground in the valley, below St. Christoval, the enemy having moved on Alba de Tormes and its vicinity. Toward evening, we fell in, and crossed the Tormes by a ford, under the hill of Cabrerizos, and marched in the direction of Salamanca, the river being on our right hand. Night approached, and a German hussar passed us at full speed, and said, *"She's coming,"* meaning the French dragoons, who had pushed forward to the village of Calbarasa de Abaxo.

The atmosphere became now overspread with an unusual darkness; the thunder began to roll, the lightning was vivid, and the rain fell in torrents. During the storm a whole troop of horses galloped past at full speed, without their riders, having broke loose from fright, caused by the loud claps of thunder. Continuing our march, we soon bivouacked about two miles from Salamanca, our left wing resting on the Tormes, and in vain attempted to screen ourselves from the pelting of the storm. However, the morning of the 22nd broke beautiful and serene and at six o'clock we heard to our right, and about two miles to the front, a brisk fire of small arms, which continued for an hour, and then died away. The enemy had attacked the seventh division, in a wood near the heights of Nuestra Señora de la Pena, to ascertain whether the Earl of Wellington intended to give up Salamanca. A young officer was washing his shirt in the Tormes when the order came to fall in at eleven o'clock, and was under the necessity of putting it on wringing wet.

The Light Division advanced, and took up the ground which the seventh division had occupied in the morning; the wood extended a short way to our front. The division was formed in open column, concealed from a small body of the enemy, who were stationed, in small force half a mile to our front, with two pieces of cannon, on some rocks, round the old *quinta* of Nuestra Señora de la Pena. From our situation we formed a corps of reserve, communicating with the third division placed on the top of the conical hill of Cabrerizos, on our extreme left, and rather in advance of us, on the right bank of the Tormes.

We had no sooner piled arms, than I began to look about me. A *table mountain,* or rather one of *Los dos Arapiles,* was a short way to the right, and a mile to the front, with a very large mass of troops formed behind it, in contiguous columns, with one red regiment presenting their front towards the enemy in *line* at the top of it. Large bodies of cavalry, the first, fourth, fifth, sixth, and seventh divisions of infantry, with a proportion of artillery, composed the right and centre of the army in the plain, towards Las Torres; also a corps of *Spanish Patriots.* Placed thus, who could have thought that the General-in-Chief intended that day to retreat? I *never did.* Nor could I see the reason for it: it seemed advisable to beat the French before *El Rey* Joseph coming from Madrid, and General Chauvel, who, with a reinforcement of cavalry and horse-artillery, had crossed the Duoro, near Pollos, should make their appearance with additional forces.

The arrangement of our troops was inimitable, *years* could not have improved it. Our right had been fairly turned since the 20th; the army were presenting a new front, so that the *first* or *last,* whichever it may be termed, of military movements was to be effected, that is for the contending armies to *change places.* The French could not attack our left that day; if they had, the right of their army must have been either surrounded or cut to pieces. The third division would have hung on their flank, the Light Division Would have engaged them in front, the masses behind the table mountain could have debouched on either side, While our cavalry, artillery, and the rest of the army, could have moved forward, and attacked the left of the French in the plain, which must have advanced to support such a movement.

The table mountain is the mark of the French marshal's discomfiture. Military men say the French ought to have taken possession of it: but was their army up and strong enough to maintain it? The advance of the enemy at six o'clock in the morning was not that of their whole force: I should say, that it was merely a *reconnaissance;* half a dozen squadrons of cavalry and a division of infantry must not be taken for a whole army. Nor had the French soldiers wings; for in justice to them, more could not have been done by legs. The Duke of Ragusa might have had his army in hand, and could have placed a corps of observation where his centre stood; then towards evening manoeuvred with his main body at a greater distance from our right flank, and threatened to cut us off from Rodrigo, (and thereby change positions with us) until nightfall; at the same time keeping his communications open with Alba de Tormes, in the event of his not deeming it advisable to follow up such a movement the next day. At all events, the French general would have gained time, which was precious to him, as reinforcements were on the road to join him.

The fact was, the French marshal was completely out-generalled: the table mountain puzzled him; and the third division descending from Cabrerizos at twelve o'clock, and rais-

---

* The third division did not pass through Salamanca, when they descended from the hill of Cabrerizos. They forded the Tormes, and passed within a mile in rear of us.

ing clouds of dust as they passed along the rear of our army[*], caused the Duke of Ragusa to imagine that we were drawing off, which I am confident led him to take hasty measures, forgetting that he had been manoeuvring only on *blank* ground the four previous days.

The Earl of Wellington saw his over haste and his error; knowing that to support such an extension of the left, the enemy ought to have advanced in force on the village of the Arapiles, or that they must expose their left to a flank attack, which they did. On the other hand, had they advanced towards the Arapiles in the plain in force, our right and centre would have become engaged, and the troops concealed behind the table mountain could have debouched, and hovered on their right flank.

This was the first *general action* fought on the Peninsula, where the Earl of Wellington *attacked;* which led the French marshal still farther from his reckoning. The General-in-Chief, of course, did not wish to fritter away his army in useless skirmishes, and therefore only waited for a *fit moment* to bring it fairly in contact with the enemy, to *finish* well when once commenced; and as the Duke of Ragusa brought himself to action within the precincts of Salamanca, the advantage was ours, the wounded soldiers having speedy assistance, while those of the enemy who managed to drag themselves far from the field, endured the most distressing privations. The French were formed on the heights behind the village of the Arapiles, with an extensive forest in their rear.

The field of battle generally was composed of light sand, with a few straggling blades of parched grass. A very light breeze blew towards the French, which gave them the benefit of the clouds of dust and the volumes of smoke arising from the immense masses in motion, notwithstanding the heavy rain on the preceding night. Near 1 p.m. the third division were passing in rear of ours. I was strolling about, here and there coming across a dead or wounded soldier of those who had fallen in the morning, when a Portuguese caught my attention. He was resting on his elbows with his legs extended, suffering indescribable pain from a wound in his stomach; his face pale, his lips discoloured, and stifled groans issuing from his nearly lifeless body, while an almost tropical sun was shining on his uncovered head.

Soon after the third division had reached its destination, a column of French descended a hill *en masse* on our extreme right, towards the village of Miranda. Three eighteen-pounders opened on them, which took full effect, and spoiled their regularity. The enemy hesitated, While the discharges of our heavy ordnance were overthrowing all opposition. They went to the right-about to get out of range. Our columns, formed behind the table mountain, now debouched in double time, showing the French Marshal that the long-expected crisis was at hand.

A sharp fire of musketry opened on some companies of the seventh fusiliers, supported by the light companies of the foot guards, as they broke through the village of the Arapiles at half past two. The third division had already brought up their right shoulders, and were pushing on very successfully, when the enemy's horse furiously charged the grenadiers and right of the 5th regiment, while advancing in line, which they repulsed and continued their movement. The fire gradually increasing, at half-past four the armies were well in contact. The musketry rolled without intermission, only interrupted by the still louder artillery.

The fourth division, breathless, amidst showers of grape, musketry, and round-shot, had succeeded in planting their standards on the crest of the enemy's position; but at that moment a French division, in close column, and at a run, with fixed bayonets, forced them down the hill, whilst others advanced on their left flank, which was exposed, and carried the centre of the battle again into the valley; but our heavy cavalry, in the right centre, were bearing down all opposition, driving the left of the enemy before them, and putting them into the greatest confusion. Major-General Le Marchant was killed heading this charge. Marshal Beresford, Generals Leith, Cole, and Alten, were wounded. On the part of the French that fell, were the Duke of Ragusa, Generals Fercy, Thomieres, Desgraviers, Bonnet, Clausel, and Menne, besides their losing numerous prisoners, standards, and cannon.

At six the battle was at the height—no cessation of musketry, and the cannon of both armies thundering away as if there were to be no end of it. The columns of smoke and dust were rolling up in dense volumes, so that the atmosphere became dark above the bloody scene; yet there was not a cloud to be descried, except those which arose from the battle. A Spanish peasant was looking on with his arms folded; I heard him exclaim, *"Que grandísimo mundo!"* He was the only peasant I ever saw in battle, except one who offered his services at Vittoria, to conduct our division over an unprotected bridge, when the second shot fired took off the poor fellow's head.

The inhabitants of Salamanca were crowding the places of public worship, to offer up prayers for the success of our arms. *A propos,* it was Sunday.

At half-past six, a brigade of Portuguese guns opened on the enemy, in front of our division. At seven, the Prince of Orange, one of the General-in-Chiefs aides-de-camp rode up, and ordered our division to move on the left to attack. We moved towards the table mountain, right brigade in front, in open column; having passed it, we then closed to column of quarter distance.

The enemy's skirmishers soon advanced, and opened a brisk fire. The shades of evening now approached, and the flashes of cannon and small arms in the centre and on the heights were still vivid, while the enemy were making, their last struggle for victory. An English officer of General Pack's brigade passed us, covered with dust and perspiration; he complained of the rough usage of the French. They allowed the Portuguese to approach nearly to the summit of the point of attack, then charged them, and used the bayonet without remorse, taking that part of the field under their especial protection. The enemy's light infantry increased, and retired very deliberately; the ascent was gentle. The first brigade deployed, supported by the second; the first division was marching in reserve.

Our skirmishers were obliged to give ground to the obstinacy of the enemy; and nearly ceased firing. The line marched over them, dead and alive.

Appearances indicated a severe fight, for we were near the enemy's reserves. The Earl of Wellington was within fifty yards of the front, when the adverse lines commenced firing. The General-in-Chief ordered us to halt within two hundred yards of the enemy. They gave us two volleys with cheers, while our cavalry galloped forward to threaten their right flank. At this time I heard that a musket-ball had perforated the Earl's cloak, folded in front of his saddle. As we were about to charge, the enemy disappeared, not being in sufficient force to withstand the attack. This advance was beautifully executed.

Night coming on, the firing died away. Thus ended a battle which bore on the destinies of Europe, by showing the decline of French power in Spain, and leaving the British army for the first time free to pursue their enemy at pleasure. It lasted six hours.—Our line continued its movement. A French cavalry picquet fired on us at ten; the *ruse de guerre* would not do*. We continued to advance until, midnight; and bivouacked round a village.

The Duke of Ragusa was carried off the field by a company of French grenadiers. He had manoeuvred well, from the 19th till the battle, and had moved round our flank on a half circle.

As morning dawned on the 23rd, the Light Division ad-

---

* It has been affirmed, that the firing of the French picquet of dragoons in the forest caused us to go too much to the left. On the contrary, we were moving directly towards the ford of Huerta, on the Tormes, as it was supposed that the Spaniards left in the old castle of Alba de Tormes would prevent the enemy crossing the bridge at that place. These Spaniards, however, unknown to the General-in-Chief, had surrendered the day before.

vanced, supported by the first division, and crossing the ford, near Huerta, formed *en masse* in a valley, while the heavy German dragoons ascended the hill, moving on the left of the enemy. After some time we debouched. The Germans made a brilliant charge, and broke the French rear guard, formed on the side of a hill near La Serna. They suffered much. The whole of the enemy had not formed square. I observed five hundred stand of muskets on their left, lying on the ground in line, as if they had been piled and knocked down, and the owners had shifted as well as they could; the muskets Were not grounded to the front, but lying sideways. The enemy only formed two squares. I saw a man and horse dead, the rider still in his saddle. They must have received their mortal wounds at the same instant.

On mounting the hill, the enemy's army were in full view, in one great mass. Our horse artillery threw some shot into them. The troops soon halted, and the enemy were seen no more.

CHAPTER 11

The Heart of Spain

A great portion of the French army had marched more than twelve leagues, about forty-eight miles, in thirty-six hours, (advancing and retreating from the field of battle,) and had also been engaged in hard-fighting six hours out of that time, therefore, until the night of the 23rd, they had hardly made a halt for any considerable time during two days and a night, and I think I may venture to assert, that the rapidity of their movements, before and after the action, and their ultimate escape under Gen. Clausel from the very jaws of destruction, are equally astonishing.

Early on the morning of the 24th of July, we passed Pena-Aranda, from whence the inhabitants sallied out, loaded with bread, wine, and liquors, and rent the air with their acclamations in praise of the glorious victory that we had won over the French; and even the little boys straddled out their legs and bent forward their heads in derision of the enemy's soldiers, to represent to us to what a state of distress and exhaustion they were reduced.

As we passed onwards, numerous objects of commiseration, lying by the side of the road, reminded us of the miseries of war in all its horrors: many of the French soldiers lay dead, exposed to the scorching rays of the sun, which had so blistered their faces, and swelled their bodies, that they scarcely represented human forms, and looked more like some huge and horrible monsters, of gigantic dimensions, than anything else.

It is impossible to convey an adequate idea of such spectacles, or of the sensations they must have endured during their last agonies. These, now inanimate, objects had marched over sandy plains, without a tree to shelter them, while suffering from fatigue, sore feet, and want of water; then crowding into the battle, covered with dust, and under a scorching sun, they had received severe wounds, and were finally dragged, or carried on rudely-constructed bearers, from the scene of action, during excruciating torture, and ultimately left to perish by the side of the roads, or on stubble land, with their parched tongues cleaving to the roof of their mouths, and (to complete their miseries) before breathing their last sigh, to behold, with glazed and half-closed eyes, the uplifted hand of a Spanish assassin, armed with a knife, to put an end to their existence.

These dreadful fates awaited the defeated French soldiers in Spain; it was impossible to gaze on the mutilated bodies of these our enemies without feelings of deep commiseration for our fellow-creatures, who, a day or two previously, had been alive like ourselves, and perhaps the admiration of their comrades.

The vast *campos* in Leon, the two Castiles, and other parts of Spain, are apparently interminable sandy plains, covered with corn or small stumpy vines. In summer, many of the principal rivers become very shallow, and numerous tributary streams are dried up, leaving their winding beds, or indentures, filled with pebbles. In many parts there is not a tree, a hedge, or a shrub to mark private or public boundaries, nor a drop of water to be procured. The shapeless roads, or beaten tracts, are ankle-deep in sand, and in some places fifty yards wide; at other spots branching off into three or four paths, which again join at a given point. During the excessive heat of the day a solemn silence frequently pervades these immense plains; and the high steeples of churches, or the venerable turrets of monasteries of *las villas,* or *pueblos,* alone present a land-mark, and direct the weary footsteps of the traveller.

The towns are constructed of ancient massive buildings of stone or dingy brick, (the lower windows barred with iron,) intermixed with innumerable churches, convents, and religious edifices of the most ancient construction.

During the middle of the day all shops are closed by a pair of unwieldy doors, and the inhabitants enjoy their middle sleep or *siesta*. At this hour the streets may be traversed without meeting a single person, and the great monastic edifices stand in solemn grandeur as monuments of that superstition exercised by the monks at the time of their foundation in the darker ages.

As soon as the scorching heat has somewhat subsided, the doors are thrown open, and towards evening the streets are thronged by merry dancers and songstresses; the tinkling of the guitar is heard from the casements, balconies, and verandas; the servant maids go chatting and laughing to the fountains; the muleteers lead their animals to water; the peasant girls bring in cans of goat's milk, and the shopkeepers sit at their portals without coats, having their shirt sleeves tucked up, and smoking cigars.

On the 25th we made a halt to enable the stragglers and stores of the army to come up. On the same day El Rey Joseph had arrived at Blasko Sancho, near Arevalo, with a reinforcement, principally composed of Spaniards, for the purpose of joining the Duke of Ragusa; but on gaining intelligence of the defeat his troops bad sustained at Salamanca, he countermarched in the evening towards his capital, leaving a picquet of cavalry behind at Blasko Sancho, who were all taken prisoners, while carousing in a wine-house, by a corporal's party of the 14th light horse. About this time General Sir R. Hill had moved with the second division on Zafra, in Estremadura, to observe a French force in that quarter.

On the 28th our division bivouacked round the ancient town of Olmedo, where the Earl of Wellington gave a ball, with a general *invite* to all those officers who liked to attend. The Alcalde selected the different ladies as usual, whose merry hearts and supple forms were always ready for the dance.

The following morning, an hour before daylight, we advanced, and it was a droll sight to see the officers sleeping as they rode along after the fatigues of the previous night, still dressed in their ball attire, such as crimson, light blue, or white trousers, richly embroidered with gold or silver, velvet and silk waistcoats of all colours, decorated in a similar manner: dandies ready alike for the dance and the fight; most of them had received a wound, and others more, nor can I call to mind one of the officers present at this time, including the senior officer, who had reached twenty-five years of age.

Owing to the heat of the weather, it was the fashion of the times to wear the jacket open, which was the only particle of dress left to denote to what nation we belonged; as to any other uniformity for the officers, it was quite out of the question: the fantastical dresses of those days would have confounded the most ancient or modern disciplinarians.

The enemy still continued their flight across the Douro through Valladolid, which city Lord Wellington entered on the 30th, at the head of a large body of horse. The country on the banks of the Douro is remarkably sandy, and highly cultivated with vines; we forded to the left bank of the river on that day within two leagues of Valladolid. While our baggage was crossing, a batman and pony got out of their depth, and were carried down the stream a considerable distance; and so determined was the soldier to hold on, that he disdained, at the risk of his life, to quit his charge, and continued swimming until a rope was thrown, to him, by the assistance of which he conveyed the little animal and his master's portmanteaus safe on shore.

We had no sooner heard of the large town in the vicinity, than we began to prepare for the visit; however, it struck me that it would be very refreshing to enjoy a swim first, and also wishing my horse to participate in the luxury, I stripped myself and mounted its back, and together we plunged into the stream; but, as ill luck would have it, for a moment, the provoking animal hardly made any exertion, so down he went, and thinking there was no time to be lost, I sprang from his back; but owing to his plunging I received a slanting kick on my chest, such as most probably would have proved fatal, had the full weight of the blow struck me direct. The animal, however, soon recovered itself, and swimming with the current, it was with considerable difficulty I succeeded in getting it on shore.

Valladolid is a fine old city, with a spacious square, the inhabitants of which were glad to see us, but evinced none of those rapturous and warm expressions of delight displayed by those of Salamanca.

The next morning we crossed the river, and branched off in the direction of Madrid. Having halted a day or two, we again became in motion, and struck on an excellent road, leading to. the capital. Many exclaimed, "Is this the road to Madrid? Are we really going to the capital of Spain, the centre of romance?" My mind was filled with all sorts of illusions, and various anticipations of pleasure; my rest was disturbed, . and my dreams were of Madrid; every day's march was counted, every object brought something new, and I made up my mind to dance every night when I should arrive.

Continuing our route, we had reached within two days' march of the city of Segovia, in the kingdom of old Castile, and occupied a pine wood. On seeing an officer pass, who was likely to give me every information relative to the movements of the army, I issued from my small Portuguese tent, and entered into conversation with him, which lasted a considerable time. Being without my cap, I felt the top of my head extremely hot from the rays of the sun, and was about to withdraw several times for a covering, which unluckily I failed to do. When the dinner-hour arrived, composed of rice and boiled beef, without any bread or biscuit, my appetite failed, and I laid me down, in hopes that a few hours' sleep would restore me.

At daylight, the following morning, we were again *en route,* and had just cleared the sandy wood, enveloped in dust, when a sudden giddiness seized me, and I fell from my horse. On recovering my senses, I found myself supported by an officer. There was no water to be procured, and, on overtaking the division, I was advised to ride gently on to avoid the dust.

For the first time in Spain, I observed a Spanish grandee travelling in a carriage drawn by eight mules, escorted by fourteen servants, clothed in long yellow coats, with cocked hats, and all regularly armed, like horse soldiers. The costume of the peasantry now became somewhat different; one of that class was walking by my side, with a sort of spiral cloth cap, and clad in dark brown, who asked me if I did not admire a little girl passing on the road, whom he called a *Wappa Chica;* she wore also a stiff spiral cap of cloth, perched on the top of her head, with round balls of different colours up each side of it: her hair was plaited on each side of her head, ending in a huge pig-tail, about eight inches long, and precisely similar to those worn by British sailors; the jacket was brown, laced up the front; a yellow petticoat, reaching just below the knee, blue stockings, red clocks, shoes, and silver buckles.

Having travelled some leagues, I came to a village, where I observed one of the commissaries of our division standing at the door of a cottage, who remarked that I looked very ill, and asked me where I was going. I told him "about half a league farther on, when I intended to lie down under a tree until the troops came up, as I concluded they would not proceed much farther that day." He politely begged that I would partake of breakfast with him, as it was already prepared, which offer I thankfully accepted. My fever continued rapidly to increase, so that I could scarcely sit upright, and I soon began to talk very incoherently, which induced him to put. me to bed; the division shortly afterwards filed through the village, and bivouacked half a league in advance.

In the evening, the two other officers of the company with whom I messed, paid me a visit, and said, "Why, what is the matter?" when I replied, "That the commissary had used me very cruelly, and had been smothering me in blankets, to prevent my going on to Madrid." The assistant-surgeon having felt my pulse, asked whether I would permit him to throw some water on my head? which I readily assented to, entreating him to do anything to make me well. Then, being lifted out of bed, and divested of my linen garment, I was placed in a chair, while the doctor, standing on a table, emptied two pitchers of spring water on my crown; which produced a most painful sensation.

The following morning my companions assured me that I could not be permitted to proceed; but that, as there was a station to be established at the town of Cuellar, it would be necessary that I should go thither, when they felt no doubt that I should speedily recover, so as to be enabled soon to rejoin them. A car was accordingly procured, drawn by two fine mules, with a blanket extended over the top as an awning.

At the expiration of two days' journey, I reached the entrance of Cuellar, when a soldier came forward, and intimated that no sick could enter the town until the commandant's permission was obtained; and we were actually detained nearly two hours roasting in the mid-day sun, before a free passage was granted us. Much exhausted, and half suffocated, I at length obtained a most excellent billet in a gentleman's house, where I received the greatest attention from an assistant-surgeon belonging to one of the regiments quartered there; being unable to quit my bed.

At this time the army had possessed itself of the passes of Segovia and the Guadarama, and had moved forward on the 11th of August towards Madrid, having, in the course of their march, forced the enemy's advanced guard of cavalry to retire; but in the afternoon these again advanced from Malajahonda towards Rosas, to reconnoitre the Portuguese dragoons, who were drawn up on a rising ground above the latter village, and made a show of charging, but when they had arrived sufficiently near to observe the hardened looking visages of the sturdy French heavy horse, who displayed their long shining weapons, with brass hilts, like the Highland broadsword, with the exception of being one-third longer—at such a sight these our allies simultaneously wheeled about, and scampered off as fast as their Portuguese horses could trot and gallop, followed by their unmerciful pursuers, stabbing and hacking them down, and riding past three pieces of horse artillery that had been overturned.

The heavy dragoons of the King's German Legion took to horse as speedily as possible, amidst the confusion, and, after a good deal of savage sabring, the enemy retired, leaving at night the captured guns behind them. El Rey Joseph had retired with his followers behind the Tagus, and the following day our army entered Madrid, where the French had injudiciously left a garrison in the Buen Retiro, who surrendered themselves prisoners of war, just as part of the third division, and some other detachments, were about to escalade the works. A vast quantity of stores, powder, and ball, fell into our hands, besides one hundred and ninety pieces of cannon, principally dismounted.

About the 20th of August, a detachment of our regiment, from England, passed through Cuellar, but as they had experienced a long march during the hot months, an enormous number of them died, and the sick continued to increase from the army in such a ratio, that most of us were ordered to proceed to Salamanca. Accordingly, on the sixth day after my arrival, I was placed in a car, drawn by bullocks, to begin another tedious journey. The sixth division was on parade, having been left at that station as a corps of observation, and to protect the sick and the stores of the army.

That night I travelled a short way, and was billeted on a very clean house, where the *patron* was most anxious to have all the particulars of the late battle recounted to him; however, finding that I was not a sufficient master of the Spanish language to satisfy his curiosity, he was determined to make up for it by entering into the history of his own country. It was in vain that I exerted all my patience, and requested he would have the goodness to leave the room, pleading my indisposition in excuse for my apparent rudeness.

Having maintained silence for a few minutes, he offered me everything in his house, inquired if I was better, and recommenced his volubility to such a degree, that I almost became distracted, and was under the painful necessity of calling in my servant who in half fun and half earnest, turned him out of the room by the shoulders.

The next day I reached Arevalo, where the market was filled with fresh vegetables, a sight only to be appreciated by those who have travelled over a dry country, devoid of vegetation. A smiling *muchacha,* who sat by the side of a well-made young Spaniard, jumped up, and handed me a large bunch of grapes, with a dignified air of affability and frankness, so peculiar to the lower orders of that country.

I obtained a billet on a very handsome house, situated in a luxuriant garden; and, on being supported out of the car, I was so weak that I fell down, and continued in fainting fits for some time, my servant all the while sousing me with water in imitation of *the Doctor.* The fascinating *Señorita* of the house, about seventeen years of age, very kindly administered every attention; and at night, with a small lamp, remained in a recess, in readiness to offer me liquids, for which I continually inquired.

My recollection did not entirely forsake me, but my head was in a bad state, so that I fancied I saw groups of monkeys grinning at the foot of my bed; and, as I was unable to endure the slender rays of the lamp, I begged of the young lady to retire. At such a request her countenance portrayed every mark of disappointment: whether she considered me as one of the deliverers of her country, or whether so young a girl, residing in so sequestered a spot, fancied me under her especial protection, I know not; but I do know that her amiable solicitude and her lovely eyes made such an impression, that she continued the mistress of my thoughts, and heroine of my fancy, for a long period afterwards.

Taking my farewell on the following morning, and apologizing to the little *señorita* for my want of gallantry, I proceeded on my journey, and at the end of four hours reached the middle of an extensive plain, when one of the bullocks became dead lame, and the enraged driver declared vehemently that he would go no farther; my servant, therefore, dismounted from my palfrey, and placed me on its back. We made for the distant steeple, which skirted the horizon, as the point of our destination. At the expiration of a toilsome ride, we reached the *Pueblo,* and there sojourned until the next morning. In two more days we reached Alba de Tormes; I was quartered at an *apothecary's shop,* where I lay on the mattress for twelve hours in a sort of stupor; on recovering, in some degree, my servant fancied that I was dying, and proposed sending for the Spaniard, which I would by no means consent to, from the apprehension that he would bleed me to death.

The next day, while quietly passing through a wood, at a lonely spot, my horse made a sudden start, and, on looking to the right, I observed a dead man, perfectly naked, placed against a large piece of rock. He had been killed at the battle of Salamanca. His hair was long and grey; his beard had grown to a considerable length; and his arms and legs had been placed in an extended position; in fact, he was in an exact fencing attitude, in an extraordinary state of preservation, and presenting, of course, a dreadful spectacle.

I noticed during the period that I was in Spain, that those soldiers killed in action, who were exposed to the rays of the sun, immediately became a mass of corruption, but of those, on the contrary, who fell under trees or in shady places, exposed to heavy dew or rain, the skin became as hard as leather, and they would remain in that state for a very considerable period, unless they were devoured by wild animals or birds of prey. I have often seen vultures feeding on dead horses, that had been killed in battle, so fat, that they could scarcely take wing, or raise themselves from the ground.

On reaching Salamanca, I obtained a billet, on presenting which, I was treated with the greatest insolence by the man of the house, who declared that Í might enter, but that he had no accommodation for my servant; under these circumstances, I was under the necessity of sitting down in the street, until the soldier went to seek elsewhere for better success. After some farther delay, he procured me another on a public notary, where I was civilly received; but in the middle of the day my *patron,* smelling of tobacco and garlic, came in to take a *siesta,* in one of the two beds in a large recess. I asked him if he intended to sleep there; he replied *"Si, Señor."* To such an arrangement I objected; but he would not give up the point; a struggle then ensued between us, which lasted some minutes, although eventually I made him surrender. He was merely a diminutive old man; but I had become weak from the effects of my fever; and the scene was so amusing, that his own son, with a smiling countenance, was quietly looking on.

A hospital mate being put in requisition, the first dose administered to me was an *emetic,* and whenever I complained, the same dose was repeated; therefore, whenever he visited me, I invariably declared *that I was better.*

Our army had now occupied the heart of Spain, and the enemy, with rapid strides, were endeavouring to concentrate in the distant provinces round our centre, blowing up magazines, and eating up all before them, like a swarm of locusts. Napoleon was at this period traversing the wilds of Russia with his grand army, and his magnificent and highly-appointed Imperial guard. *The banners of Austria, Prussia, Italy, and the Germanic States, were marching under his control.* The *north* and *south* of Europe were in a blaze, and had become the extreme points of contest, which were ultimately to decide this mighty struggle for supremacy. The victory of Salamanca had shaken the combinations of the enemy in all parts of Spain, and put the whole of them in motion. On the 25th of August they destroyed their works before Cadiz, leaving behind them stores, heavy artillery, and mortars, many of the latter having been cast at Seville, by the order of the Duke of Dalmatia, for the purpose of throwing shells into the town of Cadiz. Some Spaniards and British immediately advanced from the lines, and took forcible possession of Seville.

On the 29th of August, Sir R. Hill, with the second division, entered Illerena, and pushed on to Ayllones, on the borders of Estremadura; but, finding the French were retrograding on Cordova and Granada, for the purpose of communicating with Joseph, who, in like manner, was forming a junction with the Duke of Albufera, intending to make Valencia the centre and the base of his future operations against Madrid; Sir K. Hill, thereupon, by a flank movement, marched toward the city of Medellin, on the left bank of the Guadiana, so as to he in readiness to act wherever his presence might be required, or to open his line with the third, fourth, and light divisions, cantoned in the vicinity of Madrid.

The General-in-Chief no sooner saw a probability of his right flank being cleared of the enemy, than he set off from Madrid, and concentrated the first, fifth, sixth, and seventh divisions round Arevalo early in September, and with a force of cavalry and artillery, passed the Douro, and retook Valladolid, which had been reoccupied by the enemy for a short time. On the 19th he crossed the river Arlanzon, and laid siege to the old castle of Burgos, bristled with cannon and the bayonets of its hardy defenders. Various attempts by escalade, mining, explosions, and breaching were tried for a month without success, owing to the want of a sufficiency of battering artillery, and to the obstinate defence made by the enemy, who firmly lined the walls, and threw their baits and bullets with deadly aim against the assailants. The enemy's vanguard was at Briviesca, and his main body behind the river Ebro, during the greater part of the siege.

In the mean time the second division had moved, in the middle of September, across the river Guadiana, through Truxillo Jaraceijo, towards Almaraz, and then crossed the Tagus by a pontoon bridge, and continuing its movement on the right of that river, passed Talavera de la Reyna, and arrived on the 30th at Toledo, occupying both banks of the river Tagus. General Sir Rowland Hill pushed forward his advance to Yepes and its vicinity, taking the command of the right wing of the army, composed of the second, third, fourth, and light divisions, besides cavalry and artillery stationed in the vicinity of Madrid.

CHAPTER 12

Skirmishes in the Woods

For my part, I had no sooner contrived to get out of bed at Salamanca, than I began to pace up and down the room, and in a very few days gained sufficient strength to be enabled to inhale the fresh air in the cool of the evening. While walking slowly along I met one of the staff doctors of our division, who expressed much regret that he had not been aware of my being sick in that town, and offered every assistance in his power; I expressed my thanks, but informed him that I intended to join my regiment.

He asked me if I were mad, and insisted on my giving him a promise not to think of prosecuting so wild a scheme for the present; which I was necessitated to acquiesce in, from a fear that he would effectually stop my rambles: however, two days afterwards, I presented myself to the medical board, which sat daily to examine officers: the group of *medicos* were seated round a table, and, having eyed them particularly, I experienced great relief at finding the worthy doctor did not form one of the party. I felt considerable agitation, from a fear that they would not sanction my departure, which gave me a colour; in fact, I reported myself in perfect health, and obtained permission to proceed to rejoin the army with a strong detachment, who were about to depart for that purpose.

At five o'clock next morning, the day before I was to recommence my journey, my servant entered my quarter, and announced that my mule had been stolen during the night, out of the stable, and that my horse had been running about loose, with the door wide open. This unwelcome intelligence caused me to tremble so violently, that I sank down on the bed, nor do I ever recollect being so agitated in my life, for I had no means left to supply its place, and I could not have walked in my weak state half a league. Fortunately an officer, who had just come from England to join us, relieved my anxiety, by offering to carry my baggage on one of his animals.

At daylight the next morning we started. The spangled dew still hung on the trees, the morning breeze refreshed my body and mind, and with exhilarated spirits I felt as if new life and fresh vigour had been conveyed throughout my frame. The dead French soldier was still stationary in the wood, and in exactly the same position already described. On re-entering Alba de Tormes, I passed the *apothecary's shop*, with exultation, which only four weeks before I had entered in such a miserable plight.

When we passed through Arevalo, one of the narrow streets leading to the Plaza was choked up with cars from the city of Burgos, crammed to overloading with exhausted, speechless, and wounded Highlanders, covered with hot sand, and many of them slumbering unto death; their pallid countenances portended the speedy dissolution of their lingering sufferings, while their sable plumes and torn tartans hung loosely on the pointed stakes, which formed the temporary sides of the rude vehicles.

I searched in vain, through every narrow avenue, and amongst the numerous convents and monasteries, for the house of the young lady who had been so attentive to me in that town. I well recollected the high walls of one of those fabrics enclosing one side of the garden; I was, therefore, in hopes that in some spot of difficult access, I should find the fair object of my solicitude. The whole of the following day (during our halt) was passed, however, in fruitless search.

Continuing the march, our little column consisted of three hundred and fifty men, and when within sight of the distant villages, which were surrounded by extensive plains, the church bells rang merry peals. Almost the whole of these places had been entrenched by temporary works, and the churches loop-holed by the French posts of communication, to protect their small detachments from being destroyed or cut off by the *guerrillas,* or surprised by the infuriated peasantry. Shortly before we reached the Guadarama mountains, we struck into the high road to Madrid; for many miles there was scarcely a house to be seen. At length we came to a *venta,* on the right of the road, but the house had been thoroughly gutted, and it was impossible for the owners of it to procure anything for us to eat.

The country bore a very solitary aspect until we began to ascend the pass by a paved road, cut in a zigzag direction up the face of the mountain, on the top of which stands a marble fountain. The prospect from this point is very grand, commanding a distant view of Madrid, of the palace of the Escurial, and of the rugged mountains extending towards Segovia, which are covered with snow during the greater portion of the year. The poor village of the Guadarama is situated in a valley at the foot of the grand pass, in the kingdom of new Castile.

Towards evening, our horses being in some degree refreshed, we rode into the park of the Escurial, which is of considerable extent, and lies adjacent to the village, producing pretty good pasturage, but infested by prowling wolves and wild boars. The trees are generally of small growth, consisting of oak, carob, ash, and cork. The front of the palace of the Escurial looks towards the mountains of the Guadarama, and is built of a grey granite, in the shape of a gridiron. This culinary utensil is represented in the books of mass, on the doors, and in various parts of the building, which is perforated by innumerable windows. The pantheon of the palace is octagonal, composed of marble; about fourteen niches are occupied by embalmed kings and queens; and there are a variety of other curiosities worthy the observation of the traveller.

Returning towards the village, the old man of the house assured us the effect of the extraordinary edifice we had explored was nothing to the wonder and astonishment we should experience at the grand bullfights of Spain. The tears rolled down his furrowed cheeks as he ran about the room, (which was paved with red tiles,) representing the wild Andalusian bull staring with surprise on first entering the arena; and then, getting astride of a chair, showed us how the *Picador* received the bellowing bull on his lance, and the way he was frequently tossed, mangled, and killed, by the infuriated animal. Then again, he skipped and danced about the room to represent the men insinuating the pointed darts and crackers into the animal's neck; and finally gave us the *graceful Matador,* with a red cloak slung over one arm, and a short sword in his hand, making his obeisance with a profound bend to the *señoras* and *caballeros,* who excite him by countless *vivas,* and the waving of the white hands, and whiter pocket-handkerchiefs, to dispatch the staggering bull at one thrust. At length the ancient *caballero* became so much exhausted by his exertions and feelings, that he fell back motionless in his chair, exclaiming, *"Oh, los ladrones Franceses!* They have eaten up all our Andalusian bulls, killed our poultry, corrupted all our *mozas,* and knocked all our *Santa Marias* from the altars, and out of their *sacred niches* by the roadside."

During this rhodomontade we remained quiet spectators, quaffing the excellent wine which our host had extracted from a concealed deposit.

Taking our departure the next morning, two of us being some short distance behind the detachment, at a very lonely spot, we observed a Spaniard of most ferocious aspect, with huge mustachios, a capacious *sombrero,* and clad in a leathern jacket, like a cuirass, with a short broad sword by his side, and a brace of pistols in his broad belt, which was buckled round his waist. We were instantly convinced that he was a robber on the look out, in the capacity of a spy, for his hidden *camarados;* however, saluting him as we passed, which he returned by a cold and distant bend of the head, the few baggage animals being in sight, we thought it necessary to warn the soldiers in charge to be on their guard, although, generally speaking, the British might pass all over the country without danger; yet some robberies had been committed in Spain and Portugal also by *banditti*.

This day we halted at the village of Rosas, about two leagues from the capital. The country is bare and hilly, and even when within half a mile of Madrid, the traveller might fancy himself in a bare wilderness, as the town stands isolated in the midst of a rugged plain, skirted on the north side by distant mountains. On the next morning we continued our journey towards the capital.

Madrid is a compact town; the lower windows of all the monasteries and houses are defended by iron bars; many of the streets are spacious, and the whole of them are remarkably clean. The Plaza Major is a square of lofty houses, many of them stained of various colours, the windows are very close together, out of which hang mats and drapery of a variety of striped patterns, to shade the rooms from the mid-day sun. Here is the principal market for vegetables and other commodities, and it invariably presents a bustling and busy scene.

The Royal Palace is of a square form, and surrounds an interior court-yard, which has two gateways. The grand staircase rises out of the courtyard near the principal entrance; it is a most splendid work, wide and lofty, leading into the principal suite of rooms, magnificently furnished. As we passed through them, I noticed the man in charge locking the doors after us: when, therefore, the curiosity of the admiring spectators was satisfied, we were ushered into another, and again made prisoners for the time being. A picture, beautifully executed, represented Napoleon in his younger days crossing the Alps, at the head of his bare-footed army and was considered, by those who had seen him, to be an exact likeness; the face was extremely handsome.

The Callé Major and Alcala are the principal streets of the

town; the latter is wide and spacious, lined by large buildings, leading direct into the *Prado*, which is much admired for its broad walks, divided into avenues by rows of trees, and running the whole length of one side of the town, being terminated at each end by gates leading from it. On the north side stands the Buen Retiro, encompassed by temporary works, which had been thrown up by the French, gardens, and pleasure grounds.

The fountains stand at certain distances from each other in the middle of the walks, and are framed after antique models. The water from one of them is esteemed the best in the town; the broad walk in the centre is adorned by these cascades, and is crowded every evening by the best company. It is here the stranger may examine, with advantage, the costume, style, and gait of the Spanish ladies. Their dress is composed of a *mantilla* or veil, gracefully thrown over the head, a long-waisted satin body, black silk petticoats, fringed from the knee downwards, white silk stockings and kid shoes, of white or black; they carry a large fan in their little hands, which they open and shut as they glide along; it serves to shade them from the sun, or to salute their different acquaintances as they pass, which they do by shaking the fan rapidly, and simpering an affable smile.

At sunset the bells of the convents and churches give notice for offering up the evening prayer to the Virgin; instantaneously the crowd becomes stationary, the *caballeros* take off their hats and remove the cigars from their mouths, the *Señoras* cover their faces with their fans, while they inwardly mutter a short prayer.

At the expiration of a few minutes, the profound silence is broken, when all again are in motion. In this place, dedicated to pleasure, our time was so divided as to be occupied night and day, either in dancing or at the *tertulias;* public balls were also held twice a week at the *Callé de Baños* and *el Principe.*

The officers of our division were anxious to display their powers as actors to their beloved *señoritas;* therefore, among other things, they were occupied in ordering dresses, and studying their theatrical parts. *The Revenge* was fixed upon as the tragedy to astonish the Spaniards, Capt. Kent, of the rifle corps, played the part of Zanga, in *El Teatro del Principe,* with due solemnity, and the piece went off in silence, until he began to move backwards and forwards, like the pendulum of a clock, his sinewy arm and clenched fist, cased in a black silk stocking, or glove, encircled by a shining bracelet—which caused the muleteers in the gallery to roar with laughter. The *señoras* tittered, and held their fans to their faces. During the remainder of the evening poor *Zanga* was treated more like a comic than a tragic character, and whenever he raised his arm, which he had frequent occasion to do, the same round of salutations greeted him on all sides, such as *"Arre Mulo"* &c. &c.

At the conclusion of the piece, a Spaniard and a girl danced a *bolero* in inimitable style: both of them were habited in male attire; the black hair of the female was clubbed up behind, and tied with a bunch of ribbons hanging down her back; she wore a richly embroidered silk jacket, white kerseymere breeches, fitting tight to the shape, white silk stockings, shoes, and buckles. She rattled the *castanets* exquisitely, and beat admirable time with her pretty little feet.

On the 21st of October our division was hastily concentrated, and first moved to some lonely villages, and then to Alcala de Henarez, one of the principal universities of Spain. On the night of the 21st Lord Wellington raised the siege of the castle of Burgos, and slowly retired on the Douro, followed by Gen. Souham. Joseph and the Duke of Dalmatia had also formed a junction, and were making various demonstrations on the line of the Tagus. On the 22nd, the second division was put in motion on that river to observe the enemy's movements. On the 24th, the third division, which had continued in Madrid, moved towards Pinto, on the road to Aranjuez, in support of the fourth and second divisions. On the 26th, the second division crossed to the right bank of the

Tagus, and extended its left on the Jarama. On the same day we marched four leagues and a half from Alcala, and entered Arganda, which is situated on the high road from Valencia.

The enemy continued to make such a variety of movements that it was impossible to ascertain positively whether he would attempt his grand push on the south or east side of Madrid, which obliged General Hill to show front on two sides of a square, for the protection of the great roads leading towards the capital, across the rivers Tagus, Jarama, and Henarez.

At ten o'clock at night (of the same day we had entered Arganda,) the bugle-horns sounded the assembly, which never occurred without the most urgent necessity, as it was not customary for the horns to sound when manoeuvring near the enemy, except under peculiar circumstances. The orderlies usually passed round, and gave the word to *pack up and accoutre*, no further questions being asked either by officers or soldiers, and all repaired to the alarm post, and patiently awaited further orders; and that so often without seeing an enemy, owing to the variety of marches and counter-marches in war, that such orders had ceased to be a novelty or any surprise to us.

The division soon fell in: I had to precede the column on duty with another officer, who was mounted on a sorry lank pony, which, on being touched on the near or off side, kicked out with one leg at every mule that passed him, in the most singular manner. I never recollect laughing more heartily; the muleteers cursed and swore, and particularly one who received a severe kick on the leg.

This class of men wear a large hat, or a pocket-handkerchief of various colours, tied tight round the head, with the corner hanging down their backs, and a sort of red Moorish sash round the loins, dark blue, or green velveteen breeches, open at the knee, and leather gaiters, with innumerable buttons up the sides, open in the middle, so as to show the calf of the leg to advantage. The mules are very gaily caparisoned, with bells at the head, and the backs closely shaved; the tails tied up in bunch, with red or other coloured worsted binding; and when they are loaded, the men sit on the top astride, singing boisterously. They usually bivouac in the woods, when the day's journey is finished, cover themselves with a tarpaulins, and allow their mules to browse about all night. These muleteers robbed the English army of hundreds of mules during the war. I lost two myself, and, during the time the Light Division was quartered in Madrid, the *ladrones* caused false keys to be made to fit the stable-doors, and actually, in the middle of the day, took the animals clear off which were never afterwards heard of.

At the end of a tedious night march, the division bivouacked in the morning on a rising ground, about a mile from Alcala, watching the right bank of the river Henarez, and the cross-road leading from Arganda; the enemy, however, did not make their appearance, and at night we entered the town. The troops lay on their arms under the *piazzas*, which run through nearly all the principal streets; the inhabitants were so fearful that we might become engaged in the streets, that they illuminated the town for three successive nights.

On the 30th we crossed the Jarama at a bridge near St. Fernando, which was already mined to blow up, and continued our retreat on Madrid. A slight affair also took place more to the right, at Puente Largo, between the van of the enemy and our troops, who had formed a junction with us from Cadiz. The General-in-Chief, on the same day, made a movement to his left towards Ruêda, on the left of the Douro, causing the bridges to be destroyed, right and left, on that river, to guard his flanks, to enable him to keep open his communication with his right wing at Madrid, and to cover its rear and left flank while retrograding from that place, through Arevalo to Salamanca.

Towards nightfall, as we approached Madrid, a slight rain fell, and when within a league of the town, the whole of the dismounted cannon taken from the enemy in the *Buen*

Retiro were blown up with a tremendous explosion, which quite convinced us that a retreat was decided on. We hastily traversed, by column of companies, the long walks of the *Prado,* which reverberated with the tramping of the soldiers' footsteps, and on passing the last gate of the town without a halt, we observed the bright fires of a portion of our army in bivouac on the distant hills, on the road leading to the Guadarama, which sight completed the gloomy thoughts of many who had formed attachments, and had, until this moment, cherished hopes of once again passing a short time in the society of the fair objects who had captivated their hearts in Madrid.

We filed to the summit of the comfortless bleak hills, and as our baggage did not reach us until two hours before daylight, we passed a tolerably uncomfortable night.

At nine o'clock in the morning, with gladdened hearts, we received orders again to advance on Madrid, but our anticipations were of short duration, as we merely halted without the walls to cover the troops who had been marching all night from the direction of Arganda and Aranjuez.

Many of the ladies came on the walks to take their last farewell, and just as we were moving off, forming the rear guard, in the afternoon of the 31st, a beautiful girl, lightly clothed, refused to leave her lover, an English officer in the Portuguese Caçadores, who dismounted, tied his silk handkerchief round her neck, and placed her sideways on his horse. Towards evening the wind blew keenly, and I saw her enveloped in a soldier's great-coat. Many females left their homes in a similar manner with the French officers, and travelled about with the army, on horseback, and astride, clad in uniform of the Polish lancers, or hussars, splendidly embroidered, with crimson trousers, made very wide, in the Cossack fashion. The ladies of Spain frequently ride astride, with pantaloons and hessian boots, with a habit buttoning up before and behind, and, when they are on horseback, it is unfastened and hangs down on each side, to conceal their legs from view.

On the 1st of November we bivouacked in the park of the Escurial, where two wild boars galloped through the lines and caused great confusion; a soldier of the 52nd was overturned by one of them, which bounded over him without doing any further damage.

During the retreat the enemy did not press us, nor were our marches unusually long; in fact, everything went on so regularly, that several days' march passed with merely the usual incidents. The whole army from Burgos and Madrid were now in junction, the left marching on the heights of St. Christoval, to cover Salamanca, and the right on Alba de Tormes, to take up a line of defence on the right bank of the Tormes.

On the evening of the 7th, our division reached within a league and a half of Alba, where it drew up until temporary defences were constructed, to resist the enemy at that small town. The country was perfectly open, without a house or tree to be seen, and I was contemplating the dreary prospect, and regretting the loss of my blanket, placed under the saddle of my horse, which I had sent to the rear, sick, on the previous morning. As the night closed on us, the rain began to pour down in torrents; we were without food, or a particle of wood to light fires.

Before daybreak we stood to our arms, looking out for the enemy: what a moment for an engagement, our clothes completely soaked through! At about eleven o'clock, the order came to retire, when we filed through the narrow streets of Alba, and crossed the bridge, where we found sappers hard at work, mining, and laying barrels of powder to blow up the centre arch, if necessary. The river Tormes had swollen considerably, owing to the torrents from the mountains: therefore the fords became difficult and uncertain. Continuing our march on the left of the river, we entered a dripping wood, half-way to Salamanca, when we found our baggage waiting for us. The division being dismissed, all the trees were filled with soldiers, cutting and tearing down huge branches to build huts.

In a short time great fires blazed up in every direction, while the soldiers encircled them with joyful countenances, Having been disencumbered of our drenched clothes, and rations having been served out, we set to work making dumplings; before dark the canteens were laid with smoking tea, rum, hot puddings, and beef. This was, indeed, a relishing and luxurious meal. The whole of the spirits having been exhausted, a heavy slumber, under a tottering hut, put an end to our carousal.

The next morning, before daylight, we were again under arms, and moved towards Salamanca, to occupy that town with the first division and some Spaniards. Every morning we assembled an hour before daybreak, without its walls, waiting the approach of the enemy. I noticed the Spanish officers invariably covering their mouths, before the sun had risen, with their cloaks, and blowing the smoke of their cigars through their noses.

The Duke of Dalmatia moved slowly and with great caution, and evidently wishing, if possible, to force us to retire without coming to blows. His army had been collected at vast trouble, and by enormous marching; many of his troops had marched, within the last three months and a half, over seven or eight hundred miles of ground. On the 10th, the enemy made a strong reconnaissance in front of Alba de Tormes, but, after a heavy firing of artillery, they drew off at finding they could make no impression. On the 12th, some musketry was distinctly heard in the direction of the position of San Christoval. Our division had been dismissed as usual early in the morning, but was again formed, and ordered to crown those heights, where we remained the whole day, the alarm having been occasioned by a few Spanish *guerrillas* firing at the French cavalry.

On the 14th, we all left Salamanca, and moved by the left bank of the Tormes, on the road towards Alba de Tormes, the enemy having crossed the river by some fords, two leagues above that town. As soon as this movement was ascertained by the General-in-Chief, he made a reconnaissance under a fire of cannon, and found the enemy strongly posted on the left of the Tormes, at Mozarbes; the second division remained near Alba.

In the evening our advance fell back, and the whole army was collected in the neighbourhood of the Arapiles, and showed front in the same direction as at the previous battle; it was supposed during the night, by everyone, that a great action would be fought on the following day. The country was illuminated for miles around from the quantity of fires, which marked the line of our bivouac. All hands caroused until nearly midnight, being fully determined to make themselves happy previously to the supposed approaching struggle; then, stretching themselves under the trees or around the fires, they tranquilly slept until an hour before daybreak, when we formed and stood to our arms, and were again dismissed.

At noon the baggage animals were ordered to the rear, and soon after we observed great masses of our army, moving in dense columns from the right by echelon of divisions towards the great forest. The enemy had laboured hard to strengthen Mozarbes, as a *point d'appui,* under cover of which they continued to extend their left at a distance, to outflank our right, and to threaten our communications with Ciudad Rodrigo. At about two o'clock in the afternoon, our division followed the movements of the army.

The rain had begun at mid-day, and now fell in torrents, and we passed a miserable night under the trees. As soon as the road was distinguishable in the morning, we were again on the march, ankle-deep in mud, which tore the shoes from off the soldiers' feet; in this manner we trudged along the whole day; towards evening we saw the enemy on our left flank, when a little cannonading took place. One hour after nightfall, we drew up under the trees, hungry, and in the most miserable plight; the fires were kindled with difficulty, and while roasting on one side, we were shivering and perishing on the other, the rain still pouring down most unmercifully, as if the very floodgates of the heavens had opened on us; for we were literally flooded.

On the morning of the 17th, not having received any orders to move, we were in groups roasting acorns to satisfy the cravings of hunger, when an officer who had ridden a short way to the left, came unexpectedly on the French heavy horse, who were stealing through the wood, and would have made a prisoner of him, had it not been for the speed of his English horse, which was at full gallop as he passed us, calling out, "The enemy's cavalry! Fall in! Join the ranks!"

The division were only waiting for orders to move off, and instantly seized their arms and debouched from the wood, and formed contiguous columns, with our horse-artillery filling up the intervals. A few of the enemy's horse, with polished helmets, and covered with white cloaks, appeared moving backwards and forwards amongst the trees, looking at us. Two officers of infantry, mounted on English horses, went to reconnoitre them, when the enemy tried to decoy them into the thicket. A troop of light horse were formed on our left flank, with sloped swords, but they did not throw out any skirmishers to feel the enemy in front.

After a short time, the division retired, and crossed a narrow rivulet, and re-formed. One company of our regiment was left amongst some old houses on the margin of the stream, when some French dragoons slowly came forward to look at us; one in particular went to our right, as if he intended to cross the stream, when a German hussar, I believe an orderly, went towards him, and challenged the Frenchman to single combat, provided he would cross the water. The Frenchman laughed, and made a similar proposal to him, as he approached quite close to the edge of the water: thereupon the German advanced, but instead of fighting they entered into a jocular conversation, and parted very good friends.

Our division again went to the right about, and moved off to the rear; fortunately the road continued very wide, which enabled us to march in column of quarter distance, with screwed bayonets, and ready to form squares. The soldiers of the division bore the wet and privation with unexampled fortitude; nor did they lose their organization. At three o'clock in the afternoon, things began to look black; we heard that all the baggage had been captured, and that Lieut.-Gen. Sir E. Paget was taken prisoner; all this having occurred on the very road which it was absolutely necessary for us to traverse.

Lord Wellington at this time joined us, and continued riding on the left flank, and quite close to our column, for he could not well join the main body of his army, as the enemy's horse scoured the road, and all our cavalry had retired. It was one of the chances of war, and could not be wondered at in a forest of such an amazing extent, that the army was three days passing through it. The French heavy horse continued to accompany us on each flank amongst the trees, and frequently spoke to the soldiers in the ranks. We made two halts, to keep the men fresh, and in good order to engage, and then resumed a quick march, but not so rapid as to cause any soldiers to be left behind. The column preserved a profound silence; not a shot was discharged, for, had we begun to fire, the noise would have brought from all quarters the enemy, who could not be aware otherwise of our isolated march.

Just before we reached a break in the forest, at four o'clock, it was absolutely necessary to detach a few skirmishers to prevent the audacious French horse from almost mixing in our ranks. The enemy's infantry were now coming up, mixed with their cavalry. Owing to the reverberation in the wood and dense atmosphere, the report of each musket sounded as loud as a three-pound mountain gun. Lord Wellington made a sweep round the column, to examine for the best fighting ground, while a lively firing of musketry took place close on the left, and in rear of our column, intermixed with the shouting of our assailants and the whizzing of bullets.

As we emerged from the forest, to our surprise we were saluted on the left by a number of the enemy's cannon, posted on a high hill just above San Muñoz. The division broke into double time across the plain, about half a mile, and made for the ford of the river Helebra. The second brigade branched off to the right to cross elsewhere, to extend a line of defence behind its banks. The seventh division was already formed in close columns on the other side of the river, near San Muñoz, and suffering terribly from the effect of the round shot.

Two squadrons of our heavy dragoons came forward to protect us over the valley. We had no sooner reached the river, than we plunged in up to our middles in water, under a sharp fire of artillery, and we were obliged to scramble up the steep bank, having missed the ford, by which the troops were thrown into a momentary malformation. While we were forming up in a hurried manner behind the horse-artillery, who were drawn up to protect the ford, Lord Wellington rode up in front of the left of number one company, and looked placidly at them, saying, "The enemy must not cross here."

At this moment a round-shot carried away one of our officer's legs, and knocked a German hussar from his horse, leaving his hands hanging by a few shreds or sinews, notwithstanding which he got up and walked off, with an agonized countenance, and his head bent forward, resting on his breast.

The three companies of our regiment who had been left in the opposite wood, now issued out at full speed, pursued by the enemy, and were obliged to run the gauntlet across the plain, with the round shot of both armies flying over their heads. The second brigade, which had already formed on our left, were keeping up a sharp fire of musketry, to oppose the French crossing the river. A Portuguese regiment was stationary, in close column, two hundred yards behind us. I saw three cannon-balls strike in precisely the same spot, carrying away a number of men each time. The firing of artillery and musketry continued until after dark, and then gradually died away, when the soldiers of the contending armies approached the river for water, and amicably chatted to each other in their different languages.

The French infantry wore broad-toed shoes, studded with nails, wide trousers of Spanish brown, a brown hairy knapsack, a broad leather-topped cap, decorated with a ball, and shining scales, and fronted by a brazen eagle, with extended wings. In action they usually appeared in light grey great coats, decorated with red or green worsted epaulettes, belts outside, without any breastplates, with short sleeves, slashed at the cuff, to enable them to handle their arms, and prime and load with facility. Their flints were excellent, but the powder of their cartridges coarse; that of the British army was remarkably fine, but their flints were indifferent.

During this day the rain had held up for eight hours, but after dark it again fell heavily, beef was served out, without biscuit; our cooking was speedily made, as we toasted it on ramrods.

After another wretched night, about two hours before daybreak, the soldiers began to clean their arms, by the light of the fires, to prepare for the coming morning. Day broke, but the enemy made no attempt to molest us, and for two tedious hours we continued without any order to move, owing to a stream, four hundred yards, behind us, which had detained the other division some hours in crossing it.

As we moved off, the dead and the dying lay under the trees, the trunks of many of them in flames, pale and shivering, with their bloody congealed bandages, imploring us not to leave them in that horrible situation, in the middle of the forest in the depth of winter. However, to attempt to afford them assistance was impossible. Every individual had enough to do to drag himself along, after three days privation. The stream we had to cross was only a few yards wide, but so deep that the soldiers were forced to cross it by single files over a tree, which had been felled and thrown across; had the enemy been aware of such an obstacle, we should have had a terrible struggle at this point; but the French army had suffered so much during the pursuit that they could no longer follow, and became glad of a halt; and we equally glad to get rid of such disagreeable neighbours.

Numerous soldiers from the other divisions of the army, which retired in three columns, fell out, and kept up a heavy firing, right and left, in the wood at wild pigs, or any other animal they could see. Many hundreds of these exhausted men fell into the hands of the enemy, and when they arrived at Salamanca, El Rey Joseph gave the English prisoners a *pecêta* each.

During this day's march the weather was fine, but the road was overflowed, and up to the men's knees for many miles. Two hours after dark we drew up on a bare hill, clear of the forest, the atmosphere became frosty, but there was scarcely any wood to be obtained, and we spent another shivering night, without rations, gazing at the starry heavens, and counting the dreary hours.

Early on the 19th we moved off. The twentieth Portuguese regiment, eight hundred strong, which had come from the south with Col. Skerret, and had been attached to our division the morning we left Madrid, could only now muster half that number of men in the ranks, owing to the cold and not being accustomed to campaigning, and they were obliged to fall out of the column of march to halt for their stragglers. The Light Division still continued in wonderfully good order, and reached Rodrigo on that day, and bivouacked a mile from the walls of the town, without suffering scarcely any loss, except from the enemy's balls the day they were engaged.

Six divisions of the army entered Portugal for winter cantonments; the second division crossed the Sierra de Gata, and took up its quarters in the vicinity of Coria, in Spanish Estremadura, and the Light Division remained near Rodrigo, on the left bank of the Agueda; the headquarters of the first brigade being at Gallegos, and those of the second brigade at Fuente de Guinaldo. Lord Wellington established his headquarters at Frenada, in Portugal, as usual.

CHAPTER 13

Towards Vittoria

Early in May, 1813, the Light Division, commanded by Major-Gen. Baron C. Alten, formed line in the plain, near Gallegos, with one regiment of the German hussars, and a brigade of horse artillery, for the purpose of passing in review before Lord Wellington, who appeared on the ground encircled by a numerous and brilliant staff.

During the winter we had remained cantoned by regiments on the Spanish frontier, on the left of the Agueda, in the different villages, during which period we, as well as the whole army, had received various reinforcements from England, the greater proportion of whom had continued in their quarters in Portugal, and near Coria, in Estremadura. The 10th, 15th and 18th hussars had recently landed at Lisbon, and also the Household Brigade , consisting of two regiments of Life Guards and the Royal Horse Guards. Every effort had been made by the General-in-Chief to make the infantry as effective as possible, and the great depot was removed from Belem to, Santarem. Previously to our advance, the great coats belonging to the soldiers were delivered into store, it being considered that the blanket was a sufficient covering for them at night, the more particularly as tents were served out for the use of the whole army, in the proportion of three to each company, to be carried by the mules that had formerly conveyed the iron camp-kettles for cooking;* instead of which a light tin kettle, between every six men, was substituted, to be strapped on their knapsacks, and carried alternately on the march.

Each man was provided with a reasonable supply of necessaries, including three pairs of shoes, and an extra pair of soles and heels, in his knapsack. The daily allowance of rations for soldiers and officers consisted of one pound of beef, one of biscuit, and a small allowance of rum or wine; the former was invariably preferred by the old soldiers, although frequently much adulterated by the mischievous *capitras*.**

The left of the army being already in motion from the interior of Portugal, the second and light divisions concentrated on the 20th of May; the former crossed the Sierra de Gata, near Baños, the following morning, which brought it in communication with our right; our division forded to the right bank of the Agueda the same day, and encamped on the skirts of the extensive forest situated between Rodrigo and Salamanca.

The German hussars rode up, smoking their pipes, and singing some delightful airs, their half squadrons at intervals joining in chorus. We had heard that the hussar brigade was

---

* The iron kettles were very heavy, and were carried on the backs of mules, one of which was attached to each company; but, when near the enemy, and the baggage had been sent to the rear, these unwieldy and capacious kettles were not at all times to be laid hold of. Besides, it occupied the soldiers a considerable time to cook their rations, particularly in the extensive plains, where only stubble could be procured; and also during the rainy season, when the forest trees were damp. I have often observed these ponderous kettles turned bottom upwards, (at a time when there happened to be a scarcity of provisions,) and encircled by ten or twelve weather-beaten soldiers, who, with empty stomachs, stepped forward, one at a time, and each of them in turn rubbing his blacking-brush on the sooty part of the kettle, blacked his dusty shoes, cap-peak, canteen strap, and knapsack.
** A muleteer, so called from having the charge of five mules, for the use of which he received five dollars daily, and one for himself. The biscuit, rum, and reserve ball-cartridge, were carried by the mules; under charge of the above men the lean Barbary bulls and bullocks followed the different divisions on their line of march—the whole originally provided by, and under the superintendence of commissaries.

to supersede these veterans, and to act with our division: the whole of us left our canvas, and lined the road to greet our old friends and companions of outpost duty. The hussars became so much affected by our cheering, that tears rolled down many of their bronzed faces. "Oh!" said they, "we are always glad to see the old *lighty division,* who will ever live in our hearts."

On the third day we had arrived near San Muñoz, and encamped on the river Helebra. Many of the forest trees were covered with beautiful blossoms, and the plumaged tribe hopped from branch to bough, while here and there a solitary skeleton lay bleached, and reminded us of those starved, drenched, and wounded victims, the recollection of whose cries for help still rang in our ears, as we had marched past them on our retreat from Burgos and Madrid the previous winter.

Now, how changed the scene! The inmost recesses of this extensive wood resounded with many voices, and a long line of animated troops continued to thread its mazes and winding roads. On this day the Household Brigade of cavalry came up; their horses' backs were in a very bad state, owing to the heat of the weather. In the evening, while sitting at our tent door, we observed one of the Germans making up his fat horse for the night, and afterwards employing himself in sharpening his sabre with a stone. "That man," remarked an officer, "seems to be preparing for single combat."

Early on the 26th we halted on the verge of the wood, within a short distance of Salamanca; our cavalry and some guns pushed onwards, and crossed to the right bank of the Tormes by two fords above the town, where they found three thousand French infantry preparing to retrograde. Our cavalry made a demonstration to charge them, but the enemy presented so firm a front, and then retired in such good order, that it was thought advisable not to attempt to break them, until a few discharges of artillery should have shaken the resolution of these veterans; which that course failed to accomplish. They at length formed a junction with a part of the French troops retiring from Alba de Tormes.

Our dragoons were then drawn off, and the enemy continued to retreat without farther molestation. In the afternoon our division moved forward and took up their ground in a wood immediately overlooking the left bank of the Tormes, a league below Salamanca.

The next morning, as there had not been any order for the troops to move, I mounted my horse, and, in company with, some other officers, rode into Salamanca. The inhabitants expressed their congratulations on seeing us again, although our reception was not of that warm character shown towards us in the preceding summer and, indeed, it would have been out of all reason to expect to find countenances decked with joy, when contending armies had trampled down and destroyed their corn over a fertile plain of many leagues in extent.

On entering the great square, we observed the principal inhabitants, full-dressed, flocking towards the cathedral, a very handsome stone structure, where we alighted, and, following the crowd through the. grand entrance, found a great multitude waiting the arrival of Lord Wellington, who soon entered, escorted by a numerous retinue of Spanish generals and other staff officers, in a variety of uniforms magnificently embroidered.

I was much struck with the simplicity of Lord Wellington's attire, who wore a very light grey pelisse coat, single-breasted, without a sash,, and a white neck-handkerchief, with his sword buckled round his waist, underneath the coat, the hilt merely protruding, and a cocked-hat under his arm. He stood with his face towards the altar during the prayer offered up for the success of our arms in the approaching struggle, (for during this time the divisions of our centre were branching off and marching over dusty plains towards Miranda de Douro, to support the extreme left, under General Sir T. Graham, which had crossed to the right bank of the Douro, east of Lamego, had passed through the defiles of Tras os Montes, and was marching on the right of that river through Leon, towards Carvajales, and Tabara, to out-flank the enemy;) the deep-toned organ played some fine pieces during the ceremony, and at the conclusion, the ladies, by way of a benediction, dipped their delicate fingers into a marble basin at the door, *and sprinkled us with holy water.*

At daylight on the 28th, we forded the Tormes, and continued a forward movement along a winding road, through a rich valley compassing the base of a hill, on the summit of which stood a number of videttes belonging to the Household Brigade; and although the men and horses looked gigantic, and bore a fine appearance, still the idea of outpost duty for the heavy cavalry caused much merriment in the ranks. At the expiration of a long march, we encamped in the vicinity of Aldea de Figueras, on the high road to Toro, where we halted four days; the second division, under General Hill, besides Portuguese and Spanish auxiliaries, were encamped half a league to our right, for the purpose of keeping in check and watching the movements of the enemy stationed on the right of the Douro, and also at Pollos and Ruéda, situated about two leagues from Tor-de-Sillas, on the left bank of the river, where the French still remained in some force, hovering on our right flank.

Under all these circumstances, it became necessary to be vigilant, as the left and centre of the army were now moving to pass the river Esla, under the immediate orders of the General-in-Chief, who had left Salamanca to join them, and to superintend this delicate movement in person, which he had caused to be executed for the purpose of turning the enemy's right, and to threaten his northern line of communications.

Owing to this manoeuvre, the French army was thrown on two sides of a square, and only possessed the chance of extending a line on the Esla, by throwing their left forward against General Hill at the moment when he was separated from the bulk of our army; (thereby making Madrid the base of their operations). However, El Rey Joseph had not concentrated his army, and showed no inclination to keep open his communication with that capital; and therefore he gave up the line of the Esla and the Douro without a blow.

The passage of the Esla having been effected on the 31st, without opposition, Lord Wellington moved on Toro, where he arrived on the 2nd of June, and the hussar brigade fell in with a strong body of the enemy's heavy horse between that town and Morales, where they overthrew the French, after a very vigorous charge, and made upwards of two hundred prisoners. Our division on this day made a forced march over a bare country, halted to cook during the heat of the day, then resumed its movement, and reached the vicinity of Toro in the evening, where we encamped among some luxuriant, well-watered vegetable gardens on the left bank of the Douro, the sight of which proved very refreshing after a long, sultry, and weary march; and it was most gratifying to observe with what zest and relish the officers and soldiers devoured the raw cabbages, onions, and melons.

The next morning our division crossed the fine stone bridge. The centre arch of it had been blown up and entirely destroyed. The soldiers, therefore, in the first instance, descended by ladders placed close together, communicating by planks thrown across to the steps of the opposite ladders, by which the men again ascended, thereby surmounting the obstacle with little difficulty, and then marching through Toro, which is situated on high ground on the right bank of the river, and commands a fine prospect for some leagues over the surrounding country.

The artillery and baggage forded one hundred yards above the bridge, without difficulty; the water being only knee-deep at this season of the year. We encamped half a league from the town. In the afternoon I walked in to see the prisoners who had been taken by the English hussars on the previous day, all of whom bore a very martial appearance, and many of their countenances were so covered with hair, that it was difficult to distinguish their features: one man, in particular, had a long red beard which reached down to his middle; he wore a brass helmet, surmounted with tiger's skin, with a bunch of horse hair hanging down his back from the *casque*.

One hundred of these French dragoons, who bad not been wounded, were assembled to march to the rear. Their officer maintained a profound silence, and looked angry and highly indignant, with a large stick over his shoulder, stuck through the middle of a four-pound Spanish loaf. The, whole of the captured, raw-boned horses, were huddled together in a courtyard, and bore evident marks of bad provender, escort duties, marches, and counter-marches; and nearly the whole of them had the most horrible sore backs, almost frying in the sun, while innumerable flies settled on and irritated the poor animals.

A number of English medical officers were busily employed dressing the wounds of the French cavalry; some of them were of a most shocking description, from sabre cuts on their heads and faces. A Frenchman, of enormous stature, lay extended with a dreadful thrust from a pike, which had been inflicted by a cruel *guerrilla*, some hours after he had surrendered himself a prisoner. A medical officer was on his knees trying to bleed him, and held his wrist, moving his arm gently, having made an incision in hopes of causing the blood to flow; but every effort to save his life was useless; the dying soldier nodded thanks to the doctor, and soon after expired.

On the 4th the whole army being concentrated*, it moved in three columns, the centre in the direction of Palencia. The country was beautifully diversified, studded with castles of Moorish architecture, realizing the descriptions given in the

---

* The British army was composed of eight divisions of infantry, as usual. The first, of two brigades of Guards, with two of the King's German Legion; the second, three brigades of British, and three of Portuguese; the third, two of British, and one of Portuguese; the fourth, fifth, sixth, and seventh, the same, the Light Division of two brigades. Total, seventeen brigades of British infantry, two of Germans, ten of Portuguese; besides other detachments. The cavalry consisted of four brigades of Heavy, and four of Light Dragoons, and two of Portuguese.

chivalric days of Ferdinand and Isabella. The sun shone brilliantly, the sky was of heavenly blue, and clouds of dust marked the line of march of glittering columns. The joyous peasantry hailed our approach, and came dancing towards us, singing and beating time on their small tambourines, and, when we were passing through the principal street of Palencia, the nuns, from the upper windows of a convent, showered down rose-leaves on our dusty heads, and the inhabitants declared, by way of compliment, that the Oxford Blues were nearly as fine as the Spanish royal horse guards. Our division took up their ground close to the town, and on the exact spot where the French had bivouacked the same morning.

Continuing our advance towards Burgos on the 12th, the right of our army made a demonstration to attack the enemy, who had taken post there, while our division brought up its left shoulder, and hovered, with the hussar-brigade, on their right flank; the left of our army halted, until the effect of this movement was ascertained, by which the enemy were again thrown on two sides of a square. The day was remarkably cold and cloudy.

Towards morning on the 13th, we heard a great noise, which we considered distant thunder, but it was soon known that the enemy had blown up part of the works of the Castle of Burgos, and had retreated. The left of our army was now pushed on in echelon, to turn by a flank movement the line of the Ebro, while our right and centre hung on the enemy's rear, ready to engage them in support of this movement. The country here was extremely wild and mountainous*.

On the 15th we descended by a narrow pass, about a league in extent, which had the appearance of being scarped; the road was extremely rugged, and, winding suddenly, we found ourselves in the valley of the Ebro, which extended some dis-

---

* The enemy left in the Castle of Pancorbo, (which commands the narrow and tremendous pass through which the high road runs towards Miranda,) a small garrison, who soon afterwards surrendered themselves prisoners to the Spaniards.

tance to our right. The beauty of the scenery was far beyond description, and the rocks rose perpendicularly on every side, without any visible opening to convey an idea of any outlet. This enchanting valley is studded with picturesque hamlets, orchards, of cherry trees, and fruitful gardens, producing every description of vegetation. We crossed the river by the Puente Arenas, where we saw a number of sturdy, thick-legged women, loaded with fresh butter, from the mountains of the Asturias. I had not tasted that commodity for more than two years, therefore it will be unnecessary to describe how readily I made a purchase, and carried the treasure in front of my saddle, until we had encamped; but as ill luck would have it, there was not any biscuit served out on that day.

The next morning we ascended by a most romantic winding road for a league, and obtained a view of the tents of the fifth division, who had made a detour to outflank the enemy, and to secure the passage of these narrow defiles. While passing a village, I asked several of the inhabitants to sell me some bread; a shake of the head was the only answer returned. I at last caught a glimpse of a priest, and, as I was determined to have bread to eat with the fresh butter, I made towards him, saluted him by a most gracious bend, pulled out a *pecêta,* and requested he would procure me a loaf, he very good-naturedly acquiesced, and soon again made his appearance with a three-pounder, and also returned half my money: he seemed pleased, so was I, and, more courteous salutes having been exchanged between us, I rejoined the ranks. Travelling onwards, we perceived a large building on the side of a hill, with something white waving at each window, which, on a nearer view, we perceived to be a convent, and the nuns shaking their white handkerchiefs to greet our approach. On taking up our ground for the day, the baggage made its appearance, and ample justice was done to the bread and butter by myself and companions.

On the 18th, while we were advancing left in front, along a narrow road, shrouded by overhanging woods and high mountains, a hussar informed us that the enemy were at hand. On reaching a more open space, we observed a brigade of the French drawn up behind a rivulet, and their front covered by a few houses.

Two battalions of the rifle corps, supported by the 52nd, instantly attacked them, and, after some smart firing, the enemy gave ground. During this skirmish our regiment turned off the road to the left, and formed line on a hill, as a rallying point, in case of need; when, to our astonishment, we observed the head of another column of the French issuing, by a road parallel to us, out of an opening between two perpendicular rocks and in rear of our second brigade, already engaged.

The other regiments composing our brigade scrambled over the rocks, to endeavour to attack their left, which the enemy perceiving, turned off the road, and made for a hill: the 62nd brought up its left shoulder, and actually formed line facing to the rear, at a run, and encountered the enemy on the crest of the hill, who, the moment they met that regiment, turned round, and, throwing off their packs, fled to the mountains, keeping up a running fight. The second brigade was now engaged front and rear.

During this desultory *fusillade,* the baggage belonging to the French division debouched from the already described outlet. The whole of the enemy's escort huddled together, and made a most desperate resistance amidst the rocks, while their affrighted animals ran loose, and were seen on the highest pinnacles of precipices. Nearly the whole fell into our hands, besides three hundred wounded and prisoners. The position of the division became singular after the fight, with its centre at the village St. Millan, and keeping a look-out to the front and rear. The enemy had also attacked the left of our army, near Osma, in hopes that, by causing such a delay, it would enable these two brigades, marching from Frias, to form a junction with their main body.

On the 19th we moved forward, and, at about ten o'clock in the morning, part of the fourth division became engaged with the light troops of the enemy. Our division then made a short detour, and turned the left of the French, who precipitately retired towards Vittoria.

The next day we halted, and the army took up a line on the river Bayas, after long and arduous marching. Lord Wellington approached the river Zadorra, which covered the enemy's position, for the purpose of examining the ground they occupied, and pointing out to different generals the various debouches, and their necessary line of attack, in the event of the French continuing to occupy the same ground on the following day.

On the 21st, we stood to our arms, and moved forward in darkness, some time before daybreak. A heavy shower of rain fell; but, as morning dawned, the clouds dispersed, and the sun arose with fiery splendour. A towering and steep ridge of mountains rose abruptly from the valley on our right, which the Spaniards climbed early in the morning, at first unopposed; the ascent was so steep, that, while moving up it, they looked as if they were lying on their faces, or crawling. They were supported, and soon followed across the river Zadorra, and through the town of Puebla de Arlanzon, by part of the second division, for the purpose of attacking the left of the enemy, who were posted on the heights above Puebla de Arlanzon and Sabijana de Alava, where the contest, at the former place, began at nine o'clock, amongst deep ravines, rocks and precipices.

The second division becoming heavily engaged with the enemy, under all these disadvantages it could only maintain the ground already won, and the firing seemed to die away in that quarter. Our right centre, composed of the light and fourth divisions, continued to advance, as also the great bulk of our cavalry.

At about ten o'clock, on ascending a rising ground, we observed the French army drawn out in order of battle, in two lines, their right centre resting on a round hill, their left centre occupying a gentle ascent, and their left hid from view on the heights of Puebla; the river Zadorra ran at the foot of this formidable position, and then took a sudden turn, embracing and running parallel to their right flank, towards Vittoria.

El Rey Joseph, surrounded by a numerous staff, was stationary on the hill, overlooking his own right and centre. The French army was unmasked, without a bush to prevent the sweeping of their artillery, the charging of their cavalry, or the fire of their musketry from acting with full effect on those who should attempt to pass the bridges in their front, and which it was absolutely necessary to carry before we could begin the action in the centre. When within a short distance of the river, five of the French light horse advanced on the main road to look out, and were overtaken by an equal number of our dragoons, when they wheeled about and attempted to make off, without effect; they were assailed on the near side, when three instantly fell from their saddles, covered with sabre wounds, and their affrighted horses galloped at random.

The Light Division left the road when within one mile of the river, and drew up in contiguous close columns behind some shelving rocks near Olabarre, with the hussar brigade dismounted on the left; the fourth division made a corresponding movement, by branching off to the right, and took post opposite their intended point of attack; the greater part of our heavy cavalry and dragoons remained in reserve, to succour the central divisions, in case the enemy should advance before the third and seventh divisions should have taken up their ground on the enemy's right flank.

The first and fifth divisions, with two brigades of Portuguese, a Spanish division and two brigades of dragoons, were making a detour from Murguia, to place themselves on the line of the enemy's retreat, towards St. Sebastian; the sixth division remained some leagues in the rear of our army to guard the stores at Medina. Gen. Clausel's division was manoeuvring on our right, but not sufficiently near on this day to give much cause of apprehension.

All the movements of our army required the nicest calculations, both for the attack and defence; for at this time the four great columns advancing were separated by difficult rocks and a rugged country, interspersed with deep gullies, narrow roads, and scattered hamlets. The enemy were again under the painful necessity, for the third time in one month, of manoeuvring on two sides of a square; and the first cannon fired by General Graham, at Abechucho and Gamarra Major,* must have been to Joseph and Marshal Jourdan, (his Major-General,) like a shock of electricity: all in an instant was riot and confusion in Vittoria; the baggage stuck fast, blocking up all the roads, and even the fields.

At half-past eleven o'clock Lord Wellington led the way by a hollow road, followed by the Light Division, which he placed unobserved amongst some trees, exactly opposite the enemy's right centre, and within two hundred yards of the bridge of Villoses, which we understood was to be carried at the point of the bayonet.

I felt anxious to obtain a view, and, leisurely walking between the trees, I found myself at the edge of the wood, and within a very short distance of the enemy's cannon, planted with lighted matches ready to apply to them. Had the attack begun here, the French never could have stood to their guns so near the thicket; or at least the riflemen would have annihilated them. The General-in-Chief was now most anxiously looking out for the third and seventh divisions to make their appearance.

We had remained some time in the wood, when a Spanish peasant told Lord Wellington that the enemy had left one of the bridges across the Zadorra unprotected, and offered his services to lead us over it. Our right brigade instantly moved to its left *by threes,* at a rapid pace, along a very uneven and circuitous path, (which was concealed from the observation of the French by high rocks,) and reached the narrow bridge which crossed the river to Yruna. The 1st rifles led the way, and the whole bri-

* We could not see the extreme right of the enemy, stationed near Arunnez, in front of Abechucho and Gamarra Major.

gade following, passed at a run, with firelocks and rifles ready cocked, and ascended a steep road of fifty yards, at the top of which was an old chapel, which we had no sooner cleared, than we observed a heavy column of French on the principal hill, and commanding a bird's-eye view of us.

However, fortunately, a convex bank formed a sort of *tete de pont,* behind which the regiments formed at full speed, without any word of command. Two round shots came amongst us; the second severed the head from the body of our bold guide, the Spanish peasant. The soldiers were so well concealed, that the enemy ceased firing. Our post was most extraordinary, as we were at the elbow of the French position, and isolated from the rest of the army, within one hundred yards of the enemy's advance, and absolutely occupying part of their position on the left of the river, without any attempt being made by them to dislodge us; scarcely the sound of a shot, from any direction, struck on the ear, and we were in, momentary expectation of being immolated; and, as I looked over the bank, I could see El Rey Joseph, surrounded by at least five thousand men, within eight hundred yards of us.

The reason he did not attack is inexplicable, and, I think, cannot be accounted for by the most ingenious narrator; Gen. Sir James Kempt expressed much wonder at our critical position, and our not being molested, and sent his aide-de-camp at speed across the river for the 15th Hussars, who came forward singly, and at a gallop, up the steep path, and dismounted in rear of our centre. The French dragoons coolly, and at a very slow pace, came within fifty yards to examine, if possible, the strength of our force, when a few shots from the rifles induced them to decamp. I observed three bridges, within a quarter of a mile of each other, at the elbow of the enemy's position. We had crossed the centre one, while the other two, right and left, where still occupied by the French artillery; at the latter, the enemy had thrown up an earth entrenchment.

We continued in this awkward state of suspense for half an hour, when we observed the centre of the enemy drawing off by degrees towards Vittoria, and also the head of the third division rapidly debouching from some rocks on our left near the hamlet of Mendoza, when the battery at Tres Puentes opened upon them, which was answered by two guns from the horse artillery on the right of the river. Some companies of the rifle corps sprang from the ground, where they lay concealed, and darted forward, opening a galling fire on the left flank of the enemy's gunners, at great risk to themselves of being driven into the water, as the river ran on their immediate left, while the French cavalry hovered on their right; however, so well did this gallant band apply their loose balls, that the enemy limbered up their guns, and hastily retired; and the third division, at a run, crossed the bridge of Tres Puentes, cheering, but unopposed.*

The enemy withdrew the artillery from the bridges in their centre at two o'clock, p.m., and were forming across the high road to Vittoria. The third division had no sooner closed up in contiguous columns, than General Picton led them forward in very handsome style, in column, by a flank movement, so as to place them exactly opposite the French centre. The fourth division directly after crossed the river by the bridge of Nanclara, and were ' hurrying forward to support the right flank of the third division; the seventh division also crossed the bridge of Tres Puentes, supported by the second brigade of the Light Division and faced the

---

* The French did not defend any of the seven bridges across the Zadorra, except the two lying north and N.E. near Vittoria, although it was their original intention to do so, The able manoeuvres of the General-in-Chief threw the French generals into doubt: they knew not whether to defend their left, their right, or their centre; so they gave up one after the other, in conformity with the threatened attacks of Lord Wellington—which was exactly what he wished, and most accommodating of his opponents, who thus left this intended great battle without beginning or without end; for the French infantry were not half beaten, before disjointed orders and crowds of baggage blocking up the different roads, completed their confusion past all remedy.

small village of Marganta. Our heavy horse and dragoons had deployed into line, on the other aide of the river, so as to communicate with the rear of the second division, (in the event of their being driven back from the mountains,) or to support the centre of the army, in case of any disaster. They made a brilliant display of golden helmets and sparkling swords, glittering in the rays of the sun.

Three divisions being in motion, the centre and left supported by the Light Division and the hussar brigade, the battle began by a terrible discharge on the third division, while they were deploying into line. We closed up to them behind a bank, when, with loud *huzzas*, they rushed from behind it, into the village of Ariyez, with fixed bayonets, amidst flashing small arms and roiling artillery, and after a bloody struggle carried it. The enemy's artillery was within two hundred yards of us, ploughing up the ground in our rear; fortunately, the bank nearly covered us, during the time it was necessary to remain inactive, to support the front attack, if needful.

A Portuguese regiment, attached to our brigade, had been detached for a short time, and rejoined in close column; but, just before they reached the cover, some round shot tore open their centre and knocked over many men; and such was the alarm of a Portuguese officer, at the whizzing of balls and bursting of field shells, that he fell into an officer's arms, weeping bitterly.

For ten minutes at this point, what with dust and smoke, it was impossible to distinguish any objects in front, save the shadows of the French artillerymen serving the guns, and the shouts of troops while forcing their way into the village. The smoke had no sooner cleared away, than we came on the bodies of many dead and gasping soldiers, stretched in the dust.

The sharp fire of musketry and artillery in the centre, announced it to be the point of contest. The "advance" of the second division had been severely handled on the mountains to our right, but they were now getting on as speedily as the nature of the ground would admit, it being composed of deep ravines, and such natural obstacles, as almost to delay their progress unopposed.

The first and fifth divisions were engaged at Gamarra Major and Abechucho, in front of the bridges over the Zadorra. These villages were carried after a smart action, by which a position was gained threatening the enemy's line of retreat by the high road to France, running N.E, some distance close on the left of the river. The bridge was attempted, but was found to be impracticable, until our centre bad-forced the enemy to give up Vittoria.

The different divisions in the centre were exposed to a desultory fire, while passing the villages of Gomecha and Luazu de Alava, and over broken ground, forming lines, columns, or threading the windings of difficult paths, according to the nature of the country, or the opposition of the enemy. The fourth division pushed back the left centre of the French, and were fighting successfully, and performing prodigies of valour, among crags and broken ground. The seventh division now came in contact with the enemy's right centre, which. resisted so desperately, and galled them from a wood and the windows of houses with such showers of bullets, that victory for a short time was doubtful; however, the second brigade of the Light Division coming up fresh and with closed ranks, assisted by the seventh division, broke through all opposition at a run, and routed the enemy at the point, of the bayonet.

The four divisions of the centre continued to gain ground, shooting forward alternately, leaving the killed and wounded scattered over a great extent of country. At six o'clock in the evening, by a sort of running fight, with hard contests at certain points, the centre of the army had gained five miles in this amphitheatre; for General Hill's corps was on the mountains, and General Graham was still on the right of the Zadorra.

Lord Wellington was in the middle of the battle, vigorously driving the enemy, to finish that which the wings had so well begun. First, General Hill's movement in the morning had caused the enemy to weaken his left centre; then General Graham's attack induced him to give up the front line of the Zadorra, without a shot (hardly) being fired.

At half-past six we were within one mile of the city of Vittoria, the capital of Alava, situated in a fruitful valley; but the French army now drew up, and showed such an imposing array in front of the town, that our left centre facing *Ali* was completely kept at bay, owing to the blazing of one hundred pieces of cannon vomiting forth death and destruction to all who advanced against them. This roaring of artillery continued for more than an hour on both sides, with unabated vigour: the smoke rolled up in such clouds, that we could no longer distinguish the white town of Vittoria; the liquid fire marked the activity of the French gunners.

During this momentous struggle, the left centre of the French covered a bare hill, and continued for a considerable time immoveable; while, pouring their musketry into the now-thinned ranks of the third division, it was doubtful whether the latter would be able to keep their ground, under such a deadly fire from very superior numbers: however, they maintained this dangerous post with heroic firmness, having led the van throughout the thick of the battle.

At this period of the action, it was absolutely necessary to strain every nerve to win it before nightfall. The fourth division, on our right, shot forward against a sugar-loaf hill and broke a French division, who retired up it in a confused mass, firing over each other's heads, without danger to themselves, owing to the steepness of its ascent. I was laughing at this novel method of throwing bullets, when one struck me on the sash, and fell at my feet, thereby cooling my ardour for a short time: however, when a little recovered from the pain, I picked it up, and put the precious bit of lead into my pocket.

The scene that now presented itself was magnificently grand: the valley resounded with confused sounds like those of a volcanic eruption, and was crowded with red bodies of infantry and the smoking artillery, while the cavalry eagerly looked for an opening to gallop into the town. On one side of the field rose majestically the spiral and purple-capped mountains, rearing their pinnacles on high; on the other ran the glassy waters of the Zadorra: and the departing sun threw his last beams to light up the efforts of those struggling in dangerous strife for the deliverance of Spain.

The enemy sacrificed all their cannon, with the exception of eight pieces, while withdrawing the right of their army behind the left wing, under cover of this tremendous cannonade, which was the only chance yet left them to quit the field in a compact body. This movement being executed in strange confusion in and about Vittoria, their left wing retired by echelon of divisions and brigades from the right, while delivering their fire; and finally, their last division quitted the field with nearly empty cartridge-boxes, and taking the road towards Pampeluna.

The greater portion of our army then brought up its left shoulder, or rather wheeled the quarter circle to its right; which movement brought us on the road to Pampeluna. The French managed to drag the eight pieces of artillery across the fields for nearly a league; but, coming to marshy ground, they stuck fast, and three of them rolled into a ditch, with mules struggling to disentangle themselves from their harness. Two pieces the enemy carried clear out of the action, leaving their numerous cannon behind them, owing to the roads being so blocked up with wagons.

The dark shades of evening had already veiled the distant objects from our view, and nothing of the battle remained, save the lightning flashes of the enemy's small arms on our cavalry, who continued to hover and threaten their rear guard.

The road to Pampeluna was choked up with many carriages, filled with imploring ladies, wagons loaded with specie,* powder and ball, and wounded soldiers, intermixed with droves of oxen, sheep, goats, mules, asses, *filles de cham-*

---

* Some excesses were committed, although the greater part of the booty, as usual, was bagged by the followers of the army.

bre, and officers. In fact, such a jumble surely never was witnessed before; it seemed as if all the domestic animals in the world had been brought to this spot, with all the utensils of husbandry, and all the finery of palaces, mixed up in one heterogeneous mass.

Our brigade marched past this strange scene (I may well assert) of domestic strife, in close column, nor did I see a soldier attempt to quit the ranks, or show the most distant wish to do so; our second brigade had not yet joined us, when we bivouacked a league from Vittoria, on the road towards Pampeluna. The half-famished soldiers had no sooner disencumbered themselves of their knapsacks, than they went to forage; for even here the sheep and goats were running about in all directions, and large bags of flour lay by the side of the road: in fact, for miles round the town, the great wreck of military stores was scattered in every direction.

Night put an end to the contest: the growling of artillery ceased, the enemy were flying in disorder, the British army bivouacked round Vittoria, large fires were kindled and blazed up, and illumined the country, over which were strewed the dead and suffering officers and soldiers: strange sounds continued throughout the night, and passing lights might be seen on the highest mountains and distant valleys.

CHAPTER 14

The Bidassoa

On the morning of the 22nd the atmosphere was overcast, and, being without either cloaks or blankets to cover us, our uniforms were very damp, owing to the heavy dew which had fallen during the night; notwithstanding this, we arose from the ground exceedingly refreshed, and gazed around, in mute amazement, at the prodigious wreck of plundered Spain; for, beneath the French caissons, tumbrels, and brass cannon, lay scattered *los doblones de oro, of the same virgin gold* which had been extracted in former times from the peaceful Incas of the new world, by those vindictive Spanish adventurers, whose avaricious veins boiled at that epoch with the hot blood of the Moors.

At nine o'clock the rolling of the tenor and bass drums, and the clank of cymbals, beating the marching time, announced that the leading regiments of the division were in motion for the purpose of following the enemy. During the rest of the day we marched through a valley, enclosed by highlands, but did not overtake the enemy; the corn was trampled down in many places, which showed they had moved in three columns, whenever the ground would admit of it. Soon after dark, the division bivouacked in a wood, a drizzling rain began to fall, and we laid down under a tree to enjoy a nap, until the arrival of our sumpter mules, heavily laden with flour and livestock, which we had industriously scraped together from the refuse of Vittoria's field. At midnight we were awakened,

with keen appetites, by the well-known neighing of the horses, and braying of donkeys; but none of the baggage animals
came our way, and during our anxious and broken slumbers
the night passed away, and the morning was ushered in by a
sweeping rain, which thoroughly saturated the troops before
they began their march.

As I chanced to be for the duty, of bringing up any stragglers who might happen to lag behind, and my hungry
messmate being also for the baggage guard (of those who
had come up), we journeyed together along the sloppy road,
when the conversation naturally turned on the splendid victory gained over the French legions two days before, and
we remarked how gladdened the people of England would
be on the receipt of such a piece of glorious intelligence,
while they would little imagine that the greater portion of
the victors would willingly lay down half their laurels for a
good breakfast.

At the close of the evening we came to the remains of
a French bivouac, consisting of doors and window shutters
torn from a neighbouring village by the enemy, and propped
up to screen them from the inclemency of the weather. The
sole person to be seen was a draggled-tailed old woman, with
a ragged petticoat, who, without noticing us, or once raising
her eyes, continued to pursue her interesting employment of
stirring up with a stick the mud (which was interspersed with
fragments of books and French novels,) or handling the broken fragments of earthenware pots.

Our curiosity was so much excited, that we reined in
our steeds to watch the progress of the wrinkled and cop-
per-coloured old dame, who, stretching out her bronzed and
shrivelled arm, at last laid hold of a whole utensil, and as she
hastily splashed off, I caught a glimpse of a chicken, resting
on one leg, behind a shutter, which somehow or other had
escaped the ramrod of the enemy, and the hawk-eyed soldiers
of the pursuing column. Unsheathing my sabre, I jumped to
the ground, and sprang forward either to grasp or maim the

destined prize; however, the ground was in such a slimy state, that my speed availed not; on the contrary it hastened my fall. My companion, disdaining to take warning at my mishap, must needs himself begin a hot pursuit; however, the practical experience convinced him of the slippery obstacles; he soon lay sprawling on his face, plastered with mire: suffice it, the bird escaped, and we resumed our wet saddles, in a condition and appearance nowise enviable.

Soon after dark we came to a river, but as the enemy had not sufficient time to blow up the bridge, they had set fire to many of the houses in the main street of the town, which were still in flames, in hopes of blocking up the way with the burning rafters, which they had hurled from the roofs of the houses, in expectation of preventing our artillery from passing through, and thus harassing our retreat. The rain still falling in torrents, by degrees extinguished the red embers of the smoking ruins, and presented the place from being entirely consumed to ashes.

The soldiers of the division crowded the houses, and huddled under cover wherever they could find shelter. We were obliged to content ourselves by squeezing into a small hovel, where the smoke found egress through the broken roof; the floor was composed of slabs of rocks, in some places rearing their primitive heads amid flints and loose stones. During the night a ration of meat and six ounces of mouldy biscuit were served out, which was greedily devoured by the victorious troops. It was in vain that we scraped into a heap the stones of this macadamized lodge, for the purpose of lying down; for bumps and holes only increased our difficulties, and we were forced to ascend a broken ladder into a wretched loft, swarming with vermin, to prick for a soft plank, whereon to stretch our chilly limbs.

At dawn, on the 24th, we were again on the road; the weather cleared up, and the cheerful rays of the sun sparkled in the crystal drops, which fell on our heads as we glided beneath the wet foliage. Having advanced a few miles, we found the enemy's rear-guard posted at a bare and steep pass, which covered the highroad, two leagues from Pampeluna. The column having closed up, two battalions of the rifle corps (supported by the horse artillery) pushed forward, and, after a sharp skirmish, they succeeded in pushing back the French rear-guard; the guns then galloped up the road, and plied the round shot with such effect, that they succeeded in dismounting one of the only two cannon which the enemy had extricated from Vittoria's entangled field. They had rolled the gun over a steep bank on the right of the paved causeway, on which were regular league stones, and the first I had noticed in Spain. One round shot had struck down seven of the enemy on the left of the road, some of them were dead, others still alive, with either legs or arms knocked off, or otherwise horribly mutilated, and were crying out in extreme anguish, and imploring the soldiers to shoot them, to put an end to their dreadful sufferings. A German hussar, in our service, assured them that they would be kindly treated by our medical officers. "No! No!" they vociferated, "we cannot bear to live. Countryman, we are Germans, pray kill us, and shorten our miseries."

Continuing onwards, we soon after drew up on the slope of a hill, within sight of Pampeluna, the capital of Navarre; it is well fortified, with a strong citadel, and situated near the banks of the river Arga, in a fertile plain abounding with wheat, the ears of which we rubbed between our hands to satisfy the cravings of hunger. Just before our arrival, the enemy's scattered army had clustered beneath the ramparts of the fortress, where they were in hopes of entering to obtain rest and provisions; but the place was so scantily supplied, that the gates were ordered to be barred against all intruders.

From this place an excellent road branches off in a north-westerly direction to Tolosa; but as General Graham, with his corps, was marching direct on that town, by the great road to France, it was of no avail to the main body of the enemy, who were obliged to continue their retreat into France, by Roncesvalles and other roads, merely leaving a rear guard in the valley of Bastan.

The following morning we filed over a rugged and flinty mountain, south-west of Pampeluna, from the summit of which we almost commanded a bird's-eye view into the very heart of the town, garrisoned by four thousand of the enemy. This place, well provisioned, should have been fixed on for the grand base of Joseph's defensive and offensive movements; for, had he made it the pivot of his operations, and opened his line on Aragon, (and the strongholds in Catalonia, held by the Duke of Albufera), his flanks would have been secured by the Ebro and the Pyrenees, and would have thrown our army on two sides of a square, and entangled it between two strong fortresses, and the labyrinths of the Pyrenees. Most probably such a movement would have kept the war from the immediate frontier of France, whence fresh troops, under favourable circumstances, could debouch and attack our left face. From political reasons, the time had not arrived for the decided invasion of that country; besides, if it had, such an invasion could not have been executed, so long as the enemy hovered in force on our right flank.

Continuing our route, we crossed the river Arga, and entered the town of Villalba: our baggage at last came up, and the *casa* in which we were quartered was enclosed by a good garden, well stocked with vegetables, which was considered a piece of good fortune in those times. This day, the 25th, General Graham overtook General Foy, retiring from the vicinity of Bilboa, who, on hearing of the unhappy extent of the French disasters at Vittoria, made an effort to block up the passage through Tolosa, but the victorious English broke through all obstacles, and continued to advance. In a few days the small garrison of Los Passages surrendered themselves prisoners. Thus it was that the left wing of the army had hardly halted since issuing from the *bowels of Portugal,* until the precipitous bank of the river Bidassoa (which divided France and Spain), put a stop for a time to its memorable, march and victorious career.

On the 26th we had an idea that we should halt, but during the day we were again under arms, (marching by an excellent road running S. S. E., leading direct on Tafalla,) accompanied by the third and fourth divisions, with a proportion of cavalry and artillery, to endeavour to cut off General Clausel's corps, which had approached Vittoria the day after the battle; but he also, being made acquainted with the total route, of El Rey Joseph, immediately countermarched on Logroño, and thence to Tudella.* During the movements of the right and left wings of the British army, General Hill, with the centre, showed front, and *masked* Pampeluna.

The weather now cleared up, but continued variable during the whole summer; the seasons here being totally different from the dry and scorching heats in the more southern provinces, where the sun-burnt mountains and vast plains, are covered, at this time of the year, with a parched vegetation, or the remains of many cindered forests.

Continuing our movement, we became once again extricated from the mountainous regions, which had everywhere enclosed us for more than a fortnight. The country was now open, and highly cultivated, with groups of bold peasantry lining each side of the way, and greeting us by crying *Vivan los Coluros, y viva el Rey Fernando séptimo*, and, while moving in the direction of Tudella, our enthusiastic hopes were raised to the highest pitch, at the probability of reaching the venerable and renowned city of Saragossa; but our line was all at once changed, and by a forced march we entered the province of Aragon, passing through a barbarous-looking country,

---

* There he gained information of our movements, which forced him to follow the right hank of the Ebro, until he reached Saragossa, where, crossing the river, and leaving a small garrison behind, he moved towards the pass of Jaca, and entering France on the 1st of July, he at last succeeded, after a round-about march, with the loss of the greater part of his *matériel* in forming a junction with the French army.

barely peopled, (the forlorn *pueblos* lying wide asunder, the poor dwellings being mostly constructed of dried mud, and plastered over with the same substance;) and at the expiration of five days we reached Sangueesa, and encamped.

Here we halted one day,* and, while promenading the town in the evening, the soft notes of music floated in the air, and on a nearer approach to the place whence the sounds issued, we were agreeably saluted by the scraping and cheerful notes of violins. A crowd of Spaniards had assembled round the door of the *casa*, and on being questioned by another officer and myself whether the ball was public, *"Oh si señores,"* answered they, *"es muy público:"* so, bustling up the stone steps, and feeling our way along a dark passage, we found ourselves, on opening a massive door, amongst many *señoritas*, with a scarcity of *caballeros*. A staff-officer, who was the promoter of the dance, expressed his gladness at so opportune an arrival. Although a friend, we apologised to him for the apparent intrusion; but he was a man of no ceremony, and declared it to be a lucky mistake; which turned out to be the case, for we beat good waltz time during the whole night, to the great satisfaction of the *señoritas*.

On reaching the camp the following morning, the tents were already struck, and the troops moving off on their return to Pampeluna. What with the overpowering rays of the sun, the rising clouds of dust, and our overnight's exertion, we were so overcome, that had it not been for the kindly arms of the soldiers, we should have dropped from off our horses, while fast asleep, dreaming of black-eyed *señoras, waltzing, and precipices!*

In two days we reached Pampeluna by a more direct road, but the men began to flag, owing to irregular and poor feeding; besides which, we had been marching for thirty-two

---

* There was a great scarcity of wood in the neighbourhood of this place, and as the third division followed ours, Sir Thomas Picton cast his eye on a pile ready cut, and, as soon as he had dismissed his division, sent a regular party, with a *cal*, to secure it, when, lo! it had all vanished!

days, with only two regular halts, since quitting our camp between Toro and Salamanca; therefore, those plagued and suffering from sore feet were under the painful necessity (unless totally unable to proceed), of going on until they got well again, I have often seen the blood soaking through the gaiters, and over the heels of the soldiers' hard shoes, whitened with the dust.

The General-in-Chief having cleared his right flank, and again condensed his right and centre round Pampeluna, debouched thence on the 4th July, for the purpose of taking possession of the passes of the western Pyrenees and pushing the enemy's van-guard out of the valley of Bastan into France; which was executed by part of the second division, on the 7th. Our division, forming the left centre of the army, flanked this, movement.

Our route at first lay through verdant and luxuriant valleys, abounding with apple orchards, groves of chestnut trees, and small fields of Indian corn; from thence we ascended by broken roads, over rugged mountains, which were cracked in many places into vast chasms, overhung with oak trees of enormous magnitude, whose ponderous and wide spreading branches cast their dark shadows over the dried watercourses and natural grottos, formed by the intricate mazes of the underwood, entwining around the peaked and overhanging rocks, which in many places were garnished with wild strawberries.

The third day after leaving Pampeluna, we descended from the mountains into the compact little town of St. Estevan, situated on the rocky and woody bank of the clear stream of the Bidassoa, over which a good stone bridge communicates with the opposite side of the river: here we halted, with full leisure to explore the lovely scenery, which on every side encircled this secluded valley.

Our curiosity was much excited by the peculiar-method of washing in this part of the country, the women squatting, or rather sitting on their bare heels, with their lower garments tightly pulled about them, whilst others stood in the river rinsing the linen, with their only petticoat tied in a knot very high up betwixt their legs, displaying the most perfect symmetry; and it was morally impossible to refrain from admiring the natural and graceful forms of these nymphs.

The dress of the Basque peasantry is totally different from that of other provinces, and many of the females possess very fair complexions and are extremely beautiful, being a happy mixture of *las brunas y las blondas;* their hair is combed back without any curls, and plaited into a long tail, which hangs down below the hips; their jackets are of blue or brown cloth, and pinned so exceedingly tight across the breast, that the bosom seldom swells to any size; the woollen and only petticoat worn by them is of a light or mixed colour, reaching to the middle of the calf of the leg; and, with the exception of the bosom being so compressed, they are divinely formed. They are also remarkably nimble of foot, and always carry their little merchandize on the top of the head; they seldom wear shoes or stockings, except on Sundays and saints' days.

The men go bare-necked, and wear a blue cap, or bonnet, (precisely similar to those worn in the highlands of Scotland,) with bushy hair hanging in ringlets on their shoulders. In hot weather they usually carry the short blue, or brown jacket, slung over the left shoulder, and with long and rapid strides, or at times, breaking into, a short run, they traverse the steep acclivities with their shoes and stockings frequently slung on a long pole, which they either carry sloped over the shoulder, or grasped in the middle like a javelin, and use it for the purpose of assisting them in scaling or descending the crags, or frightful precipices. Their waistcoats are double-breasted, without a collar; the breeches are of brown cloth, or blue velveteen, fitting tight over the hips, (without braces), and reaching to the cap of the knee, where they are usually unbuttoned, to give full play to the limbs; a red sash is twisted round the loins, They are a gaunt, sinewy, and remarkably active race of men, of sallow complexions; their limbs are admirably proportioned, and they are as upright as a dart.

After a rest of two days, we marched towards Bera by a narrow road, running parallel on the right bank of the river Bidassoa, the greater part of the way being blocked up with large stones, or fragments of rock, which had tumbled from the overhanging cliffs, that were rent in many places into terrific chasms, partly choked with huge trunks or roots of trees, through which overwhelming torrents gushed from the mountains during the heavy rains and formed vast cataracts, often swelling the river into a foaming and angry torrent. Its rocky bed is fordable at this time of the year, and varies from thirty, to more than a hundred yards in breadth. Owing to the badness of the road, a number of infantry soldiers were employed in clearing away obstacles, or lifting the wheels of the cannon, with handspikes, over the loose fragments or projecting slabs of rock, which, at every few paces for three leagues impeded their progress.

During the march we passed near the bridges of Sunbilla, Yansi, and Lazaca, which cross to the left bank of the river, where some Spanish sentinels were posted on the cliffs, who called out to us, *"miren ustedes, miren los Franceses,"* and on casting our eyes upwards, we observed three of the enemy's *chasseurs à cheval,* looking down on us as if from the clouds, Part of the division had been already detached, for the purpose of keeping a look out up the narrow road to the right leading to the heights of Echalar.

Just before we reached the mouth of this contracted defile, a buzz from the head of the column proclaimed the enemy's infantry to be at hand, and the musketry had no sooner commenced, than an officer, who had been amusing himself by the perusal of a volume of *Gil Blas,* hastily placed it under the breast of his grey pelisse: almost at the same instant a musket ball buried itself in the middle of the book, and displaced him from his horse, without inflicting any further injury; it is a curious fact, that the exact pattern of the silk braiding of the pelisse* was indented in the leaden bullet.

Our front being speedily cleared of the enemy's skirmishers, the firing ceased, and we entered a pleasant valley, within half a mile of Bera, which on this road is the frontier town of Spain, and is situated at an elbow, on the right bank of the Bidassoa: it has a good church with a lofty steeple, and consists of one long straggling street, a quarter of a mile in length, and immediately at the foot of the mountain de Comissari, over which a steep road, three yards broad, crosses the summit, which is called the *puerta de Bera,* and leads N. N. E. to St. Jean de Luz, in France; two other roads, if they may be so designated, branch off right and left from Bera, the first running easterly along the valley, (parallel with a small rivulet which empties itself into the Bidassoa), and passes between the great rock of La Rhune and the opposite mountain of St. Bernard, to St. Barbe and Sarré, into France; at this point the rugged defile is very narrow, and almost causes a complete *break* or *separation* in the western Pyrenees: the other road from Bera runs across the Bidassoa, over a narrow stone bridge, four hundred yards from the town, to Salines, thence branching off . through gloomy forests and over steep mountains to Oyarzun, Passages, and Saint Sebastian.

From Salines there is also a narrow rugged pathway, which traverses N. N. W. by the winding current, on the left bank of the Bidassoa; it is intersected with loose stones, and in many places ascends the steep and difficult acclivities over the naked rock, and finally enters the great road beyond Irun, which leads across the Bidassoa (where the enemy had broken down the bridge) into France, thence passing over the river Nivelle

---

* Many of the officers of our corps wore red and grey pelisses, similar to those of the Hussars. The bullet which I have described was afterwards shown as a curiosity, and I examined it myself; the silk braiding had been carried into the compressed leaves of the book, and remained twisted tight round the ball.

to St. Jean de Luz, and on to Bayonne, a distance of about twenty-four miles from Irun, which is the frontier town of Spain by that route.

The right of the enemy immediately opposed to us rested on a nearly perpendicular rock, at an elbow of the Bidassoa, and overlooking the small marketplace of Bera, so much so, that, if inclined, they might have smashed the roofs of the houses, at the west end of the town, by rolling down upon them huge fragments of rock. This post was decorated with a variety of fancy flags, or strips of cloth, of various colours, tied at the top of long poles while groups of French *tirailleurs*, who encircled them, sounded their small shrill trumpets, *and jocosely invited us to the attack*.

Their centre or reserve, composed of black columns, crowned the heights on each side of the *Puerta de Bera,* and also the wooded heights extending to the base of the rock of La Rhune, on which their left was stationed in an old ruin.

The ground having been fully examined, and the picquets properly placed, we re-entered the mouth of the pass, and, having cut down two or three small fields of Indian corn, and stored it up as provender for the animals, we encamped on the stubble close to the river. The day was fine, but during the night the rain descended in torrents, and continued to fall so heavily for two days, as to swamp the ground on which our tents were pitched, and it was with the utmost exertion that we could keep them upright, owing to the frequent gusts of wind tearing the pegs out of the liquid mud. In these damp and chilly regions the tents proved of incalculable service to the army. The. weather again clearing, our first brigade ascended the bare heights of Santa Barbara, the second brigade occupied a rising ground to protect the entrance of the defile leading to St. Estevan, and the picquets were pushed into the town of Bera, (within half a stone's throw and beneath those of the enemy), and into the farmhouses in the valley, enclosed by orchards.

The stupendous and lofty chain of the western Pyrenees being now taking up for the purpose of covering Pampeluna and St. Sebastian, the second division occupied the various rugged paths and passes winding up the steep sides of the mountains near Roncesvalles and Maya; the seventh division those of Echalar; the Light Division the heights of Santa Barbara, and the road leading to St. Estevan, opposite to Bera; and the first division and Spaniards guarding the left bank of the Bidassoa to the sea-coast. The latter troops helped to block up the numerous *gaps,* all along the crest of the position, such as mountain paths, goat tracks, and dried water-courses, as well as the numerous fords across the Bidassoa. This extended position is about thirty-eight miles in extent, as the crow flies, running north west from Roncesvalles to the town of Fontarabia, (which is situated near the mouth of the Bidassoa, where this river empties itself into the sea,) but necessarily following the rugged and zigzag flinty roads, along the winding or crooked valleys, or over difficult mountains, intersected with deep glens, chasms, craggy defiles, tremendous precipices, and through almost impenetrable forests. The distance may be fairly calculated at sixty miles for troops to march from right to left.

On the 13th, the Duke of Dalmatia came from the north for the purpose of taking the command of the French army. The 15th being the anniversary of Napoleon's birthday, the enemy at night illuminated their bivouac, by ingeniously festooning the branches of the trees with thousands of paper lamps, which produced a very bright glare, and of course presented a very novel appearance.

Four days after this, the fifth division began to dig the trenches at St. Sebastian, for the purpose of erecting batteries to batter *en brêche.* The third and fourth divisions, which had been kept in the neighbourhood of Pampeluna in reserve, and also to assist the Spaniards in drawing a line of circumvallation round that place, for the purpose of hemming in and starving the garrison into a surrender, now moved forward (leaving a Spanish corps to guard the lines); the former went to Ol-acque, and the latter to Biscarret; the sixth division was at St. Estevan: *these three divisions being the reserve,* and ready to suc-cour at those points where their assistance might be required. The cavalry and artillery were cantoned in rear of the centre and left of the whole army.

One evening, while reclining on the parched and sun-burnt turf at the tent door, our milch goat nibbling particles of hard biscuit out of my hand, on looking around, I was much struck with the beauty of the scenery; the azure sky was reddened and glowing with a variety of brilliant tints, reflected from the glare of the setting sun, whose bright rays glided the rugged peaks of the towering and great bulging mountains which every where inclosed us. A long line of grey-coated French sentinels lined the opposite ridge, and one of their bands was playing a lively French air. In the valley below us, the little active Basque boys and girls were pelting each other with apples,* between the hostile armies, while the straggling and half-starved Spanish soldiers, who dared not pluck the fruit) pretending to enjoy the sport, but in reality were picking up the apples, and carefully deposit-ing them in their small forage bags.

---

* This was a usual pastime among them, throughout the mountains, which abounded with vast quantities of apple trees. One day another officer and myself were enjoying a rural walk, when we met two of our friends, whom for amusement we pelted with apples, and drove them at full speed out of the orchard. All of a sudden, we were assailed by a number of the Basque boys, led on by a girl, who had witnessed our sport at a distance, and, although we piqued ourselves on being pretty good throwers, we found it a difficult matter to contend with them, from their dexterity in dealing out such irritating blows on our faces and legs; until, being ashamed to ask for quarter of such diminutive and laughing antagonists, we made a last effort, and succeeded in hitting one of their leaders on the bare heel, when they all ran away, to our exceeding satisfaction. My companion had been a Cadet at the Royal Military College at Marlow, and declared that he had never experienced a warmer rencontre in his more juvenile affrays at that place.

In the background sat our tanned and veteran batman,* employed in mending a pack-saddle, after a long day's forage, and casting an eye of affection towards his animals, which were tied round a stake, feeding, with ears turned back, on some fresh heads of Indian corn. In the meanwhile my mess-mate was conversing with, and drawing a caricature of, a dowdy woman,** (from the Asturias,) loaded with an oblong basket of fresh butter, with her arms akimbo, and her nut-brown knuckles resting on hips which supported no less than four short coarse woollen petticoats; from underneath these branched out a pair of straddling legs, of enormous circum-ference, the feet being wrapped in brown hairy skins, by way of sandals.

In this position of things my contemplative mood was all at once interrupted by an officer of the *rifle corps* riding up, who, with a mysterious air, whispered me, by way of a profound secret, that he had become acquainted with a Spanish family, residing in the town of Bera, and offered to introduce me, provided I would agree to limit my attentions to the eldest daughter, Maria Pepa, who, he acknowledged, was endowed with very ordinary attractions, whereas her sister, *Ventura,* of seventeen, possessed charms of a far superior description.

As a matter of course, not wishing to throw any impedi-ments in the way of so liberal an offer, I readily acquiesced in the proposal, and forthwith accompanied him to the destined

---

*The batmen of the army were hard-working and privileged characters, who, after unloading at the end of harassing marches were obliged to go a great distance in search of forage, and armed with a sickle ready to cut down even rushes, or anything they could lay their hands upon, for their famished ani-mals. If all happened to be right, after a long day's journey when questioned by the anxious officers (no matter of what rank), they would negligently turn away, and scarcely give any answer; but if one of their horses or mules hap-pened to be lame or suffering from a sore back, or had cast a shoe, they would fret, fume, curse, swear, throw the ropes about, and give such a catalogue of evils, as to terrify the master with the idea that all was going to rack and ruin.
**These hardy women are in the habit, thus heavily loaded, of walking thirty or forty miles a day.

casa, for as such I may justly nominate it, as I may affirm that this introduction was subsequently the means of the life of a wounded brother officer being preserved, owing to the kind attention of its inmates, who watched over his mattress night and day, until he was out of danger: his hurt in fact was so severe, that when a doctor was asked how he found the patient, he replied: "Pretty well, but no man can ever recover from such a wound."

On alighting from our horses we entered the house, and having ascended the staircase, we found *el Padre, la Madre, y las dos hijas* seated in a spacious apartment, with the casements open, and a French sentinel, who was posted on a projecting grey rock, so thoroughly overlooking the house, that we could almost fancy he could overhear the lamentations of the anxious parents, who, devoutly crossing themselves, prayed that the siege of St. Sebastian might be speedily brought to a conclusion, to enable them to return to their house at that place, and secure the valuable plate and property, which they had been forced to abandon in great haste, to escape being confined in that town during the siege. Having passed some hours with them in a very agreeable manner, we took our departure, with a promise of shortly renewing our visit.

The left and main body of the French army, being now concentrated, formed a line at the foot of the Pyrenees, in the vicinity of Forage and St. Jean Pied de Port, in France, with its right wing occupying the mountains from the Rock of la Rhune to Bera, thence by the right of the Bidassoa to Andaye, and flanked by the Bay of Biscay. This ridge immediately covers the country in front of St. Jean de Luz and Bayonné.

Preparatorily to offensive movements, the French marshal issued a flaming proclamation, to his troops, in which he reminded them that the standards of Britain waved aloft, and that her army, from the summits of the Pyrenees, proudly looked down on the fertile fields of France—an evil which he attributed to the want of decision in the late French commanders.

"Let us then," said the Marshal, "wipe off the stain from our faded laurels, by chasing the English beyond Vittoria, and there celebrate another triumph, to add to the many victories which have so often decorated your brows, in all parts of Spain, *and on*

CHAPTER 15

The Battle of Pampeluna

The Duke of Dalmatia, on the 25th of July, assaulted the passes in the neighbourhood of Roncesvalles,* and the Count d'Erlon that of Aretesque, four miles in front of Maya. The result of this day's combat obliged Generals Cole, Byng and the Spanish General Morillo, to fall hack from Ronceavalles; owing to which retrograde, the British army were taken in reverse.

The fifth division, at day-break, had stormed the breaches of St. Sebastian without success; two thousand men had fallen, or were made prisoners, at the various points of contest; and General Hill fell back, during the night, from the pass of Maya. So far everything seemed propitious to the views of the French marshal. Under all these circumstances, General Campbell, (who was stationed with a Portuguese brigade at the pass of Los Alduides,) finding his flanks laid bare, retired from that post, and, during the 26th, formed a junction with General Picton, who, by a flank movement to the right, had marched from Olacque to Lizoain, for the purpose of succouring the troops falling back from Roncesvalles.

During these operations, General Hill had taken up a strong position at Irrueta, sixteen miles from the pass of Aretesque,

---

* Pampeluna is about thirty-five miles from the extremity of the principal pass at Roncesvalles, forty-five from that of Aretesque, in front of Maya, and fifty miles from the pass of Bera; all these points it was necessary to occupy on the right of the Bidassoa; which clearly demonstrates the advantage the enemy possessed by attacking principally at Roncesvalles.

where he opposed, for the time being, the farther progress of the Count d'Erlon. This position covered the flank of General Picton's column, retrograding from Zubiri, and prevented the Count d'Erlon from uniting with the Duke of Dalmatia, and also enabled the sixth division to march direct to the rear from San Estevan, and to unite at the well-arraged point *d'appui,* five miles in front of Pampeluna, where, on the 27th, the General-in-Chief joined those troops which had retired from Zubiri, under the command of Generals Picton, Cole, Byng, Campbell, and Morillo, and who were now drawn up on a strong ridge in front of Pampeluna, and flanked by the rivers Arga and Lanz.

General Picton was in a manner thrown back on the left of the Arga, in front of Olaz, and supported by General Cotton, with the cavalry in reserve, for the purpose of preventing the enemy from taking the right of the army in reverse by the road from Zubiri. The enemy, who had followed the march of the troops by that road, had no sooner arrived opposite the third division, than by an oblique prolongation to their right, they began to extend their line across the front of the General-in-Chief, under a fire of small-arms—by which manoeuvre they succeeded in cutting off General Hill's retreat by the Maya road, running through Ortiz; he, therefore, having passed through Lanz, hedged off diagonally in a westerly direction, and, by an oblique march, formed a junction with the seventh division (from St. Estevan) at Lizasso, thence to co-operate, if possible, with the left of the General-in-Chief, whose position in front of Pampeluna was about eighteen miles from that place.

During these various movements, General Graham, with the first and fifth divisions, and a corps of Spaniards, remained stationary on the left bank of the Bidassoa, for the double purpose of covering St. Sebastian, (the siege of that place was now converted into a blockade, and the battering train embarked at the port of Los Passages,) and watching General Villate.

The latter lined the opposite bank of the river, to be in readiness to assume the offensive, for the purpose of raising the siege of St. Sebastian, or hanging on General Graham's rear, in the event of the Duke of Dalmatia gaining a victory at Pampeluna, or succeeding in cutting off in detail the various divisions of the British army, now thrown into echelon, and extending from the banks of the Bidassoa, in front of Irun, to seven miles in an easterly direction beyond Pampeluna; a distance of at least sixty miles for the army to unite to either flank, (between two fortresses, whose ramparts were garnished with the cannon and small-arms of the enemy,) on an irregular quarter circle: amid multifarious barren rocks, towering mountains, and extensive forests, over whose inhospitable regions it was necessary, amongst other things, to convey provisions, ammunition, and biscuit bags, for the daily consumption of the moveable divisions—an operation attended with great difficulty under such circumstances.

Although the right of the army had been retiring for two days, the Light Division still tranquilly remained unmolested in front of Bera; but on the morning of the 27th, on finding that the seventh division had quitted the heights of Echalar, and uncovered our right flank, the first brigade quietly descended from the heights of Santa Barbara, and the whole division concentrated behind the defile on the road to Lazaca, the picquets being left to mask this movement, and form the rear-guard.

As soon as the division had got clear off, the picquets evacuated the farmhouses in succession from the right; and lastly, at ten o'clock, a.m., quitted the town of Bera within pistol-shot of the enemy's sentinels, who pretended not to notice this retrograde, probably being apprehensive of bringing on an action without being able at this point to display a sufficient force to assume offensive movements, and also conjecturing that the division might meet with a reception little anticipated, on reaching the neighbourhood of Pampeluna.

The Duke of Dalmatia, at this moment, was still pursuing the troops from Roncesvalles and Zubiri, and actually within a few hours of the vicinity of Pampeluna, *two days' march behind the second and seventh divisions, and. three in rear of the Light Division,* and even *threatening to intercept the sixth division* from St. Estevan.

As I was left with the picquets at Bera, I had a good opportunity of witnessing the *sang froid* of the French outposts. They made no forward movement, and as I was loitering behind, within a short distance of the bridge of Lazaca, over which the troops had crossed to the left bank of the Bidassoa, I observed the Spanish family, (with whom I had recently become acquainted,) with rapid strides trudging along the flinty road, having rushed from their only dwelling through fear of the French, the instant they perceived the sentries retiring from their posts.

They now presented real objects of commiseration, clad in thin shoes and silk stockings; the glossy ringlets were blown from off the forehead of *la señorita Ventura,* and a tear from her dark blue eye, (shaded with raven eye-lashes), rolled down her flushed cheek, into the prettiest pouting lips to be imagined; a *mantilla* loosely hung across her arm, fluttering in the breeze, and a black silk dress, hanging in graceful folds around her delicate form, gave her, with all her troubles, a most enchanting appearance. *El Padre* accepted the offer of my horse, and, sticking his short legs into the stirrup leathers, composedly smoked a cigar.

The mother took my arm, the other I offered to *Ventura,* who smilingly declined, saying, "It is not the fashion for *las señoritas* to take the arm of *los caballeros,*" but politely offered her hand. While crossing the bridge, "Here," said the little heroine, why do you not call back *los soldados,* and tell them to *tirar las balas a este Puente?*" I endeavoured to explain that our flank was turned, and all the grand manoeuvres of an army; little to her satisfaction, for she could not comprehend any other than the front attack.

On entering the town, the family stopped at a large stone mansion of a relation, where they intended to take up their abode for the present: the parents urged my departure, through fear that I might fall into the hands of the enemy. I then took my farewell of them, (as I thought, for the last time), and galloping through the town, soon came within sight of the division, threading its march up a steep defile, enclosed on all sides by an extensive forest. Towards evening we encamped, one league and a half W. N. W. of San Estevan, on the mountain of Santa Cruz, from whence we still commanded a view of the French bivouac. Here we halted during the night.

On the following day, the battle of Pampeluna took place thirty miles in our rear, but, being entangled amongst the mountains, we did not hear of the event until three days afterwards.

The combat began in a singular manner; the sixth division, under Gen. Pack, while on its march over a rough country, intersected by stone walls, within a few miles of Pampeluna, suddenly encountered the grey-coated French columns in full march, debouching from behind the village of Sauroren for the purpose of out-flanking the left of the fourth division. The consequence of these two hostile bodies clashing was, that the enemy's van were driven back by a hot fire of musketry. The French, being thus foiled in this manoeuvre, turned their grand efforts against the front of the heights on which the fourth division was stationed, commanded by Sir L. Cole. The valour of the red regiments shone transcendent, and Lord Wellington repeatedly thanked the various corps, while they were recovering breath to renew fresh efforts with the bayonet, in driving the enemy headlong from the crest of the rugged heights; thus forcing them, after a most sanguinary and furious contest, to desist from farther offensive movements on that position.

The General-in-Chief could only collect, at the end of three days, two brigades of the second division, General Morillo's, and part of the Count d'Abisbals Spaniards, and *the three reserve divisions,* to oppose the Duke of Dalmatia; which clearly demonstrates the great difficulty of occupying such a vast and rugged range of country. The *first, second, fifth, seventh,* and *light divisions,* were too far distant to join in the action of the 28th; and even the third division, only a few miles to the right of the field of action, could not take part in it, as the enemy had a corps of observation opposite General Picton, backed by a numerous train of artillery and a large body of cavalry, in readiness to engage him, should the *sixth* and *fourth* divisions lose the day.

The Light Division continued in position at Santa Cruz during the whole of the 28th, having completely lost all trace of the army; and, during these doubtful conjectures, at sunset we began to descend a rugged pass, leading W. S. W. near Zubieta, to endeavour to cut in upon the high road between Pampeluna and Tolosa, as it was impossible to know whether General Graham, by this time, was not even beyond the latter town.

To add to our difficulties, the night set in so extremely dark that the soldiers could no longer see each other, and began to tumble about in all directions; some became stationary on shelvings of rocks, or so enveloped in the thicket, that they could no longer extricate themselves from the trees and underwood. The rocks and the forest resounded with many voices, while here and there a small fire was kindled and flared up, as if lighted in the clouds by some magic hand.

For myself, I at length became so exhausted and out of temper, at the toil of lugging along my unwilling steed, that in a fit of despair I mounted, and keeping a tight rein, permitted the animal to pick its own steps. The branches of the trees so continually twisted round my head that I expected every minute to find myself suspended; at last the trusty horse made a dead stop, having emerged from the forest into a small hamlet, where I encountered a few harassed soldiers, enquiring of each other where the main body had vanished to, or what direction to pursue, for they no longer knew whether they were advancing or retiring; and, without further ceremony, they began to batter with the butt-end of their firelocks the strong and massive doors of the slumbering inhabitants, demanding, with stentorian voices, if any troops had passed that way?—a difficult question for people to answer who had just risen from their mattresses, and now timidly opened their doors, in considerable alarm, being apprehensive that we had come at midnight hour to rob and plunder them.

At last a resolute Spaniard* threw a large *capote* over his shoulder, and, stepping forward, said, "*Señores Caballeros,* only inform me whence you came or whither you are going, and I will be your guide;" but we were so bewildered, owing to the crooked path, and the intricate windings of the forest, that no one could take upon himself, to point towards the direction of the bleak mountain we had come from, or the name of the place we were going to; as a matter of expediency, therefore, we patiently awaited the coming morn.**

At daybreak, a scene of complete confusion presented itself, the greater part of the division being scattered over the face of a steep and woody mountain, and positively not half a league from whence they had started on the previous evening. As soon as the various corps had grouped together, they followed the only road in sight, and soon met a mounted officer, who directed them towards Leyza: near that place one-half of the division were already bivouacked, having reached the valley before the pitchy darkness had set in.

---

* It was a frequent custom, when in want of a guide, to employ a peasant, who received a dollar at the end of his day's journey. These *Pizanos,* being accustomed to pastoral lives, were well acquainted with every inch of ground or by-path for leagues around their habitations, as well as the various fords across rivers and tributary streams, the depth of which depends on the season of the year, or the quantity of rain that might happen to fall at uncertain periods on these mountains.
** On the 29th, at the end of four days' fighting, both Marshals desisted from hostilities in front of Pampeluna. The French employed themselves in edging off to their right to assist the Count d'Erlon, who had followed the march of General Hill by Lanz. Lord Wellington, on the other hand, was drawing in the seventh division to insure a communication with General Hill, and also watching his adversary's movements, to take advantage of what might accrue on the morrow.

It was now the third day since we had retired from Bera, and Gen. Baron C. Alten became so uneasy, that he ordered some of the best-mounted regimental officers to go in various directions to ascertain, if possible, some tidings of the army, with which he had had no communication for three days, being now isolated amongst the wilds of the Pyrenees, on the left of the river Bidassoa, half-way between St. Sebastian and Pampeluna.

At six o'clock the same evening we again. broke up and marched two leagues in the direction of Arressa, and then bivouacked in a wood, with an order not to light fires, thus to prevent any of the enemy's scouts or spies ascertaining our route. Two hours after nightfall, the troops were again put in motion, and I was left in the forest, with directions to continue there all night, to bring off in the morning any baggage or stragglers that might happen to go astray. At daylight on the 30th, having collected together a few women (who dared not again encounter another toilsome night-march along the verge of precipices); it was a droll sight to see this noisy group defiling from the forest, many dressed in soldiers' jackets, battered bonnets, and faded ribbons, with dishevelled locks hanging over their weather-beaten features, as they drove along their lazy *borricas* with a thick stick; and, when the terrific blows laid on ceased to produce the desired effect, they squalled with sheer vexation, lest they might be overtaken, and fall into the hands of the enemy's light horse.

Having travelled for two hours as a sort of guide to these poor women, I perceived an officer at some distance in front, and, on my overtaking him, he expressed the greatest joy at seeing me, and declared that he had been wandering for some hours in the most agitated state of mind, not knowing whither to bend his footsteps. The division had drawn up again during the night, and he having, lain down on the flank of the column, had fallen into a profound slumber, out of which he had awoke at broad daylight, with the rays of the sun shining full on his face; and, when somewhat recovering his bewildered recollections, he wildly gazed around for the column which had vanished, and springing on his feet, hallooed with all his might; but no answer was returned, a solemn silence reigned around, save the fluttering of the birds amongst the luxuriant foliage of the trees; the morning dew no longer bespangled the sod, nor did the print of a single footstep remain to guide his course: at length, in a fit of desperation, he hastily tore a passage through the thicket, and luckily reached the road, and at random sauntered along in no very pleasant mood, until I overtook him.

Soon after this we heard to our left sounds like those of distant thunder, as the sky was perfectly serene, we concluded that the noise must be caused by a heavy firing of musketry.* On reaching Arriba, we found most of the doors closed; however, we succeeded in purchasing a loaf, and then seated ourselves on the margin of a clear mountain-stream, where we devoured it, and forthwith solaced ourselves with a hearty draught of the refreshing beverage. This stream looked so inviting, that we threw off our clothes and plunged into it. Notwithstanding the cooling effects of the bathe, the feet of my companion were so much swollen, owing to previous fatigue, that with all his tugging he could not pull on his boots again; fortunately mine were old and easy, so we readily effected an

---

* This firing was near Lizas so, where the enemy endeavoured to turn General Hill's left flank by the road to Buenzu, and while the Count d'Erlon was striving to execute this movement, the Light Division, unknowingly, were marching on his right flank: however, the General-in-Chief being still in position in front of Pampeluna, finding that the Duke of Dalmatia had weakened his left and centre, to support the Count d'Erlon, immediately counter-manoeuvred, and attacked the right of his opponent with the sixth and seventh divisions, under Lord Dalhousie, and the left with the third division, and then pierced the centre of the enemy with the fourth division and General Byng's brigade of the second division, and thus before sunset pushed back the enemy beyond Olacque. By this attack the left flank of the Count d'Erlon became uncovered, which obliged him to fall back during the night, towards the pass of Donna Maria, to avoid tailing into the snare originally intended for his adversary.

exchange, and then followed the road across a high mountain, from whose summit we saw the division bivouacked to the right of the broad and well-paved road (near Lecumberri) which leads from Pampeluna to Tolosa; from this position we could march to either of those places, being halfway between them; here the division awaited the return of its scouts the whole of the following day.

The French army being completely worn out, and having suffered terribly in killed and wounded, continued to retreat during the 31st, followed by the five victorious divisions of the British in three columns, by the roads of Roncesvalles, Maya, and Donna Maria.

On the evening of the same day, although obliquely to the rear of the pursuing columns, we received orders, if possible, to overtake the enemy, and attack them wherever they might be found. Accordingly, in the middle of the night we got under arms and began our march.

Towards the middle of the following day, the 1st of August, having already marched twenty-four miles, we descended into a deep valley between Ituren and Elgariaga, where the division drew up in column to reconnoitre the right flank of the enemy, who were still hovering in the neighbourhood of San Estevan. After an hour's halt, we continued our movement on the left of the Bidassoa, and for three hours ascended, or rather clambered, the rugged asperities of a prodigious mountain, the by-path of which was composed of overlapping slabs of rock, or stepping-stones. At four o'clock in the afternoon a flying dust was descried, glistening with the bright and vivid flashes of small-arms, to the right of the Bidassoa, and in the valley of Lerin. A cry was instantly set up "the enemy!"

The worn soldiers raised their bent heads covered with dust and sweat: we had nearly reached the summit of this tremendous mountain, but nature was quite exhausted; many of the soldiers lagged behind, having accomplished more than thirty miles over the rocky roads intersected with loose stones; many fell heavily on the naked rocks, frothing at the mouth, black in the face and struggling in their last agonies, whilst others, unable to drag one leg after the other, leaned on the muzzles of their firelocks, looking pictures of despair, and muttering, in disconsolate accents, that they had never "fallen out" before.

The sun was shining in full vigour, but fortunately numerous clear streams bubbled from the cavities and fissures of the rocks, (which were clothed in many places by beautiful evergreens,) and allayed the burning thirst of the feinting men. The hard work of an infantry soldier at times is beyond all calculation, and death, by the roadside, frequently puts an end to his sufferings—but what description can equal such an exit?

At seven in the evening, the division having been in march nineteen hours, and accomplished nearly forty miles, it was found absolutely necessary to halt the second brigade near Aranaz, as a rallying point. Being now parallel with the enemy, and some hours ahead of the vanguard leading the left column of our army, our right brigade still hobbled onwards; at twilight we overlooked the enemy within stone's throw, and from the summit of a tremendous precipice: the river separated us; but the French were wedged in a narrow road, with inaccessible rocks enclosing them on one side, and the river on the other: such confusion took place amongst them as is impossible to describe; the wounded were thrown down during the rush, and trampled upon, and their cavalry drew their swords, and endeavoured to charge up the pass of Echalar, (the only opening on their right flank,) but the infantry beat them back, and several of them, horses and all, were precipitated into the river; others fired vertically at us, whilst the wounded called out for quarter, and pointed to their numerous soldiers, supported on the shoulders of their comrades in bearers, composed of branches of trees, to which were suspended great coats clotted with gore, or blood-stained sheets, taken from various habitations, to carry off their wounded, on whom we did not fire.

Our attention was soon called from this melancholy spectacle to support the rifle corps,* while they repulsed the enemy, who had crossed over the bridge of Yanzi to attack us, to enable the tail of their column to get off. Night closed on us, and the firing ceased; but, owing to our seizing the bridge, we cut off the whole of their baggage, which fell into the hands of the column of our army following from St. Estevan.

In this way ended the most trying day's march I ever remember. On the following morning, soon after daylight, we filed across the bridge of Yanzi, held by our pickets, and detached a small force to guard the road towards Echalar, until the troops came up from the direction of San Estevan, which had hung on the enemy's rear for the then three previous days. Continuing our march, we once more debouched by the defile opposite Bera, where the French sentinels were still posted, as if rooted to the rocks on which they were stationed the day we had taken our departure.

As soon as the second brigade came up, we again ascended the heights of Santa Barbara, where we found a French corporal, with a broken leg, his head resting on a hairy knapsack, and supported in the arms of a comrade, who generously remained behind to protect the life of his friend from the *cuchillo* of the Spaniards. As soon as he had delivered him to the care of the English soldiers, he embraced the corporal, saying, *"Au revoir, bon camarade Anglais"* and, throwing his musket over his shoulder, with the butt-end *en l'air,* he descended the mountain to rejoin the French army on the opposite range of heights. Of course, no one offered to molest this *simple soldat,* who easily effected his escape.

As our picquets could not enter the valley until our right was cleared, and the enemy pushed from the mountain of Echalar, as soon as another division attacked those heights, the 1st rifles moved on and clambered the mountain of St. Bernard, supported by five companies of our regiment. The soldiers had been for

---

* One of the first I saw wounded was Capt Perceval, of the rifle corps. "Well," said he, "I am a lucky fellow, with one arm maimed and useless by my side from an old wound, and now unable to use the other."

two days without any sustenance, and were so weak that they could hardly stand; however, an excellent commissary had managed to overtake us, and hastily served out half-a-pound of biscuit to each individual, which the soldiery devoured while in the act of priming and loading as they moved on to the attack.

The summit of the mountain was wrapped in a dense fog: an invisible firing commenced, and it was impossible to ascertain which party was getting the best of the fight; the combatants were literally contending in the clouds. When half-way up the side of the mountain, we found a soldier of the rifles lying on his face, and bleeding so copiously that his haversack was dyed in blood: we turned him over, and, being somewhat recovered before he was carried off, he told us, in broken monosyllables, that three Frenchmen had mistaken him for a Portuguese, laid hold of him, thrust a bayonet through his thigh, smashed the stock of his rifle, and then pushed him from off the ledge of the precipice under which we discovered him.

The second French light infantry were dislodged, before twilight, from the top of this mountain; but the sparkling flashes of small-arms continued after dark to wreath with a crown of fire the summits of the various rocks about Echalar.

Thus, after a series of difficult marches, amongst a chaotic jumble of sterile mountains, the enemy were totally discomfited, with an enormous loss, by a series of the most extraordinary and brilliant efforts that had been made during the Peninsular War. For three days the French indeed had the vantage ground, owing to their superiority of numbers at a given point; but on the fourth day, the same divisions which had so heroically fought while falling back, sustained, with their backs to a hostile fortress, (whence the enemy sortied during the battle,) a most desperate assault made by the Duke of Dalmatia, over whom Lord Wellington gained a memorable victory, and ceased not in turn to pursue the French marshal, until he was glad to seek shelter from whence he came.

The standards of Britain again waved aloft, and flapped in the gentle breeze over the fertile fields of France.

CHAPTER 16
Second Assault on St. Sebastian

Whenever in the vicinity of the enemy, it was customary to turn out an hour before daybreak, and for the troops to stand to their arms until objects at a short distance became visible. On these mountains we were terribly annoyed by the toads. Many officers possessed mattresses or covers, (the latter being usually stuffed with dried fern,) but if they happened to be left in the tent two or three days without removing, or taken out to dry, which was often the case, owing to heavy rains or dense fogs, we were sure to find one or two bloated speckled toads under them, as large in circumference as a small dessert plate.

Towards the end of the month, we could distinctly hear the heavy thundering of the battery cannon at St. Sebastian, and an order was issued for the first, fourth, and light divisions to send a certain number of volunteers, to assist the fifth division in storming the breaches at that place, as soon as they should be considered practicable.

By some mistake, we were informed that two officers were to proceed from our regiment with the volunteers, accordingly Lieut. John O'Connell and myself offered our services, and marched off and formed with the rest of the volunteers of the division, in front of General Alten's quarters, which was about a league in rear of our encampment; but as more officers had proffered their services than the proper quota, I, amongst the rest, made a surplus, and Lieut. O'Connell, be-

213

ing my senior, remained. This officer had formed one of the storming party at Ciudad Rodrigo, and at Badajoz, where he was badly wounded, a ball having passed in at the top of his shoulder and came out at the elbow joint: he was ultimately killed on the sanguinary breach of St. Sebastian.

Lieut.-Col. Hunt, of the 52nd, took the command of the volunteers of the division. Major W. Napier had also volunteered, but not being required on this occasion, both he and myself returned to camp. On the following day, myself and three other officers obtained permission to proceed across the mountain to be *spectators* of the assault. The weather was extremely fine, and we enjoyed a tranquil ride over the mountains, many of which were entirely covered with oak trees, aromatic plants, fern, and evergreens. For more than two leagues there was scarcely a house to be seen. The day being far advanced before we left our camp, darkness overtook us, and, on making enquiries at a cottage, we were informed, by a peasant, that there was an encampment at a short distance, which we soon discovered to the right of the road, and found it to be the 85th light infantry, just arrived from England. We received a hearty welcome, besides *aguardiente y vino tinto,* and then wrapping our cloaks around about us, we enjoyed a few hours repose in Major Ferguson's tent.

At daybreak we went on our way through an open, hilly, and sandy country, towards St. Sebastian, and in a few hours took post in the trenches cut through the sandbanks, on the right bank of the river Urumea, and within six hundred yards of the town, which stands near the river, or rather on a small peninsula, between two arms of the sea. The place consisted of twenty streets, besides churches, convents, and monasteries; and is enclosed on three sides by ramparts, bastions, and half-moons. The castle is built on the top of a bare rock, and overlooking the sea; the entrance of the harbour, on the west side, is between two moles, and is capable of containing a few small vessels.

During our stay in the trenches, just below a mortar battery, the enemy hardly fired a shot from the fortress, in the walls of which were two breaches eighty yards asunder. The principal and wide-mouthed breach had crumbled into a vast mound of sand, rubbish, and broken masonry. A breach is indeed an awful mound of dilapidation to look on, or rather a heap of disagreeable rubbish, particles of which sparkle brightly in the sunbeams, while the whole seems to the amateur easy of ascent, but the wary veteran knows it to be a deceitful slope, re-entrenched from behind, and most probably cut off from all communication with the interior of the town. Well may it be called "the deadly breach:" all fighting is bad enough, but when the valiant soldier sees insurmountable obstacles before him, and finds all his efforts unavailing, and death jostling him on every side, his foot, perhaps, planted on the body of an expiring comrade, whose bleeding mouth is filled with dust, and whose trampled uniform at last becomes identified with the rubbish, and the human form no longer distinguishable; and every instant the heap of the slain accumulating, without any possibility of carrying the place—then, indeed, comes the "tug of war;" for, as a distinguished officer very justly observed, "A breach may be made the strongest part of a fortification, since every combustible, and power of defence, are brought to a known focus."

Having remained in the trenches a considerable time, we made for the small town of Renteria, where we put up, with two convalescent officers of our own corps, until the next day.

On the 31st the morning broke hazy. Meanwhile before starting for St. Sebastian, we were introduced to Lieutenant Folliet, a young officer of our regiment, who had just come from England for the first time; he expressed much regret at not being able to witness the assault, as he very properly considered it incorrect to leave his detachment, which was ordered to march that morning for Bera. This circumstance I mention, owing to the premature death of this officer.

At half-past ten o'clock, a.m., we took post within cannon

range of the ramparts of St. Sebastian, immediately overlooking the river Urumea. The troops of the fifth division were already formed in the trenches cut across the isthmus, within a short distance of the body of the place, ready to move forward as soon as the tide should be sufficiently low to admit of a passage. It was so well known that the assault was to take place, that numerous inhabitants had flocked from the adjacent towns and villages, dressed in their holiday attire, and were already seated on the hill which commanded a panoramic view of the town.

Many of the women were clothed in dresses of English calico, and in fact composed a motley group and mixture in dress and appearance, such as I had never before seen in Spain. Two pretty Spanish girls were seated on the slope of the hill, and offered us some of their sugar drops, whereupon we thought we might as well place ourselves beside them as elsewhere. A few minutes before the troops moved to the assault, all within the town seemed tranquil; no noise issued from its walls, nor was a single French soldier visible on the ramparts.

Soon after eleven o'clock, the "forlorn hope," headed by Lieut. MacGuire of the 4th regiment, sprang out of the trenches, followed by the storming party, and a brigade of the fifth division;* but, owing to the difficulty of extricating themselves from the trenches, and to their *extreme* ardour, they ran towards the *great breach*, discharging their firearms to the left, to keep down the musketry of the enemy, who galled them by a terrible flanking fire from a bastion which projected nearly parallel, and enfiladed their left flank while moving towards the breach.

Lieut. MacGuire wore a cocked-hat, with a *long white feather,* to make himself conspicuous. He was a remarkably handsome young man, active of limb, well-made, and possessing a robust frame. He ran forward, amid projectiles and

---

* The fifth division led the attack, *not the volunteer from the army.*

a shower of bullets, with such speed that only *two* soldiers could manage to keep within five or six yards behind him; and he actually jumped over the broken masonry, at the foot of the breach, before he fell. In a moment afterwards he was hid from our view by the column bounding over his body* to climb the breach. They had no sooner gained the crest of the breach, than they found the enemy strongly entrenched at each flank of the *terre-plein* of the rampart and the interior slope, composed of a scarped wall, nearly thirty feet deep, so that the brave soldiers who mounted the breach fell a sacrifice to their valour, by an overwhelming cross-fire.

The enemy had cleared away the rubbish some feet from a *round tower*, nearly in the centre, and on the crest of the great breach, which they maintained, and it was from this apparently trifling and *imbreached spot* that the troops sustained their principal loss—standing up to their knees in rubbish, and losing their lives without any probability of success. As the French, however, could not well fire on their left flank without hanging over the parapet, our soldiers were enabled to keep their station on the slope of the breach, at the expense of a great number of officers and men.

Had the enemy been able to flank the slope of the breach, all the troops must have been annihilated. The slaughter, however, was so great, as to cause the most serious apprehension, and the wounded and dying were suffering dreadfully, and languishing in the most horrible torments, for want of water, without being again able to regain the trenches, owing to the cross-fire of musketry through which they had to run the gauntlet while advancing to the assault.

With the exception of the guns in the castle, the enemy hardly fired any artillery from the walls, either from their being principally dismounted, or that they were unable to depress them sufficiently to do much execution. At this time

* He was killed. I knew him intimately; he possessed naturally gentle manners, with a soldier-like deportment.

hardly a word escaped the lips of the astonished spectators; and many of the women were drowned in tears at so doleful a spectacle.

At twelve o'clock General Graham, seeing affairs in this desperate state, ordered the guns from the batteries to open, to oblige the enemy to keep down, and to shield the troops for a short tune, from their fatal bullets, and to give them a little breathing time, so as to enable the wounded who could yet walk to regain the trenches. The fire from the batteries was terrific, and the troops retired four or five yards down the slope of the broach, while the heavy shot passed over their heads, skimming the round tower, the ramparts and the crest of the breach with a precision truly astonishing, so that the enemy could not show their heads, or discharge a single firelock.

Never was artillery better served, or opened at a more seasonable moment; and without doubt this was one of the principal causes of carrying the day; for indeed, had it not been for this seasonable relief, the troops must have been inevitably sacrificed by piecemeal. The volumes of smoke arose in dense clouds, and the reverberation was amazing. The iron balls rattled into the devoted town, unroofing the houses, knocking up the dust and rubbish, and thundering against the walls with a tremendous crash, as if the ramparts were cracking and every stone broken, and the whole tumbling into a mass of ruins. All the edifices seemed tottering to the very foundations, and it was as though every living creature within were about to be swallowed up in the vortex and buried amid the utter desolation.

When first the assault took place, the sun shone forth brilliantly; it was now twelve o'clock, and the clouds blackened and gathered together, foreboding the coming storm.

The blazing of the heavy artillery lasted more than half an hour, during which time General Graham let loose the volunteers and the reserve of the fifth division against the large breach and *adamantine round tower*. The Spanish girls near us ejaculated (while shedding a few pearly tears, and unfolding the little papers containing their sugar-drops,) *"pobre Sebastiano! pobre Sebastiano!"* We asked them why they did not say, *poor soldiers,*—*"Oh si, si"* answered they, *"pobres soldados tambien!"*

As soon as the fire of the heavy calibre had ceased, fresh efforts were made against the breach, and the sharp fire of the deadly small arms was resumed. At half past twelve o'clock a Portuguese regiment led on by Lieutenant Colonel Snodgrass[*] moved along the sands and began to ford the river Urumea, the water at low tide being at this spot about two hundred yards in width. As soon as they reached the middle of the stream, a gun from an embrasure exactly opposite to them discharged a round of grape shot, which fell into the middle of the column, and knocked the men down in every direction: some of them sank to rise no more, others floundered in the water, and called out for help in the most pitiable manner.

The enemy fired a second discharge before the Portuguese could extricate themselves from the stream, (which reached up to the hips), and again inflicted dreadful havoc in their ranks. The smoke of the last round created considerable surprise among us, as it was of a reddish colour, as if red ochre had been mixed up with the powder. The excellent and steady conduct of the 13th regiment of Portuguese was beyond all praise. Having cleared the river they closed up, moved forward and ascended the small breach, eighty yards from the larger one.

At this time we also observed part of the 85th regiment a short distance out at sea (in large boats) apparently threatening the back of the rock, on which stands the Castle of La Motta, but this threat of escalading the rocks was relinquished owing to the impracticability of such an enterprise; the troops in the

---

[*] The Portuguese troops forded the river Urumea directly after the firing of the cannon ceased from the English batteries; and the great explosion to the right of the large breach, (to the left of the breach as we looked towards it,) did not happen until half an hour after this event. It cannot, therefore, be said that our artillery caused that explosion.

breaches became fixtures as before, and no further progress towards the capturing of the fortress appeared to be made.

At last I saw several soldiers quitting the large breach and running to the right to assist the Portuguese at the small one; and a brave bugler sounded the advance several times. Confused cries of assembled voices echoed from the ramparts at that point, and we could hear sounds like the battering of fire-locks against doors or barricades, intermingled with occasional firing of musketry. Still, no very serious impression was visible to us.

At one o'clock a violent explosion took place on the rampart behind the French traverse to the right of the large breach, and, before the fragments blown into the air had fallen, or the smoke cleared away, the troops nobly pushed forward, and, at the same time, the crowd of spectators on the hill rose simultaneously with joy beaming on every countenance; and when the hollow sounds of the firing were heard within the interior of the town, we became satisfied that the place was taken.—The explosion was supposed to be caused by accidental sparks, or loose cartridge paper falling on the train. Probably no one living knows the real cause. However, all the French soldiers near the spot were blown into the air, and fell singed and blackened in all directions; and the dead soldiers lay so thick on the slope of the breach that it looked, to the naked eye, as if the mass of troops were still stationary.

Soon after, we saw the French issuing from the town, and firing down upon the British troops from behind some old walls running in zigzags up the castle hill. There cannot be a shadow of doubt that the place would not have been carried, had it not been for the decision of General Graham, who, persisting in a constant attack to the last, kept the troops in that honourable post to take advantage of any contingencies that might chance to throw open the door to victory.

The enemy lost seven hundred men, prisoners taken in the town, who were unable to reach the castle. The fifth division and the volunteers from the British army lost two thousand men and officers, killed and wounded; amongst the latter Generals Leith, Oswald and Robinson were wounded, and Colonel Fletcher commanding the engineers was killed by a musket ball, just before the assault took place.

At half past one p.m. a heavy mist began to fall, which caused us to bend our course towards Renteria, and, before we reached half a league, the rain descended in torrents; but none had fallen during the storming of the breaches.

CHAPTER 17

The Passage of the Bidassoa

On the same day that the assault of St. Sebastian took place, the Duke of Dalmatia, with the right wing of his army, crossed the Bidassoa, opposite to the heights of St. Marzial, and another division forded the river two hundred yards below Bera (under cover of the high rock, which rises abruptly over the west end of the town) and immediately moved forward to attack the heights above the village of Salines, occupied by part of the seventh division, with whom and the Portuguese the enemy were engaged the greater part of the day.

The French repeatedly endeavoured to climb the heights of St. Marzial without effect. The ascent was so difficult, that the Spaniards had little more to do than to deliver their fire, by which they managed, in the presence of Lord Wellington, to beat the enemy.

The French marshal, when he saw his soldiers giving way and plunging into the Bidassoa, became perfectly furious, for, owing to this unsuccessful attack, the French above Salines were obliged to grope their way down the uneven and slippery mountain, in search of the ford which they had previously crossed (in the morning) in good order, and in the highest spirits. When, however, they now reached the river after exceeding toil and in total darkness, they found it so swollen, owing to the floods from the mountains, that they could not attempt to cross it.

The wind howled fiercely; the roaring torrents, and vast

bodies of water, poured down the sides of the mountains, rocks and water courses, swelling the river into an. overwhelming flood, which rushed through the narrow arches of the bridge of Bera, with irresistible fury. In short, a perfect hurricane raged over the mountains, and swept throughout the valleys, in boisterous whirlwinds, that carried away in their fearful blasts branches of trees, and bellowed furiously over the tops of the forests.

During this awful convulsion of the elements, a few stragglers of the French division succeeded in overpowering a corporal's picquet, and rushed over the bridge of Bera; but a company of the second battalion of rifle corps, which occupied the shell of a house, immediately forced them to re-cross the bridge. Again the enemy several times attempted to cross the bridge at the *pas de charge*, but were as often beaten back by the well-plied bullets of the rifles; and, strange to relate, this picquet and the French division continued engaged within five hundred yards of the French post above Bera, and not more than twice the distance from the second brigade of the Light Division which occupied the rising ground in front of the debouche of San Estevan—the first brigade having crossed to the left bank of the Bidassoa on the previous day, in support of the seventh division. When too late, another company arrived to their assistance; but morning dawned and the odds were too great; the captain commanding, when in the act of mounting his horse, was shot through the body, and the French rushed across the bridge. This was a most extraordinary fight, while the storm was so tremendous that the musketry could hardly be heard; and neither the French nor the English army gave an effectual helping hand to their comrades during this wild contest.

On the morning of the 1st of September we started from Renteria, to return to our division, and had only travelled a short distance when we met and questioned some wounded Spaniards, who gave a very vague account of the fighting on the preceding day, and all that we could extract from them was *"Oh! señores mucho combate ayer."*

We pursued the rugged road, and met an English soldier, who told us that there had been some sharp fighting all along the ridge of the mountains on the left of the Bidassoa; but he could not inform us whether the enemy had advanced or retired. This piece of intelligence made it advisable to keep a sharp look-out. We soon, however, met Lieutenant-Colonel Gordon, one of the General-in-Chief's aides-de-camp, who gave us every information, and told us that the road of communication was now quite open to Bera.

Having travelled another league, we arrived, by a wild and crooked road, at the summit of a mountain covered with oak trees, where we saw a soldier of our regiment standing by the side of a goatherd's roofless hut, who told us that his master, Lieut. Folliet, had been mortally wounded four hours after we had taken leave of him on the previous day. A body of the enemy had pushed through the forest beyond the left flank of a brigade of the seventh division, and, rushing furiously through the wood towards the little detachment with loud shouts, and a rattling fusillade, had succeeded in scattering these young soldiers.

On entering the hut, we saw the youthful sufferer, deadly pale, lying on his back, with his uniform, sash, sword and cap, died in blood and strewed about on the loose stones or rock, which formed the floor of the miserable hut. On seeing us, he extended his hand, and a momentary gleam of joy passed across his pallid features, as he mildly informed us that he was dying from a wound in the abdomen, which had caused him excruciating torture until mortification had ensued. He was quite resigned to his fate, and begged that we would not give way to melancholy, for that he was quite happy, and only hoped we thought he had done his duty; that the only grief he felt was from not having seen the regiment, the summit of all his ambition—before he expired.

In a few hours he was no more; and having been enveloped in a blanket, he was interred under the wide-spreading branches of an oak tree, by the side of the ruined hut.

Little at that time did my three companions anticipate that, before the expiration of three months, two of them would be buried in regions equally inhospitable. Lieut. Baillie was shot through the head, Captain Murchison in the groin, and Lieut. James Considine was dangerously wounded.

In the evening we rejoined our brigade, which had returned to Santa Barbara, when we felt considerable pleasure in hearing they had not been engaged during our five days' absence.

During the month of September, the enemy worked hard in sawing and felling timber to form abattis, and in constructing entrenchments. The right and left of our own army were employed in a similar manner.

Towards the end of the month, I observed one of my messmates winding along the crest of the mountain, on his way from England, having recovered from a terrible wound. Our joy at meeting was very great; his at finding me still in the land of the living, and mine at seeing an old friend, whom, when last we parted, I never cherished the hope of meeting again.

The baggage being unpacked, his soldier servant, who had accompanied him, came up with a good-tempered smile; and, while unfolding a dingy pocket handkerchief, intimated that he had brought me a present from England.

"Well! What is it?" said I, my curiosity being somewhat excited; but he continued to unfold his offering, wrapped in layers of paper, without making any express reply, and at length brought forth a piece of bread, which he had taken from a dinner table in England. This he handed to me, certainly in a very mouldy state, owing to the length of the voyage, but the compliment was equally appreciated. I thanked him for his kind recollection of me, and ate it on the spot.

On the 6th of October, it was intimated that the enemy were to be attacked on the following morning; such information, however, made no difference either in our conversation or reflections.

This day Lieut. Fry,* of the rifle corps, dined with us. The soup was made with bullocks' tails; the spiced minced meat was of bullocks' heads, and the third course consisted of a bullock's heart.

Soon after dark an orderly entered the tent, and informed me that I was ordered to descend into the valley before daylight, with a reinforcement to the picquet, destined to begin the attack on the morrow.

"Ah, now that is very strange," ejaculated one of the party; "for last night I dreamed that you (meaning myself) were killed skirmishing up the opposite mountain." I returned thanks to him for this pleasant piece of intelligence.

On reaching the valley, at the appointed hour, before daybreak, I found the officers of the company in a profound slumber, stretched on the floor, and the commander lying on a table in a small farmhouse; but, as I had no inclination to sleep, I stirred up the dying embers of the wood fire, and purposely made so much noise, that I thoroughly aroused the sleepers into a conversational mood; and one of them announced the pleasing information that he could supply us with coffee—which was carefully boiled in a pipkin, and which we partook of with considerable zest, to fortify our stomachs for the morning combat.

The passage of the river Bidassoa began at daylight, by the extreme left of the army, personally directed by Lord Wellington. The fifth division crossed near the mouth of the river, and the first division began the attack early in the morning. Lord Aylmer's brigade, and a corps of Spaniards, also forded the river at various places, covered by some pieces of cannon stationed on the heights of St. Marzial. Here a sharp contest took place, particularly against the fifth division, while ascending the steep and difficult mountains. The enemy, being attacked at so many points at once, by the various fords, were outflanked right and left, and were finally beaten off this tre-

---

* Our friend of the rifle corps was shot through the leg the next morning.

mendous range of mountains: the fourth division were in reserve behind Bera, and also deployed on the heights of Santa Barbara, to support the Light Division.

An hour after daylight, the whole of the picquets of the Light Division in front of Bera, first began the attack of a detached ridge, called the Boar's Back, from its jagged summit. It was necessary to carry this before the division could debouch through the town of Bera, for the attack of the main position, covered by forts and abattis. The 3rd rifles began to skirmish up one end of the Boar's Back, and we on the other; it was only defended by a small body of French troops, and was speedily carried.

The second brigade, under Sir John Colborne, began a sharp attack on a great tongue of the mountain, which sloped down towards Bera; but the first effort proved unsuccessful against a square fort, which the enemy held with great resolution, and not only beat off the attack, but in their turn sallied from the works, and drove, with the bayonet, numbers of the assailants over the rugged precipices.

At this critical moment, the 52nd regiment, being in reserve, advanced in column, and bore against the stragglers in such good order that they not only pushed them back, but drove them pell-mell into the fort on one side, and out at the other; in fact, they appeared literally to walk over the entrenchment. I had an admirable view of this affair from the top of the rock already carried, and from which it was necessary to descend before we could ascend the principal ridge.

The second brigade continued to advance; but the ground was so difficult, that at every step they met with a severe loss, in killed and wounded. At the end of three hours, when they had nearly gained the summit of the mountain, the enemy rolled (from a strong entrenchment) large stones down upon them, and by this mode of warfare, with a sprinkling of balls, kept them at bay for a considerable time.

In the meantime the first brigade, under General Sir James Kempt, had pushed through Bera to support the skirmishers, who moved parallel, with the second brigade, or rather branched off by degrees a little to the right, and engaged the enemy up the mountain leading into France.

The obstacles on each side of the way rendered the mountain fearfully difficult of ascent; and it was, indeed, so intersected with rocks, trees, brushwood, and prickly briars, that our hands and limbs were pierced with thorns, and the trousers were literally torn in shreds from off our legs. When halfway up the mountain, we emerged from the entangling thicket, fatigued and deluged with perspiration, and found the enemy plying bullets from a small fort.

As soon as a sufficient number of men could be scraped together, we gained possession of that post by a charge of the bayonet: from thence we overlooked a very small field, enclosed by rocks, wherefrom the enemy, consisting of three or four hundred men, could no longer extricate themselves, and fell into our hands, or, more properly speaking, were left in a trap, in a valley between the first and second brigades. These captives may be fairly ascribed as prisoners to the first brigade, since they were within point blank of us, and not within a mile of the second brigade, who did not discharge a single shot at them, but on the contrary had quite enough to do, independently of that affair, in clearing the ground of the enemy opposed to them, from whom they took three pieces of cannon, which were abandoned in the entrenchments.

After three hours' toil and clambering from rock to rock, we arrived within two hundred yards of the summit of the *Puerta de Bera,* which was defended by a few hundred of the enemy; the remainder of their face was extended in order to oppose the second brigade, and to the right, along the wooded ridge, as far as the rock of La Rhune, distant about two miles from the extreme right of our division, to oppose the Spaniards. The rolling of musketry was now incessant on all sides.

It was here I saw the remarkable death of one of the rifle corps, who had killed a French soldier, and who, before he had taken his rifle from the level, received a ball through his body, which caused him such excruciating agony, that his face was all at once distorted, his eyes rolled, and his lips, blackened with the biting of cartridges, convulsively opened. His teeth were tightly clenched; his arms and legs were thrown into an extended position, and he held out his rifle, grasped at arm's length, and remained stationary in this extraordinary attitude for a few moments, until he dropped down dead, as suddenly as if struck by a flash of lightning.

As soon as the skirmishers had gained the top of the mountain, Sir James Kempt rode up amongst the flying bullets, and expressed his approbation of all that had been done; for the skirmishers alone had grouped into a compact body, and forced the pass at the point of the bayonet, and the French were now running in all directions.

To attempt to express our boundless delight at the grandeur and extreme beauty of the surrounding scenery would be impossible. Behind us lay the prodigious mountains and gloomy fastnesses of the Pyrenees, whose rocks, cast in nature's roughest mould, towered one above another as far as the eye could reach. To the north, the dark blue waters of the tranquil ocean glittered in the sunbeams; and various distant white sails skirted the remote horizon. Beneath us lay the supposed sacred fields of France, the towns of Bayonne and St. Jean de Luz, the rivers Nivelle, Nive, Adour, and innumerable tributary streams, which laced and meandered near vine-clad hills, through verdant valleys, whose banks were decorated with a luxuriant foliage; whilst the country was studded with countless spires of churches and red-topped villages, chateaux, farm-houses, and rural white cottages, enclosed by gardens, and shrouded by fruit trees and plantations.

The Spaniards made several attempts to climb the mountain of La Rhune, crowned by a tremendous bare rock, which rose in frowning majesty above their heads. They endeavoured to hide beneath the various shelving rocks, or behind the forest trees, from the dreadful effects of the fragments of rock, or loose stones, hurled down upon them by the enemy, and which bounded with a terrific crash into the deep valleys.

The General quitted the skirmishers at the top of the Puerta de Bera, to bring up the reserves; but our enthusiasm was so great at the idea of taking possession of French ground, which seemed more than a compensation for all our Spanish toils, that three hundred of us descended the pass of the mountain, and pursued the enemy for a league and a half into France, where, to the left, we could distinguish the French columns retreating from Hendaye, and various other points, whence they were driven by the left of our army in the greatest confusion, and were counter-marching round the unfinished batteries in front of St. Jean de Luz, and, in a hurried manner, pointing their cannon towards the various roads, and other debouches leading respectively to them.

The various farmhouses were deserted by the inhabitants, who left their doors wide open, as if to invite the ravenous invaders to help themselves. Here we spent the day in rural delight, on the top of a pretty green hill,. encircled by orchards, on which we built a hut, and tied a pocket-handkerchief to a twig by way of a flag, within a mile of the enemy. A thousand gratifying reflections here arose in our minds, and enlivened our occupations; while the contented soldiers of Spain, with arms in their hands, brought us wines, fruits, and other delicacies, without having committed one outrageous act, or despoiling the property of the peaceable inhabitants, further than helping themselves to the excellent rations of goose, turkey and hams, already cooked, and preserved in hogs' lard; added to which, there was a plentiful supply of nice soft bread, which afforded us a most excellent repast.

The day having closed on this *fête champêtre* we kindled a few extra fires, re-formed, and re-trod our way to the top of the pass in time for supper.

The first brigade had taken possession of the boarded and well-roofed huts, constructed by the French with the utmost regularity, as if they had anticipated the occupation of them during the approaching winter. My messmates had already made themselves quite at home in one of them, and the cook was busily employed in roasting a nice piece of beef, which had been extracted out of a little cavity, dug by the late occupier, to keep it fresh and cool, no doubt for some contemplated feast. While partaking of this delicious *morceau* we failed not to remember the original provider, the French officer; while he, less fortunate, most probably spent the night in a cold bivouac, or under a gun, in the entrenchments near St. Jean de Luz.

During the whole night the fatigue parties continued to arrive from Santa Barbara, with their knapsacks, which had been left there;* and also carrying, in blankets or in bearers, the wretched wounded soldiers, whom they had discovered, by their groans, amongst chasms, cavities, or beneath the prickly briars on the broken sides of the mountains. Many unfortunate soldiers had fallen into deep ravines or hollows; and their dead bodies were subsequently discovered by those who accidentally wandered off the beaten tracts amongst these difficult acclivities.

The right wing of the army in their turn demonstrated during the combat of the 7th, guarding the mountains from Echalar to Roncesvalles; while the left wing, after the combat, held the ridge from the rock of La Rhune (which the enemy evacuated on the 8th), to the Bay of Biscay; which totally dispossessed the right of the French army from the mountains of Commissari, Mandale, and the height of Hendaye. As soon as the French had evacuated the mountain of La Rhune, the first brigade of our division moved to its right, and encamped in a forest within half a mile of its base. The second brigade took our post at *Puerta de Bera*.

In the middle of October the weather became cold and

---

* The troops always fought with their knapsacks on; and this is the only time I ever knew them left behind, except when storming breaches of fortresses, or escalading forts.

dismal, and the rains poured down in torrents. The Spaniards having seized a fort, in the French territory, in the valley below the pass of Echalar, the enemy one night retook it, by a *coup de main,* putting many of the Spaniards to death before they could recover from their surprise, or even put on their accoutrements, A desultory skirmish however continued the whole of the following day by the Spaniards, who seemed particularly attached to this mode of warfare, although the French evidently gained ground; which circumstance forced five companies of our regiment to take post on the rock to prevent the French from following the Spaniards to the top, and driving them from it. Night put an end to these *long shots,* and this waste of ammunition.

Every other day it fell to my lot to ascend this rock on duty, with a huge telescope slung on my back, to report to the General, in writing, any movements of the enemy. From this pinnacle their bivouacs might be seen from right to left. This duty was extremely disagreeable: the custom was to start at daylight from the saturated camp, attended by an orderly, and a mule loaded on one side with firewood, and on the other with a tea kettle, provisions, and a blanket. La Rhune was bare and comfortless, and often wrapped for whole days in a chilly mist. On the east and west it was inaccessible, having only one narrow pathway winding up the south; on the north side it sloped down gradually towards La Petite la Rhune being composed of tremendous overlapping slabs of rock, presenting the most desolate aspect.

One day, while on this duty, I observed a numerous retinue of French staff-officers emerge from behind La Petite la Rhune, and from their motions and gestures it was evident that they were examining the most commanding eminences for the purpose of constructing works for its defence. The whole of them were in uniform, with large cocked hats,[*] blue pantaloons, and boots with brown tops.

---

[*] The French army wore very high cocked hats; the English quite the reverse; the latter was called the Wellington hat.

Some hundreds of Spaniards* were bivouacked round the old ruins of the hermitage at the top of this mountain, where, for want of good, clothing, and owing to the cold nights, they were in the most miserable and forlorn state, and had barely a sufficiency of provisions to keep life and soul together; these necessary comforts were irregularly served out, and in such small quantities, that the cravings of hunger were seldom or ever satisfied. When they were fortunate enough to get a meal, the ceremony of eating it was very curious: the rations for twenty or thirty men were mixed in a large kettle or cauldron, round which they formed a circle and approached it, one at a time, from the right, each dipping in his spoon, and then resuming his original place, to make the most of it, until it came again to his turn. In this manner they continued to advance and retire, with the utmost circumspection, until the whole of it was consumed.

Their clothing was ragged and miserable as their fare: uniforms of all countries and all the colours of the rainbow, French *chakos* without peaks, leather and brass helmets, rusty muskets, and belts which had never been cleaned since in their possession. Some had old brown cloaks, with empty knapsacks and hempen sandals, and others were with torn shoes and almost bare-footed.

At the solitary roll of the drum, they sometimes issued from their burrows, or cavities of the rocks like so many rabbits. One day while standing on a large slab of rock like a tombstone, all at once, to my surprise, I felt it in motion, and on looking down perceived a slight smoke issuing from the crevices on each side, and, while stepping aside, the stone nearly gave way with me; several voices then cried out from

---

* General Longa's corps were by far the most miserable of any I had ever seen in the Spanish service; but, considering they were doomed to inhabit a cheerless mass of rocks in such attire, I thought them worthy of description; some of the other Spanish corps were well dressed; but the whole of the army suffered more or less, owing to an indifferent supply of rations—privations which they seemed to bear with unexampled patience.

below: *"Demonio, demonio que quiere usted!"* when, spring-ing off the ricketty foundation, to my astonishment, the slab was slowly lifted up on the heads of a dozen Spaniards, who were crouching in the cave, enveloped in the fumes of *cigarras* which they smoked to keep themselves warm, to drive away hunger, and to beguile the tedious hours!

Before the troops quitted this chilly region, many of the sentinels were so benumbed with cold, that they fell down with stiffened limbs, and were obliged to be carried from their posts.

One day, being as usual on the look-out, I saw the French hard at work in constructing three forts on La Petite la Rhune, which were built with pieces of rock and loose stones, with incredible labour; and a long string of the enemy, by single files, reached into the valley behind the small mountain, and were traversing backwards and forwards like a swarm of ants, being employed in handing up the stones from one to the other.

In the evening another officer and myself were wind-ing beneath the base of the rock of the great La Rhune, on our return to camp, when a large stone bounded over our heads, and on looking above, we observed an officer of our regiment, (who was on picquet,) pushing down the wall of the old ruin from the summit of the mountain, and calling out to us, in derision, to keep out of the way. Fortunately we found a projecting rock, underneath which we screened ourselves from the broken fragments that came tumbling down with nearly the velocity of cannon balls, making ter-rific bounds of two or three hundred yards at a time, and rolling into the distant valley with a terrible crash. We saw one piece of rock strike a tree in the forest below, and shiver the trunk asunder; and in this way our antagonist kept us prisoners until it was nearly dark, for whenever we made an effort to move, down tumbled more stones, which obliged us to run back to our hiding place.

Having, at last, effected our escape, we vowed vengeance, and on meeting him (when relieved from picquet), we got our spears in readiness to put our threats into execution. These poles or spears we carried in imitation of the Basque mountaineers, to assist us up the jagged rocks; and, after long practise, we could throw them twenty or thirty yards with great velocity, and almost with unerring aim and precision. He reminded us however, of a circumstance which induced us to let him off, namely, that a party of us had nearly drowned him in the river Agueda, two years before. He was a very expert swimmer, but he annoyed those who went to bathe to such a degree, by splashing them, that one day, when he was in the middle of the river, we sallied from behind the rocks, on both banks of the river, encircled him, and gave him such a ducking, that it was with the utmost difficulty he could reach the shore, after a lesson which had induced him to behave with more gentleness for the future.

During the month of October,* our days passed tediously, and we resorted to the most simple pastimes, whenever the weather would admit of a ramble. Sometimes we fired with ball at the eagles and vultures; and at others, chased the herds of wild ponies, which browsed in the sequestered valleys of the Pyrenees. They were hardly beyond the size of wolf-dogs, and had wiry coats, and long shaggy manes and tails. It was astonishing to see these sure-footed little animals, with small heads and wild eyes, capering, prancing, and darting through the underwood, and up and down the steep acclivities.

One day a Spanish soldier brought to our camp a pretty little fat pony for sale; and after a good deal of bargaining, he sold it to our mess for twelve dollars. The following morning a Spanish officer deliberately walked up to the tree, to which our animals were tied, and to our surprise demanded *his* pony. We assured him we had purchased it; but as he declared it had been stolen from him, and had witnesses at hand to identify the animal. We were obliged to give it up, with the loss of our twelve dollars, for we knew not where

---

* On the 31st of October, the French garrison at Pampeluna surrendered themselves prisoners of war for want of provisions, which circumstance now cleared the rear of our army, and enabled it to make offensive movements.

to search for the *picaro*, or *dispensero mayór*, who had so completely jockied us. It behoved us to put up with the loss as philosophically as might be.

While the heavy rains continued, in the beginning of November, we were obliged to construct wicker-work huts, to save the horses, mules, and milch goats from perishing during the inclemency of the weather; for days together our tents were pierced by the heavy rains, and often, being without candles and other little comforts, in self-defence, we had to lie down in our damp blankets, to endeavour to pass the tedious hours of the night.

Two or three evenings before we broke up our camp for the grand invasion of France, we were much diverted by the doleful cries of an *owl*, which had perched itself in the deep recess of an adjacent valley, and, whenever imitated by us, failed not to return our mockery in her very best and most plaintive screeches!

At this time the weather cleared up, and the three-pounders, mountain guns, passed through our wooded camp. The carriages, guns, ammunition boxes, and iron balls, were strapped separately on the backs of a string of powerful mules; and these guns could be, therefore, conveyed so as to bear on the enemy from cliffs, or craggy elevations. The sure-footed mules would ascend or descend steeps, dried water-courses, or crooked goat-tracks; and would pick their steps from rock to rock, planting their feet cautiously for a good foundation, or a firm hold.

CHAPTER 18

The Battle of the Nivelle

On the evening of the 9th of November, the division received orders to move during the night, for the purpose of taking up its ground previously to the attack on the enemy's position in France, on the following morning. The whole of the ample store of ready-cut wood, (a portion of which had been split up by the officers to keep themselves in exercise,) was piled up, and a monstrous fire kindled, which soon burst into a tremendous blaze, throwing a bright glare on the distant objects moving between the trees of the forest.

At the usual hour, the owl began to utter her notes, and continued her cries longer than heretofore; all which was construed into something ominous by Lieut. Baillie, a sinewy young Highlander, who, with an eagle's wings held on each shoulder, which he had shot with a single ball a few days before, recited those tragic lines sung by the witches in *Macbeth,* as we all joined hands and danced around the crackling faggots, and sang in chorus, which at intervals was intermingled with the screeches of the aforesaid owl. The flickering and livid glare of the flames, glancing on the scarlet uniforms, the red sparks flying over the forest, and the soldiers packing and beating their knapsacks, gave an unusual wildness to our midnight orgies.

Before striking our tent, we partook of a comfortable breakfast, after which we each secured a biscuit, of American manufacture; they were of a peculiar hardness (nearly an inch thick), so much so, that it required the stamp of an iron heel, or some hard substance, to break them. An officer jocularly remarked, while placing one of them under the breast of his jacket, that it might turn a ball—which actually occurred.*

During the darkness we got under arms, and moved silently under the north-west side of La Rhune, by a narrow pathway, which had been cut at that point to facilitate the passage of the troops to the destined point of attack, within a few hundred yards of the enemy's outposts.

We had scarcely taken up our ground, when we perceived the flash of a cannon, fired by the enemy on the high road to Saint Jean de Luz, and immediately followed by five others from the same spot. The conclusion was, that these discharges were fired as a signal; for, soon after, we heard the martial sounds of the French drums beating to arms, over a great extent of country, *au petit point dujour*; our eyes anxiously glanced towards the spot, where we expected to see the second brigade of the division already formed. But nothing seemed to be under the rough side of the mountain of Siboure, except slabs of rock, when, all of a sudden, as if by magic, the whole of the fancied rocks were in motion; and as the haze gradually cleared away, we could see the soldiers packing the blankets with which they had covered themselves, having taken up their ground long before us, as they had had a greater distance to march.

The rising of the sun above the horizon was to be the signal for the battle of the Nivelle to begin; or, if the weather proved cloudy, the heavy artillery (which had been dragged with great difficulty through the pass of Echalar,) were to open on the French occupying a fort, which had been constructed to block up the break of the ridge of the Pyrenees leading towards the village of Sare, in France.

The sky was free from clouds, and a sharp cold wind whis-

---

* A musket-ball perforated the biscuit, which caused the bullet, after passing under the fleshy part of the breast, and round the ribs, to glance off and pierce quite through the thick part of the left arm.

tled through the barren and cheerless rocks, whilst all eyes were directed towards the east, watching the inflamed orb of the sun as he rose to view. Our regiment, under Major W. Napier, then fixed bayonets, and rapidly moved forward in column to the assault of the three stone forts on the top of La Petite la Rhune; two companies rushed forward to skirmish, four formed into line, and four supported in column. The heavy guns opened at the Puerta de Echalar; part of our brigade moved further to the right; the second brigade scrambled over the rocks, precipices, and ravines, to take the enemy in reverse; and the mountain guns fired into the forts from a ledge of ragged grey rocks.

In a few minutes we reached the summit of the small mountain by a green slope (not unlike a large breach) within twenty yards of the walls of the first fort. The soldiers and officers gasped for breath: many of the former, from the weight of their, knapsacks and accoutrements, staggered and fell, and, before they could recover their limbs, were pierced with bullets to rise no more; the officers led on in a group and carried the first fort. The second was then attacked hand to hand, the French using their bayonets and the butt ends of their pieces; one of our officers gallantly jumped into the second fort, and a French soldier thrust a bayonet through his neck-handkerchief, transfixed him to the wall, and then fired his piece which blew away the officer's collar, who jumped up unhurt. Another officer, while clambering up the wall, received a most tremendous blow on the fingers with the butt-end of a firelock, which made him glad to drop his hold; and we were so hard pressed, that one or two of the officers seized the dead soldiers' firelocks and fought with them. Among others, Sir Andrew Barnard of the rifle corps joined in this hard fight.

As the enemy rushed out of the second fort, a little athletic man with red hair eagerly followed a French officer; the Frenchman parried two of his thrusts, but finding his men giving way, he turned suddenly round and made off, and the soldier, fearing his prey might escape, hurled his firelock at him; the bayonet flew through the back of his body, and he fell heavily on his face with the weight of the musket and the bayonet still sticking in him. Another French officer, who had shown a noble example of heroism, stood on the top of the wall with both his eyes hanging on his cheeks, with his short cloak flapping in the wind, and not daring to move from his perilous position, lest he should tumble headlong down the steep precipice of many hundred feet in depth.

The forts being now carried, I seized the hand of an officer to congratulate him on his escape; the next instant he was down with a horrible wound, and a ball grazed my left cheek.

Thus, in ten minutes, six companies assaulted a tremendous post, and carried three forts at the-point of the bayonet. It was one of the best contested fights I ever saw; but ten officers were killed and wounded, and nearly a hundred men. General Sir James Kempt, and his gallant aide-de-camp, the Honourable C. Gore, had urged their horses up the rocks with hats off, and were cheering us on while carrying the third fort, when the General was wounded in the wrist of the right arm.

The four companies in support had moved forward at a moderate pace and in good order, to succour us in case of need; but finding there was nothing more to be done at this point, and seeing a line of the enemy in front of a star fort, a few hundred yards distant, they became wild with impatience to share in the combat, and simultaneously burst into a run; and it was only by Sir James Kempt's galloping ahead of them that he could restrain their ardour. He was well aware the movement of the second brigade would entirely dispossess the enemy of La Petite la Rhune without further bloodshed.

From this post we had an admirable view of the fourth and seventh divisions, who had succeeded in capturing the fort opposite St. Barbe, and were now debouching on the rugged ground, and bringing up their right shoulders in succession to form a line of battle in front of the ridge of Sare. The second, third, and sixth divisions formed the right, coming down the pass of Maya.

The enemy's main position convexed in the centre, and extended about twelve miles, as the bird flew; but a greater distance to march, owing to the windings of roads, rivulets, and the steep and barren country lying towards their centre and left. Their right was posted in front of Saint Jean de Luz, amid fortified chateaux, farmhouses, villages, woods, and orchards, converted into formidable abattis, and partly defended by an inundation, and fifty pieces of heavy artillery. Their centre rested on the rocky heights of La Petite la Rhune, the ridge of Sare, and adjacent eminences which were crowned with redoubts.

Their left was stationed on the heights of Ainhoue on the right bank of the Nivelle, which was also strongly entrenched.

The extreme left of our army consisted of the first and fifth divisions, Lord Aylmer's brigade, a corps of Spaniards, with artillery and two brigades of cavalry under General Hope[*] to demonstrate and to guard the high road to Spain, while the centre and left of the army were employed in more active operations.

The firing and rolling of musketry were now vehement to our right towards the village of Sare. On the first retreat of the enemy, they had set fire to some hundreds of huts built of fern and wicker-work, near the rocks of St. Antoine, but soon returned with drums beating the *pas de charge,* to endeavour to retake them from the Spaniards. The smoke, however, was so dense, owing to the wind blowing direct in their faces, that they were forced from the contest, more from the heat of the flames and downright suffocation than the good management of their antagonists, who, as usual, plied them with, long shots.

As soon as the fourth and seventh divisions were well engaged with the enemy under General Beresford, aided by the third division moving to its left, who were combating and driving the enemy up the heights east of Sare, our division

---

[*] General Graham having gone to Holland, to take the command of a separate British force in that country.

241

descended from La Petite la Rhune, left in front for the purpose of attacking the great redoubt in the centre, on the bare mountain of Esnau, near Ascain. It was defended on all sides by clouds of skirmishers, engaged with the Caçadores and rifles of our division. Here Sir Andrew Barnard fell pierced through the body with a musket-ball amongst the light troops. The rattling of small arms was incessant and very destructive on the 52nd regiment under Sir John Colborne, which suffered a most severe loss while moving round, and to the rear of the large square redoubt. After some parleying, nearly six hundred of the 88th French, finding themselves forsaken by their main body, surrendered prisoners of war; but their commander gave way to the most bitter invectives.

After nightfall, the flashes of the firearms of General Hill's corps still brightly sparkled, while driving onwards and making their last efforts and discharges to decide the victory, and turn the left flank of the enemy—which obliged them during the night to evacuate St. Jean de Luz, and retire to Bayonne, leaving fifty pieces of cannon in their formidable lines in front of the former place. Lord Wellington directed the attack of the right of our army against the left of the French.

At night some companies of our division were pushed into a valley on picquet; and at nine we observed the heather of the camp had caught fire, illuminating the country for miles around, while the men and animals were seen gliding about, representing a sort of phantasmagoria. By degrees the fire reached the base of the hill and ignited a small forest; and two hours after midnight we were encompassed with a sheet of flames, crackling and whizzing with terrific violence; and the heat was so overpowering that we were glad to cross a rivulet, to save ourselves from being consumed by this conflagration. To add to our night's misery, my companion was groaning from excessive pain caused by the rap over the knuckles given him while we were storming the forts.

At ten o'clock on the following day our division edged off to the right and crossed the Nivelle by a small stone bridge near St. Pé. The whole army moved forward in three columns, the right marching upon Souraide and Espelette and taking post on the left bank of the Nive, at Cambo, Ustaritz, and the vicinity, to watch the enemy on the right bank of that river; the centre on Arrauntz and Arbonne, and the left crossing the Nivelle at the town and vicinity of Saint Jean de Luz, and advancing through Guethary on Bidart, eight miles from Bayonne.

In the afternoon it came on to rain, while we were marching through Le Bois de St. Pé. The roads were very deep, and we passed the night shivering and wallowing in the grass and mud of a saturated plantation.

The headquarters of the General-in-Chief were now established at Saint Jean, de Luz, an old town situated on the right hank of the river Nivelle, and within a few hundred yards of the sea coast. Through this town the high road runs from Spain to Bayonne, the latter place being strongly fortified and situated at the junction of the Nive with the Adour. The enemy occupied the farmhouses and villas three miles in front of the fortress. A morass, which was only passable at two places covered an entrenched camp which was within cannon shot of the ramparts of Bayonne.

The left of our army fronted the enemy, forming a line amidst chateaux, farmhouses, woods, heaths, plantations, hedges, swamps and ditches, as far as the sea-coast, the right being thrown back towards Ustaritz and Cambo, facing the French who lined the right bank of the Nive, as far as St. Jean Pied de Port. With the sea therefore on our left, the river Adour and Bayonne in our front, the river Nive on our right, and the lofty mountains of the Pyrenees at our backs—it may fairly be said that the army were in a *cul de sac*. The great strength of this frontier seems, particularly during the winter, hardly to be understood; for beyond the river Nive many rapid rivers cut across, and intersect the muddy country and clayey roads, so as to make offensive operations very difficult.

The advanced posts of our first brigade were in a church

behind the village of Arcangues, at a chateau two hundred yards east of it, and at a cottage half a mile further to the right, situated close to a lake, on the other side of which was the chateau of Chenie, on a rising ground, and enclosed by the small plantation of Berriots, through which a road runs towards Ustaritz. The second brigade prolonged their line towards a deep valley which separated them from the fifth division, holding the plateau, in the neighbourhood of a chateau on the high road to Bayonne, six or seven miles in front of St. Jean de Luz.

On the 23rd of November, it was deemed advisable to make some alteration in our line of posts; accordingly our first brigade formed at the chateau behind the village of Arcangues, and four companies of our regiment advanced to execute the mission entrusted to them; but, being led on by too great ardour, we came in front of a large farmhouse, strongly entrenched near Bassussarry. Here the musketry was plied on both sides with unusual vivacity. Having pushed through a small plantation to our left of the fortified house, we found ourselves within twenty yards of it. A brave soldier sprang forward before he could be restrained, and, levelling his piece, cried out, "I have been at the storming of Rodrigo, Badajoz, and Saint Sebastian; there is no ball made for me." As soon as he had fired, he fell dead, pierced with numerous bullets through his head and body.

This was *indeed* a skirmish; for in a very short time we lost ninety men killed, wounded, or taken prisoners. A brave young officer seeing things going hard (and hearing the advance sounded) rushed across a field to our left, sword in hand, and, outstripping the company, when close to the enemy, who were formed behind a ditch, was shot through the head, and tumbled into it a lifeless corpse. The officer commanding the company jumped into it, and caught him in his arms; twenty soldiers had also followed and tried to clamber the wet clayey bank, but could neither do that nor extricate themselves from this awkward position. Overwhelmed by numbers, they were obliged to surrender themselves prisoners, as well as the commander* of the company, whose uniform was streaming with blood, while he was still supporting the dead lieutenant in his arms.

We also were so near the enemy that I was obliged to give orders, in an undertone, for the men to cease firing, as the French threw twenty bullets to one. Fortunately the small trees were so thickly set, they could not distinguish us, and ceased firing, but we could distinctly see them leaning carelessly over a wall. While they were chattering away, I passed the word to our soldiers who were lying concealed amongst the small trees, and underwood, that when I should hold up my pocket handkerchief as a signal, a volley was to be fired. This took full effect.

A sergeant of ours was lying on his breast, and had scarcely taken his fusee from the level, when a ball passed in at the centre of his forehead, He instantly rolled on his back, groaned heavily, and kicked out his legs, covering the spot with a liquid stream of blood.

Sir James Kempt, ever first in the fight and last out of it, having taken his station at a house within musket-range, had now ordered a bugler to sound the "retire" after two hours' fighting; and it was quite time, for all the companies engaged had sustained a sad loss in killed and *hors de combat*.

Now came the difficulty—and how to get away without being seen. Fortunately we found a pathway shrouded by small trees, which we passed by single files, without uttering a word. On clearing it, to say that we did not feel glad would be a piece of unnecessary affectation. The men were covered with mud and sweat, and their faces and hands blackened by the biting of cartridges; and scarcely a round of ammunition remained in the pouches. The sergeant, who had been rather

---

* He was made prisoner while travelling through France on his way to Verdun, his carriage was surrounded by a party of Cossacks, who were going to pike him, when he luckily made himself understood; then being conducted to the allied army, he was most kindly treated and instantly liberated.

dragged than carried out of the wood, was lying on his back and still alive, with his eyes closed, perfectly black, and swelled up as large as a couple of cricket balls; he was frothing at the mouth, and presenting a horrible sight. The balls were again whizzing past our ears, and while spreading the blanket out of his knapsack over his trembling and agitated body, one of the soldiers said "He cannot live long," when, strange to relate, he raised his arm and waved a pocket handkerchief crimsoned with gore which he held in his hand!

An officer full of ardour came forward from the regiment to cover some of the skirmishers on the left; but he was soon shot through the leg, and the sergeant major into the bargain. The latter was a fine comely handsome man of about fourteen stone weight, who was now mounted on a soldier's back with his sword drawn, swearing all the oaths he could muster; and the sight was so ludicrous, that we were all convulsed with laughter, to see the two heroes, who had come quite fresh to cover our retreat, carried off the field in so droll a manner—while now and then a stray bullet whistled through the air, by way of a hint that it was no joke.

Our line of picquets was now advanced; which, I am quite confident, might have been accomplished without a shot being fired. In the evening we returned to the village of Arbonne with keen appetites, and heartily glad to wash the dirt and mire from off our hands and faces.

CHAPTER 19

The Battle of the Nive

The weather continued variable, intermixed with cold winds, sleet, and heavy rains. However, as we were pretty well housed, the hardships of other campaigns ceased, for we had no longer fatiguing marches, the rations were regularly served out, and, as long as our money lasted, the hordes of congregated suttlers at Saint Jean de Luz supplied us in abundance with every article of domestic comfort. When on picquet, our time was occupied chattering with the peasantry, a sort of *demi-basque* tribe. They had no decided costume: the females twisted striped handkerchiefs of various patterns round their heads according to the French custom, and wore wooden shoes or *sabots*—an article well adapted to keep out the mud in the execrable roads of this country.

On the 9th of December the army was put in motion, and the second division forded the river near Cambo, with little opposition from the enemy. Our division advanced against the French in front of Bassussary, and drove in some of their picquets; while the left under General Hope advanced on the road leading from St. Jean de Luz, nearly up to the entrenched camp in front of Bayonne. During the whole day a good deal of desultory skirmishing took place, and our army formed a sort of half-circle, the river Nive cutting through the right centre, which made the distance from right to left at least twenty miles, by roads scarcely passable. Towards evening the left of the army retired to their former line of picquets, and the main body to Saint Jean de Luz and its environs; but our division kept its ground more than half a mile in front of the village of Arcangues. The enemy seemed determined not to quit the fortified house near the little bridge, or Pont d'Urdains, and as we passed north of it, we had overlooked its enclosure, occupied by a French brigade, congregated in a noisy assemblage, while their rations were served out. Apprehensive that the sight of the loaves and wine casks might excite us to desperate expedients, one or two hundred of the enemy's *tirailleurs* extended themselves, and advanced, without much firing, to clear the ground.

After dark our sentinels were withdrawn, for the purpose of taking post on our original picquet ground. The company I commanded held a small promontory, or tongue of land, which jutted out considerably beyond all the other line of picquets; and, without doubt, was a most precarious post, as neither flank was secure and the sentinels were planted on a half-circle, to shield the main body of the picquet. Notwithstanding the ground was so disadvantageous, it was necessary to hold it, as it commanded the debouche of the road from Bayonne by Bassussary.

During the night we heard confused sounds, like the rumbling of artillery, intermixed with a good deal of hallooing and barking of dogs; but two hours before daybreak all the sounds died away, and everything was hushed and tranquil. The suspicion, however, of the field officer of the picquets was awakened, and he ordered me to feel my way towards the house of Oyhenart usually held by the French, to ascertain whether they had taken up the ground from which they had been driven on the previous day. Four soldiers accompanied me, but, as good luck would have it, I could not pass the abattis, composed of trees, which had been cut down to stop up the broad road, and to cover our picquet-house.

We then crossed into a field, and, stealing along close to the right of the road, as cautiously as possible, waited the French sentinels' well-known *qui vive*. Suddenly I felt the sergeant pulling at the skirts of my jacket, (for I had thrown off my cloak as an encumbrance,) and he whispered me to cast my eyes to the left, where I saw about a dozen Frenchmen, within six yards of us, gliding along the road towards our abattis, I think, without shoes, for they did not make the least noise. A small hedge screened us; the sergeant was about to fire, but I put his fusee down with my hand, and we all squatted in the mud, anxiously awaiting the result. Time hung on leaden wings, and they were almost entangled in the branches of the felled trees before our sentry discovered and challenged them; but not being quite certain of the cause of the slight noise, he did not fire, and presently these grey-coated phantom-looking figures came running past us, with noiseless footsteps; we then made good haste back, having been, according to our calculation, within ten or twelve yards of their sentry, who was usually planted behind a hedge which flanked their picquet-house, distant from ours two hundred yards.

At daybreak, on the 10th December, we perceived the advance of the enemy within one hundred yards of our picquet, loitering about as usual, without any outward display of anything extraordinary going on, or any signs indicating that they were about to assume offensive movements. At eight o'clock, Sir James Kempt came to my picquet-house, and, having heated himself by the fire, the assembled party consisted of Lieut. Col. Beckwith (a staff officer) of the Rifle Corps, Lieut. Col. William Napier, Major Sir John Tylden, Lieut. Maclean, and the Honourable C. Monck, of our regiment, who all entered into an indifferent conversation, without contemplating that an attack was meditated by the enemy.

Lieut. Col. Napier remarked, that he thought the French loiterers seemed very busy, which induced us to approach the window, which commanded a full view of the enemy's picquet-house, and having looked at them some time, without seeing the cause of alarm, some of the party burst into a loud laugh, and declared that it was only Napier's fancy; but he still persisted, and would not give up his point, saying, that he had seen them very often before, in a like manner, walking off by ones and twos, to assemble at given points, before making some rapid and simultaneous assault; and, sure enough, before the expiration of half an hour, these ones and twos increased considerably all along the hedges.

Although Sir James Kempt was always on the alert, (no general could be more so,) still he persisted that nothing would take place, and ordered the first brigade to return to its quarters at Arbonne, a distance of more than two miles, and over a very bad road. Lieut. Col. Beckwith remarked, that he now agreed that the French seemed to be eyeing the post, and advised Sir James to rescind the order, as it would be better to conceal the troops, and to wait until the enemy should develop their intentions. The field-officer rode off to warn the other companies in advance to be in readiness. These were formed disadvantageously, on a gentle concave acclivity, which could not be helped, from the nature and shape of the country.

Lieut. Col. Beckwith alone remained, and, before he rode off, walked round the sentinels with me, as I was ordered to defend the post, should the enemy come on, to oblige them fully to develop their intentions.

Shortly after this, one of the sentinels stationed on the most rising ground, turned his back to the French and beckoned me. On my reaching his post, he informed me that he had seen a mountain-gun brought on a mule's back, and placed behind a bush. In a few minutes the Duke of Dalmatia, with about forty staff officers, came within point-blank range of my picquet to reconnoitre the ground. During this interval, I fancied that I could hear the buzz of voices behind a small hillock, and, on clambering a fruit-tree near my picquet-house, I could just descry a column of the enemy lying down, in readiness to pounce on us.

There being no longer any doubt that they were about to attack, I instantly mounted my horse, (leaving the company in charge of the next senior officer,) and rode at full speed in search of the general, whom I met within a quarter of a mile, and told him there would be a general action fought that day, and there was no time to be lost. Sir James Kempt ordered me to send a mounted officer from the picquet to Gen. Baron C. Alten, and to be sure not to begin the firing until the very last moment. He sent also the greater part of another company to my assistance.

In two or three minutes after I had returned to the picquet, some French soldiers, headed by an officer, issued from behind the hedges, and moved round our left flank, within one hundred yards. The officer naturally thought we should fire at him; therefore, to feign indifference, he placed his telescope to his eye, looked carelessly about in all directions, and made a bow to us. Further to the left, we could also see a body of French cavalry debouching from the small thicket of La Bourdique, three miles distant, near the great Bayonne road. The French soldiers, witnessing our civility to their small party, were determined not to be outdone in *politesse,* and called out to our sentinels to retire, in French and Spanish.

At half-past nine o'clock, a.m., the enemy's skirmishers, in groups, came forward in a careless manner, talking to each other, and good-naturedly allowed our sentinels to retire without firing on them. They imagined, from their superiority of numbers, to gain this post by a *coup de mains* and the more effectually by this means to surprise, if possible, the whole line of outposts. However, when they were within twenty yards of our abattis, I said, "Now fire away."*

The first discharge did great execution. These were the first shots fired, and the beginning of the battle of the Nive. The enemy then debouched from behind the thickets in crowds; our flanks were turned right and left, and the brisk French *voltigeurs* rushed impetuously forward, (covered by two mountain-guns,) blowing their trumpets, and shouting *"En avant, en avant Français; vive l'Empereur!"*

---

* Probably such a word of command may astonish some *adjutant-major,* but I give it as it occurred: in rough ground, in rough times, and in a rough country, such expedients are resorted to in war.

251

The atmosphere was clouded, and the bright flashing and pelting of musketry sprang up with amazing rapidity. One of our companies, having held its ground too long in front of the village of Arcangues, was surrounded. The officer commanding it, asked the soldiers if they would charge to the rear, and they rushed into the village with such a loud huzza, that an officer commanding a French regiment was so surprised at their sudden appearance, as to halt the column for a few moments; and the fugitives sprang across the single street and escaped.

Two battalions of the rifle, corps being formed in columns of grand divisions, or single companies, behind the various houses, developed their skirmishers in admirable order, and fought in and round the scattered houses of Chau with great skill. So close was the combat, that Lieut. Hopwood and a sergeant of the rifle corps, were both shot through the head by a single Frenchman putting the muzzle of his piece quite close to them, while they were engaged with others in front.

In the meantime the whole of our picquets now ceased firing and retired leisurely, unengaged, took their station with the rest of the regiment, and formed in a churchyard, on our main position, more than half a mile behind the village of Arcangues,* a sort of neutral post for reserve picquets; but the village was not entrenched, was not intended to be defended, and formed no part of our main position, owing to the ground on both flanks of it being badly adapted for defence. The isolated church and the chateau called Arcangues, have been the cause of those numerous mistakes made relatively to the distant village of that name being the supposed scene of a severe conflict. The rest of the brigade already lined the breast-work of a chateau, two hundred yards to the right.

---

* On assembling in the churchyard behind Arcangues, an athletic soldier of this company being without his knapsack, told us, that while passing through the village three French soldiers had surrounded him, and one had hold of his collar; but he throwing his knapsack on the ground, knocked one man down, and the others seized his knapsack, and by this means he effected his escape.

After a protracted struggle the rifle corps retired, and formed on the position marked out for defence, but left a number of skirmishers behind some stone walls, at the bottom of the slope, from which the enemy could never dislodge them, owing to our overpowering fire from the high, ground.

The second brigade was now sharply engaged, having been in echelon to our left and obliquely to the rear, following the undulating nature of the ground. The plateau of Arcangues and Bassussarry being gained by the enemy, now became the pivot of the French marshal's operations, which, enabled his right wing to attack the fifth division, on the high road to St. Jean de Luz, where there was some, very hard fighting, in front of the batteries; and it was some hours before the first division and Lord Aylmer's brigade could come to their assistance, these troops having been peaceably in their quarters, and far to the rear, when this sudden irruption took place. The enemy's attack ceased opposite to us, with the exception of a firing of artillery within about a thousand yards, which continued to play into the churchyard, and knocked about the tombstones during the greater part of the day.

In one spot a small green mound was carried away, and also the lid of an infant's coffin, leaving the putrid remains. of the child exposed to view. However, we kept up an incessant discharge of small-arms, which so annoyed the French gunners, that, during the latter part of the day, they ceased to molest us. The walls of the stone church were cannon-proof. I saw many balls break large pieces out of the edifice, and fall harmlessly on the sod.

The assembled enemy on the neighbouring heights seemed now to meditate an assault. Two companies lined the interior of the building, the windows of which were surrounded with wooden galleries; water was taken into the church, and a strong traverse was erected opposite the door, so that, if by any accident the enemy had attacked and gained possession of it, the fire from the galleries would have driven them out again.

The rest of the battalion were stationed behind a stone wall, which encircled the churchyard, and in reserve behind the edifice, ready to make a charge of bayonets should the enemy succeed in breaking through this enclosure. Their advance were stationed behind a house, within two hundred yards of us, covered by their cannon at the brow of the hill, while we only possessed two mountain three-pounders, which were placed to the left of the church, to fire down a narrow lane which threatened our left flank.

For some days previously, trifling working parties had been employed, of twenty or thirty men, in cutting down a small plantation in front of the church, which was so intersected by the trees entangled together, that the enemy never could have penetrated them; but the other entrenchments consisted of a few shovels of earth, negligently thrown up, which the French *voltigeurs* might have hopped over; and as for flank defences, they seemed not to have been thought of.

At about one o'clock, p.m., the fourth division came to our support, and crowned a hill six hundred yards behind the chateau occupied by the rifle corps.

During the night the whole of our regiment were hard at work, in throwing up a formidable battery in front of the churchyard, and before morning it was finished, with embrasures, regular *épaulements,* (filled up with small bushes, to make the enemy believe that it was a masked battery,) and traverses. Both our flanks were secured by felled trees, strewed about, and even at the back of the burial-ground, which was now impregnable against any sudden assault; nor do I believe six thousand men could have taken it. So much for the ingenuity of infantry soldiers, with their spades, shovels, pickaxes, bill-hooks, and hatchets.

On the 11th, it was supposed that the Duke of Dalmatia intended to break the centre, by advancing against the church and chateau, (commonly called Arcangues); accordingly General Hope detached the right part of his force nearer to the left of our division; but the enemy again attacked, and obliged him to resume his original ground, where there was a good deal of firing, and many brave men fell on both sides, without any decided result. During this day, although the French advance was quite close to us, there was no firing; and we industriously profited by every moment of tranquillity to strengthen our position. At this juncture, two battalions of Nassau troops deserted into the British lines.

On the 12th, a fusillade on the left continued the greater part of the day; every now and then there was a cessation of small-arms; then a sudden rush and burst of firing, and so on. On calling the roll in the afternoon, a dozen men of our regiment were missing, and an officer being sent with a patrol to a small house enclosed in an apple-orchard, he found the enemy's soldiers and our men mixed together, in a room full of apples. The French soldiers, considering themselves prisoners, brought forth the whole of their apples as a peace offering to the officer, who merely pointed to the door, from whence they effected their escape while, on the other hand, the culprits belonging to us were brought back, with downcast heads, and their haversacks crammed with apples.

In the evening the enemy formed a strong mass of troops, within cannon range, and in front of our second brigade, but made, no further movement; while those opposite to us were, employed in throwing up the earth, as if to construct batteries. During the night, some of the rifle corps on picquet, being close to the French, observed, by the reflection of a bright fire, about thirty stand of the enemy's firelocks piled in front of their picquet-house, which the rifles determined to possess themselves of, and darted forward with such rapidity that the French sentinel had only time to discharge his piece and run away. The rest of the picquet bolted the front, and escaped, without arms, by the back door.

On the 13th, in the morning, it was found that the French Marshal had disappeared from our front, and during the night had again marched in a half-circle through Bayonne, for the purpose of attacking the second division before sufficient support or assistance could be given them, finding the three previous days' fighting and demonstrations had failed to force the lines, or oblige Lord Wellington to withdraw his right flank from the right bank of the Nive.

The sixth and third divisions supported the right of the army; the fourth division the centre; and the seventh the left centre; these four divisions being in reserve, and occasionally in motion towards those points threatened.

The company I commanded was again for outpost duty, at the identical spot which we had been driven from. We relieved a company of the rifle corps which had felt its way, *au point du jour,* to our old picquet-house. The officer whom I relieved, in a merry mood, bade us good morning, and pointed, at the same time, towards the French infantry, with knapsacks on, bayonets fixed, and aided by a squadron of hussars. The old abattis had been entirely removed, and as it was quite uncertain at what moment the enemy might make a forward movement, I ordered another abattis to be constructed at the turn of the road; and I never saw the men work with better humour. In a few minutes a sufficient number of trees were cut down, and collected, to stop any sudden ebullition of the cavalry; it would have been anything but agreeable to be attacked on both flanks, while the dragoons charged up the road.

This little defence was barely finished, when some straggling shots took place in front of General Hill's corps, occupying a concave position of about four miles in extent, between the rivers Adour and Nive; the right centre occupying the village of St. Jean vieux Monguerre. The day was fine, and in a short time the white smoke ascended in clouds, amidst peals of musketry, and the rapid and well-served artillery.

The battle was well contested on both sides, and there was no break in the musketry. Both bodies fought as if this struggle was to wind up, in brilliant style, the battle of the Nive. As fast as the grape-shot mowed down, and split the enemy's columns, they again closed up, and strenuously endeavoured to break through the brave lines of the second division, who repulsed all their attacks, and crowned the day by forcing the enemy into their entrenchments with such decision, that they no more resumed the offensive, nor was the army further disturbed by petty affairs.

The right of the French army now confined itself to the usual outposts in front of Bayonne; its right centre extended on the right of the Adour to Port de Lanne, and its left flank on the right bank of the river Bidouze, and their cavalry filled up the intermediate country as far as the small fortress of Saint Jean Pied de Port, which position embraced our army, and formed two sides of a square—our right face being on the river Joyeuse, and supported by the light cavalry.

Various acts of complaisance now passed between the vanguards of the hostile armies. A lady from Bayonne, with a skipping poodle dog, one day came to see *les habits rouges* of *les Anglais;* and while she was going through those little elegancies, so peculiarly characteristic of the French, the poodle dog came towards us, and from an over officiousness, some of the French soldiers whistled to keep it within bounds, which so frightened the little creature, that at full speed it entered our lines, and crouched at our feet. Without a moment's delay we sent it back by a soldier to its anxious mistress, who was highly delighted, and with her own delicate hand presented a goblet of wine to the man, who, with an unceremonious nod, quaffed the delicious beverage to the dregs, touched his cap, and rejoined us, with a pipe in his mouth and a store of tobacco— the latter having been presented to him by the French soldiers.

With the exception of a trifling change of quarters, and a few other occurrences, the year closed without anything to interrupt our little Christmas festivities, which were always kept in due form. On Christmas day I was on picquet, but we partook of the usual fare, and some mulled wine, with as much tranquillity as if afar removed from hostile alarms. Just before dark, while passing a corporal's picquet, an officer and myself stood for a few minutes, to contemplate a poor woman, who had brought her little pudding, and her child, from her distant quarters, to partake of it with her husband, by the side of a small fire kindled under a tree.

CHAPTER 20

Orthes

On the 3rd of January, 1814, a slight affair took place on the river Joyeuse, which caused the army to be put in motion. Our division Crossed the Nive by the bridge of Ustaritz, made a day's march and encamped; but nothing further of consequence taking place, we re-passed the left of the river, and resumed our old cantonments, in the scattered villas, farmhouses, and cottages about the village of Arrauntz. During this month the Duke d'Angouleme took up his abode with the British army at St. Jean de Luz.

The Duke of Dalmatia received an order to detach from Bayonne a large portion of his force of cavalry, artillery and infantry to the succour of Napoleon, who, since his disastrous campaign in Russia, had slowly retrograded through Germany, and after fighting many mighty battles, had been forced to re-cross the Rhine into France, and was now endeavouring with skeleton numbers, by a series of skilful manoeuvres, combats and diplomacy, to preserve the throne against a host of invaders directed personally by the three crowned heads of Europe, whose banners were at last nailed together and threatening *la ville de Paris*. There Maria-Louisa, with her infant son by her side, was issuing bulletins announcing the partial successes gained by Napoleon her husband, over the troops of her father, the Emperor Francis of Austria, the Czar of Russia, and the King of Prussia. Such was the state of events at this momentous epoch—Great

Britain still continuing the focus of resistance, and straining every nerve to keep the Holy Alliance unanimous.

The weather now became very severe, and as some reports were circulated that there was a probability of the British army advancing into the interior of France, I obtained a few days' leave for the purpose of visiting my wounded friends at Bera; and accordingly I set off in the direction of Saint Jean de Luz.

A severe frost had hardened the roads, and the ground was covered with snow, but I had scarcely travelled a league, when I heard an independent firing towards Bayonne, which almost induced me to return, under the apprehension that some portion of the army were engaged; but, on reaching a more elevated hill, I found that none of the troops were in motion, and it afterwards turned out to be the young French conscripts practising at targets. On this open heath, signal posts were erected, to communicate with the right of the army, on the right bank of the Nive. Batteries were thrown up a few miles in front of Saint Jean de Luz to cover that town on the high road from Bayonne. They appeared strong and well finished.

The narrow and dirty streets of Saint Jean de Luz presented a gloomy aspect, being filled with muleteers, cars loaded with biscuit-bags, bullocks, rum-casks, ammunition, idlers, and all the disagreeable encumbrances attached to the rear of an army. As I passed along the high road, I felt exceedingly surprised at the numerous dilapidated houses, and empty chateaux, with the orchards and all the fruit trees cut down and converted into abattis, which had been done by the French army; but every article that had been left by them in good order, the followers of our army had ransacked.

How often do the soldiers of armies bear the odium of enormities and plunderings, committed most frequently by the non-combatant wolves in the shape of men, whose crimes are of such long standing, and so frequently executed (under the cloak of night, or under the mask of hypocrisy), that at last no atrocity is too heinous for so cowardly a *banditti* to commit. They devour the rations on their way to the hungry army: they steal the officers' horses: they extort exorbitant prices for small articles, which they have stolen from the peaceful inhabitants: they strip the deserted and expiring wounded on the field of battle, and would willingly sell their bodies, could they find purchasers.

Having jogged along some miles, amongst this horde of scattered ruffians, I came to the narrow road turning off to the left, which leads across the mountains to the town of Bera, and towards evening I reached, with difficulty, the summit of the contracted pass, narrowed by the drifted and frozen snow. Here I stopped for a few minutes, (notwithstanding the piercing coldness of the frosty air) to contemplate the town of Bera, and the scattered *quintas* embosomed in the valley, now wrapped in a *death-like stillness,* and covered, as well as the surrounding mountains, with snow. The brittle branches of the trees were stiffened, fringed, and sparkling with icicles.

A few short months had produced a great change! When last I had been at this spot, the foliage was tinted with an autumnal hue, and red lines of soldiers, were formed there, their silken and embroidered ensigns waving, and their bright arms gleaming in the rays of the sun, the craggy heights bristled with bayonets, the drums beating, the merry bugle horns echoing throughout the winding valleys: every eminence was crowned with curling smoke, the vivid firing of small arms, or the occasional flash of the cannon, reverberating amid the forests in hollow caves, broken chasms, and fissures of the granite rock,—producing sounds afar off, like the rumbling of distant thunder,—and altogether giving an inconceivable life, and animation to the scenery.

On my descending from this pinnacle, to make my way down the side of the mountain, the road was so blocked up with snow, the narrow pathway in the middle so slippery, and the foothold so uncertain, that I could hardly keep myself on my legs, or the animal on its own; and, resting every now and then, I did not reach the solitary and deserted street of the town until an hour and a half after nightfall.

When opposite to the porch of the well known *casa*, (that of the before mentioned Spanish family), although shivering and benumbed with cold, I hesitated to knock for admittance. All was dark and silent; no lights issued from the casement, nor was the sound of any voice to be heard from within. In this short interval, many conjectures rushed across my mind; my friends might be gone to some distant town; the former hospitable inmates might no longer inhabit its gloomy walls, it might be occupied with strangers or be the sanctuary of the dead. With such dismal forebodings, I gave a thundering rap: the massive door was opened by a soldier, holding a little iron lamp in his hand, (filled with *aceyte* and having a small wick burning at the spout) which cast a faint glimmering light across the outlines of my cloak, and wiry-haired steed covered with flakes of snow. Without waiting for any explanation, the man was hastily closing the door, while lustily calling out, "There is no room here, this house is full of wounded officers;" but on making myself known, the portal was thrown back on its hinges, lights appeared at the top of the stairs, and the voices of my friends joyfully greeted my arrival.

In the midst of our embracings, "Take care of my side" said one of them, (still hugging me), "for it has sloughed away, and you shall see my bare ribs anon." Another was stretched on his pallet, from which he had not risen for upwards of two months, but was slowly recovering under the soothing attention, and gentle hand of *la señorita* Ventura. The former had made too free with the roseate wine at Christmas, which had caused his wound to break out anew, leaving his ribs quite bare of flesh for the space of six inches in diameter; but they were both in excellent spirits—the *braceiro* was replenished with ruddy embers, and placed at my feet, and a hot dinner speedily served up, with a bottle of sparkling wine to solace and comfort my inside, after my freezing journey.

Over this we recounted all that had passed since our separation at the battle of the Nivelle. I described fresh battles, and combats, and they all the torments they had endured while slowly carried two leagues in blankets up and down the rocks and mountains, or on the verge of terrific precipices, in momentary dread that those supporting them might slip, and let them fall on the jagged and naked rocks. Before I retired to rest, I paid a visit to a young officer of the 52nd regiment, who occupied a room at the upper part of the house; he was suffering dreadfully, and dying from a wound which he had received in the groin.

The following day, Captain Smith of the 20th regiment dined with us, who came from the neighbourhood of Roncesvalles, bringing in his train a coffin, and having performed a pilgrimage, through the intricacies of the mountains at this inclement season of the year, in search of a friend; who had been killed in that neighbourhood five months before. Three or four days passed in this manner, when a trifling circumstance broke up our sociable conviviality.

The last evening, as we were seated round the *braceiro*, I was engaged in an agreeable *tête-à-tête* with *la señorita* Ventura which seriously affected one of my wounded friends, who was deeply enamoured of her; he continued, however, to smother his anguish for a short time, and the strangeness of his manner, left little doubt on my mind that an excuse would only make bad worse, on so delicate a subject. I therefore announced the intention of taking my departure on the following morning. One of them held me by the collar, and declared I should not go, as I had introduced them to the family, and that any jealous feeling was the height of ingratitude; however, the blow was so injurious to my friend's vanity or love, that he could not endure my presence for another evening; twice, by such introductions, I had almost saved his life, yet he could not forgive, although an excellent fellow. Such is all-powerful love!

Having bidden *adieu*, myself and a friend of the rifles (who had been to Bera to see his wounded brother) re-passed Saint Jean de Luz, and soon after alighted at the quarters of a commissary, who had formerly belonged to the Light Division. While we were partaking of some refreshment, he asked us whether the division had not been surprised on the 10th of the last December; when told to the contrary, he assured us that it was generally supposed to be the case, and he was exceedingly glad to hear it contradicted, feeling an interest in all that concerned the welfare of the division, for he had made his debut with it.

Before leaving the main road, the same questions were put to us in another quarter, by an officer who had been previously in our own corps; which will give a faint idea how rapidly evil and malicious reports fly; and so evil a one as this I had seldom known hatched. However, looking to the front, we only fancied ourselves on the high road of blunders; but the most curious and laughable part of the business was, that these very reports Were in circulation by those who were so far to the rear when the battle of the Nive first began, that, had it not been for the determined resistance of the van guards of the light* and fifth divisions, the enemy would have passed all the defences, and most probably seized Saint Jean de Luz, and the bridge at Ustaritz;—and strange it is, but not less true, that the most doleful accounts float about behind an army: victory is construed into defeat and if a slight retrograde is made, off go the non-combatants as hard as they can tear, carrying away everyone in the torrent whom they can persuade to take their friendly advice.

A thaw had now set in; the cross roads, in many places, were perfect bogs and quagmires, so that we did not reach our cantonments until late at night, and were covered with mud, having been frequently obliged to dismount, to wade through the slough, before we dared trust our horses to pass through, as many animals were still sticking or lying in the liquid mud, after having floundered about until they were smothered in the mire.

---

* The reserves of the Light Division were not brought into action, but manned the main position, in case of its being attacked, which did not take place—while the main body of the army awoke from its slumbers and came to the battle-ground.

Preparations being made, early in February, for pushing into the interior of France, General Hill broke up from Bayonne in the middle of that month, and at first moved in a southerly direction as far as Hellete, driving the enemy across the rivers Joyeuse, Bidouze, and through the town of St. Palais.* These movements cut the French off from the small fortress of St. Jean Pied-de-Port, which General Mina blockaded, and obliged the right of their army to leave Bayonne to its own defence. Thence, marching along the right bank of the Adour, they crossed the river at the Port de Lanne, for the purpose of supporting their centre and left, which were retiring before General Hill, and taking post behind the river or Gave d'Oleron, with their right resting on the left bank of the Adour, and occupying the towns of Peyrehorade, Sauveterre, and the small fortress of Navarriens.

The six divisions of the army, besides cavalry and artillery, destined to penetrate into the interior, consisted of the second, third, fourth, sixth, seventh, and light divisions, which were now extending in echelon from Vieux Mouguerre to Navarriens and drawing off by degrees in succession towards the right: the first and fifth division, Lord Aylmer's brigade, and a corps of Spaniards being left behind to blockade the fortress of Bayonne under General Hope.

Our division, having passed the Nive, occupied the small town of Bastide; but, as the clothing of our regiment had reached as far as the town of Ustaritz, we once more crossed the river for it, and having halted there one day, retraced our steps to rejoin the army, the right of which had crossed the Gave d'Oleron, while General Beresford with two divisions showed front, ready to cross that river at Peyrehorade.

The right of General Hope's corps, consisting of the fifth division, having crossed to the right of the river Nive, invested

---

* All the above towns, including Bayonne, in September 1807, had been occupied by the French troops under General Junot (afterwards Duke of Abrantes) previously to their entrance into Spain under the plea of uniting with the Spaniards for the invasion of Portugal.

Bayonne on that side. On the 23rd, part of the first division passed the Adour, two hundred and seventy yards in width, on a raft four miles below Bayonne, from whence the enemy advanced to endeavour to force this small van-guard to re-cross the river, but without effect. The two following days, the whole of the first division were ferried over to the right bank of the river: Lord Aylmer's brigade, and the Spaniards in reserve hemmed in the enemy on the side of St. Jean de Luz, which completed the lines of circumvallation, drawn round the entrenched camp of this fortress and its citadel: but, owing to the intersection of the rivers, this corps was split into *three* different bodies, communicating with each other by the grand bridge of Chasse-Marées,* thrown over the Adour, and one across the Nive. Subsequently some changes of the troops took place.

On the 25th our regiment reached a village within a mile of St. Palais, and on the following morning entered that town, when, to our mortification, we were ordered to halt until relieved by some other regiment, while the 57th, whom we had replaced, marched forward to join the army. It was therefore evident that the troops were left to keep open the line of communication in rear of the army, as well as to fetch clothing.

On the morning of the 27th we heard that the 79th Highlanders were to enter the town; we therefore got under arms, and as soon as they entered at one end, we marched out at the other and towards the middle of the day passed the Gave d'Oleron,** at Sauveterre.

A fine stone bridge crossed the river; but its centre arches

---

* The sailors of Admiral Penrose's squadron assisted in boldly running these boats over the bar at the mouth of the Adour (where some of them and crews were unfortunately lost) for the purpose of forming the famous bridge of boats across that river. Admiral Collier also cooperated with the crews of his squadron in landing cannon, and working them in battery at St. Sebastian.
** Near this spot, a few days before, some light companies of the third division had forded; but they had no sooner crossed than they were violently attacked by the enemy, and forced to re-pass it under a heavy fire, losing many brave soldiers killed and drowned, before a sufficient force could cross to their support.

had been blown up and entirely destroyed: it was therefore necessary to ford the river, which was more than a hundred yards in breadth; and, although hardly three feet deep below the bridge, the current was so extremely rapid, and the bottom so intersected with loose stones, that it was thought advisable for the strongest men to throw off their knapsacks, and to join hands and form a strong chain with their faces to the current, to pick up any of the soldiers, who might chance to turn giddy or loose their foothold—for if an individual wavered to either side, the probability was, that he was whirled round by the force of the stream, and lifted off his legs, sinking to the bottom like a lump of lead, loaded as he was, with knapsack, accoutrements and sixty pounds of ball cartridge!

We breakfasted at a hotel in the town of Sauveterre, and, as the band played through it, the inhabitants stood at their windows smiling with as much indifference, as if the column had been composed of the native troops of their own country.

At this time we could distinctly hear, at some distance to our front, a heavy firing, and the rolling of musketry and cannon. Owing to its continuation we marched forward the whole of the day. The country was extremely fertile, with large farmhouses and chateaux on each side of the road. All the doors were closed, nor did we meet a single individual, from whom we could gain the least information. Towards dusk the howling of the great watchdogs might be heard all over the country; and although we bivouacked in the night in a wood, within three miles of Orthes, we were utterly ignorant of the cause of the heavy firing during the day.

At dawn on the 28th we had hardly traversed a mile when we observed the tents of the 57th regiment pitched on the top of a hill, to the right of the road, without any signs of a move. This corps had been two days from St. Palais, and in one march we were passing them. I was sent forward to gain information, and absolutely reached the old narrow bridge on the river Pau at Orthes, before I heard from an officer of engineers, who was superintending its repairs, that a battle had taken place on the previous day. The centre arch being destroyed, this officer had strict orders not to let anyone pass it, until it should be fully repaired: however, as an especial favour he had the complaisance to cause a few planks to be laid down, and, at a great risk, I succeeded in getting my horse over and entered the town—where I met a soldier of the 52nd, who could not tell me the road the Light Division had taken after the victory, and, when asked what they had been doing the day before: "Why sir," replied he, "I never saw Johnny fight better." Directly after this I saw Lord George Lennox, in a light dragoon uniform, who told me, that he feared his brother the Duke of Richmond,* a Captain of the 52nd, was mortally wounded, having been shot through the body by a musket ball, while ascending a hill with his regiment, at the close of the battle.

---

* Then Earl of March; he had been on Lord Wellington's staff for some time previously, and only joined his regiment a short time before this action.

CHAPTER 21

The Adour

It was now eight o'clock in the morning, and finding little probability of gaining the requisite intelligence of the route of the Light Division, without seeing the Adjutant-General, I made direct to his *maison,* and, being ushered upstairs, I found him in bed, comfortably reposing with the curtains drawn tightly round him. Whether he was half asleep from over-fatigue, or from some other cause, he gave me the route of the fourth division, by the road leading towards the town of Sault de Navailles.

On overtaking the tail of that division, we fell into a slow pace, owing to some obstacles and the broken bridges over the various tributary streams, which were very much swollen at this time of the year.

On this day, our hussars had an affair beyond Sault de Navailles with the enemy's cavalry; and, in the afternoon, I saw one of their officers on horseback, deadly pale from a wound in the abdomen.

After nightfall, we bivouacked in a wood to the right of the high road on the river Louts, within a short way of the town of Hagetman. Our baggage did not come up; the night was miserably cold, and the whole of the officers of our regiment took possession of a tumbledown shed, or forsaken cow-house, where, having spread out some stalks of Indian corn, some of us began to roast potatoes, when an aid-de-camp, appertaining to a General, came up to

269

the doorway (for *door* there was none), and said, "Halloo! Halloo! Who's here? Who's here?" When one of our majors coolly replied, "Officers and pigs," which created a general laugh; and the General sent elsewhere to put up his horses.—In the middle of the night, one of the officers, having suddenly awoke out of his sleep, called out with all his might, "come up, come up," fancying that a French carthorse had got amongst us.

A ludicrous scene took place—everyone for himself! till at last a heap of living heroes were piled together, each scrambling on the top of the other, and all bawling out "lights! lights!" At last, by main strength, I managed to extricate myself from a pressure nearly as bad as that in the black hole of Calcutta. The soldiers and servants, hearing such a hullabaloo, flocked into the hut, which added to, rather than diminished the disorder of the scene. At length a lighted wisp of straw being brought in, everyone stared about, with the greatest astonishment; for the object of terror had vanished, or rather had not appeared. Some crawled out from their hiding places, demanding who had taken away the horse, while the respectful and confounded servants protested, one after the other, that they had not seen a horse, nor taken any away. The alarm took place from someone kicking against the shed, which was mistaken, by the officer who created the alarm, for the hoofs of a horse shod by a French farrier, within an ace of his head! Sleep was banished, and roars of laughter continued throughout the rest of the night.

On the 29th, we got under arms very early, to give the two divisions the "go by;" but our movements had been anticipated, and we received strict injunctions not to stir from our ground, but to follow in the rear, as on the preceding day. We, therefore, again found ourselves creeping along the road as before. When we were within four miles of the river Adour, Lord Wellington rode up, he had received a blow on the hip from a spent ball at the battle of Orthes while directing the last attack on the heights, and said, "Forty-third, what do you do here?" upon which the senior officer told him that the officer commanding the column would not let us pass.

In the short space of ten minutes, the whole of the troops in our front were halted, and we marched forward, and soon after ascended a hill, and formed column in the grand place of the town of St. Sever, immediately overlooking the left bank of the river Adour. Here we found a baker's oven full of hot bread, which a commissary (with a *val* in his hand,) had laid an embargo on; and it was with the utmost favour that we were permitted to purchase a few loaves, or rather, having taken forcible possession, we were permitted to retain the bread, paying for the same; as they might have found an attempt at a re-capture rather a difficult matter from men suffering from hunger, and out of humour, on a cold hazy spring morning. To whom the bread was afterwards served out I cannot pretend to say.

The rear divisions, with drums beating, were passing near the town, and at last increased into a dense column, while forming up opposite the wooden bridge, which the enemy had set fire to. As soon as the flames were got under, and ladders placed close together to facilitate the passage of the infantry, General Sir Thomas Picton, with his usual ardour, pushed forward his division, the head of which crowded the ladders with all haste.

Our regiment now debouched from the town, with or-ders to cross, and Lieut.-Col. Ross's brigade of horse-artillery forded the river below the bridge, to accompany us, for the purpose of taking possession of the stores in the populous town of Mont de Marsan, distant twelve miles, situated on the high road to Bordeaux.

When we reached the foot of the bridge, General Sir Tho-mas Picton declined halting the third division; and it was not until he had received the most *positive instructions* to halt, that he did so. His troops were standing up and down the ladders as we passed them, when a variety of curses and imprecations

271

took place; all the battles of Spain and Portugal were fought over again, with a mixture of rage and good humour: some vociferated that they could always lead the Light Division, whilst the older soldiers were satisfied, voluntarily, to follow them: "Let us follow the Lights, it is our right; no division is entitled to bring up our rear except the fourth; we are the takers of fortified towns, and the General-in-Chief's *three lucky divisions!*"

The Duke of Dalmatia now left the high road and the fine town of Bordeaux to its fate, and retired, with his principal force, up the right bank of the Adour, to support his left flank at the town of Barcelone, and to meet General Hill's corps, which had branched off to the right, and was moving in the direction of Air, to threaten the French Marshal's communication with Toulouse; a point be could not give up, it being the pivot of his defence on the formidable river Garonne.

All the way to Mont de Marsan the road is straight and sandy. Instead of being received with hostility at that place, as we anticipated, we were agreeably surprised to see the people flocking without the town in vast crowds, to see *les étrangers.* Our clothing was old, and almost the whole of the men wore blanket trousers. The French expressed much wonder at seeing the troops of the richest nation in the world so threadbare* and poorly clad. The band struck up, and the women exclaimed, *"Ma foi! les Anglais ont de la musique! et voila de beaux jeunes gens aussi!"* The shops were open, and the inhabitants proffered their merchandize with an easy assurance of manner, as if we had been a century amongst them: so much for a divided nation; so much for honour and glory, and the extreme *bon ton of* civilization!

The seventh and our own division entered the town, where we halted two days, and then our division shifted its quarters into villages two leagues distant from it. Our regiment took possession of the large village of Brinquet. The senior officer

---

* The soldiers carried their new clothing, which they had lately received and which was not yet altered and made up, on the top of their knapsacks.

was quartered in a chateau, and invited us all to a dance; the *salle á manger* was lighted up, and the reflection shone on the highly polished floor. The band was in attendance, but unfortunately there was only one *demoiselle;* therefore, making a virtue of necessity, we waltzed with her turn and turn about, until she was quite exhausted; and we finished by partaking of an excellent supper, consisting of the choicest viands, sweetmeats, Champaign, and other delicious wines. An officer was indiscreet enough, in the warmth of the moment, to propose to the young lady to send for a few *grisettes* from the village, assuring her that in Spain the village maids failed not to attend on such occasions. She started with horror at such a monstrous proposal, saying, *"Dans la campagne, á la bonheur: mais des grisettes dans un salon, c'est affreux !"*

We halted some days at this village, and for a while the war was forgotten; and convivial dinner parties were given in this plentifully-supplied country, where provisions might be purchased for a trifle: fine capons a franc each, while turkeys, geese, ducks, eggs, bacon, milk, butter, excellent wine, and all articles of consumption were to be had at proportionally low prices.

One fine morning myself and messmate mounted our capering, snorting steeds, their ears cocked, and their carcases swelled out with good provender, to pursue our way towards Mont de Marsan, with the laudable intention of making a few purchases for an intended dinner party. Having made our selection of pastry, sweetmeats and desert, we directed the whole to be carefully packed and forwarded to a certain wine merchant, who was busily packing up, in a large hamper, several dozens of his choicest wines and liqueurs, and it was agreed that the whole was to be paid for at our quarters, to insure their punctual delivery by a certain hour—to which the wily merchant and confectioner complacently and readily assented, not having failed by the bye to charge English prices on all the commodities, that is to say about a hundred per cent above the market price.

We escorted the cart the greater part of the way to show the driver the right road, but when within a short distance of the village, we pointed it out, exhorting him to use all speed, and rode on to superintend other little preliminaries. Upon reaching the *maison de logement,* the people told us that the regiment had marched off three hours before towards Grenade, and not a vestige of anything belonging to us was left behind.

The people begged and entreated that we would take some refreshment, which we would have assented to, for our appetites were as keen as the wind, but the cart and hamper were momentarily expected at the door.

What was to be done? To pay for that which we could not consume, or carry away, would be the height of folly; therefore, confiding our predicament to the good-natured host, he embraced us, and, setting spurs to our steeds, at a hand canter, we quitted the long village at one end, as the cart drew up at the other; nor did we relax our pace, until the shades of evening brought us to a town crammed with cavalry, artillery, tumbrels, baggage and commissariat.

Here we gained some tidings from one of the heavy German dragoons of the route of our division, and alighting at a hotel, we got our horses well fed, and rubbed down, and, having partaken of an excellent bottle of wine, and a dish of stewed veal, we resumed our journey.

At eleven o'clock at night, we entered another town, filled with infantry soldiers, who were standing round the fires they had kindled in the streets, whilst others were fast asleep, sitting on the stone steps, or lying under the threshold of doorways. We would fain have passed the night here, but admittance was nowhere to be gained, although we dismounted and kicked, and thumped with all our might at the several doors. These noises had so repeatedly occurred during the night through the troops outside striving to gain an entrance, that such salutations were unattended to. Thence wandering onwards amidst darkness and uncertainty we issued from the town by a broad road, enveloped in a thick fog, for not a soul could now give us the least clue to the division; and it is impossible to convey an idea of the uncertain information in rear of an army. I have often been within half a mile of the division, without meeting a person who knew any thing of its march, and, without the least hesitation, people would give a totally opposite direction to that followed by the troops.

In half an hour, we heard a buzz of voices to the right of the road, and through the dense mist could see the glimmer of fires, and in a few minutes more found our corps, encamped in a fallow field, where we passed a shivering night. Often is the cup of happiness dashed from the lip; but certainly the conclusion of our intended *fête* was quite the reverse of what we had anticipated, when briskly and gaily starting for Mont de Marsan on the preceding day!

During this short suspension of hostilities with us, General Hill had been engaged with the enemy, on the 2nd of March near the town of Air, and, after a sharp affair, succeeded in driving them to the right bank of the Adour, and also in a southerly direction towards the large town of Pau.

From this place, we moved into wretched villages, situated on muddy crossroads in the neighbourhood of Cazeres. The weather continued frigid; the atmosphere was overcast with either miserable fogs, or heavy rains.

The peasantry in Gascony speak a sort of *patois,* or broken French. The women tilled the fields, harnessed the horses, drove and loaded carts, and handled the implements of husbandry—such, as the plough, the long spade, and dungforks—just like the men: their appearance is ugly and coarse; many of their statures are of Herculean proportions. They wear wooden shoes, and a bundle of short coarse woollen petticoats, with a piece of coarse cloth, or sack wrapped about their heads, the flaps of which hang on their shoulders, or down their backs, to keep off the inclemency of the weather, altogether giving them a most uncouth appearance. The wives and daughters of the *gros fermiers* possess a little more life and animation, and were pretty well attired; but they are a plain, innocent, plodding people, over whose morals the *Curé du Village* exercises a gentle sway, apparently more by the superiority of his education, than by spiritual exhortations.

These pastors reside in comfortable houses, decorated with the vine, the rose tree, odorous plants, &c. Their garden is generally well stocked with vegetables, or otherwise prettily arranged by some fair hand under the designation of *ma niéce*. An entrance was never gained to these abodes, unless all the other houses were crammed to excess by the soldiery.

While in this neighbourhood we frequently moved towards the high road, and stood to our arms the whole day. On the 12th General Beresford with the seventh division entered Bordeaux, where he was received with acclamations by the populace, who hoisted the white flag, and the *cocarde blanche,* crying, *"vivent les Bourbons! vivent les Anglais!"*

The Duke of Dalmatia, finding our left flank extended as far as Bordeaux, moved forward, and on the 13th made a feint by the roads of Conche, and Castleneau, (on the left of the Adour), to turn General Hill's right flank. The General-in-Chief, to counteract this movement, threatened the town of Plaisance on the right bank of the river, by this means counter-manoeuvring, and threatening the enemy's right flank, and also their communication with Tarbes. General Beresford now quitted Bordeaux, leaving the seventh division at that place under Lord Dalhousie, and the army closed up in three columns, for the purpose of ascending both banks of the Adour, towards Tarbes. Our division moved in the direction of the town of Plaisance with the hussar brigade.

One day we were with the 15th hussars on picquet at a mill to the right of the great *Chaussée.* The soldiers laid themselves down under the sheds with the horses, and the officers reposed on some sacks of flour, just over the wheel of the water mill, which kept up an eternal clattering noise throughout the night. In the morning we came out as white as millers!

On the 17th the weather cleared, the roads dried up, the

atmosphere was warm and genial, the hedges and young trees were clothed with a spring verdure, and the country looked most inviting, presenting a similar face to that of England.

On the 19th having finished our march, we encamped on a ridge of hills, about five miles East of Vic-Bigorre which lay in a valley. About two o'clock p.m. we were ordered to stand to our arms, and on reaching the summit of the hill, we saw the third division attack that town. The sun shone forth in full lustre, and a vehement fire of small arms and cannon almost enveloped with volumes of smoke, the scene of contest. We moved on the verge of the hills in a parallel line to turn the right flank of the enemy;—a heavy brigade of cavalry during the middle of the combat, turned the right of the French through the meadows close to Vic-Bigorre, and they were finally driven through the place.

I hardly ever recollect a more delightful march than that we enjoyed towards the evening. The sun was sinking behind the western hills, the surrounding country was wrapped in tranquillity, the din of war, had died away. The soldiers were tired, conversation ceased, and no sounds broke on the ear except the tread of the men's footsteps, or the planting of the horses' feet of the hussars, who were riding along in single files, or going off to the side of the road, so as not to retard our march.

CHAPTER 22

Towards Toulouse

We did not halt and encamp until an hour after dark. On the 20th in the morning we passed the road leading towards Rabastens on our left hand, where a picquet of the hussars had planted their vedettes. When within a short distance of Tarbes the hussars rode forward, and pushed their line of vedettes half-way up the hills to the left of the road, with their carbines resting on their thighs, and within one hundred yards of the French infantry, who did not fire, although stationed on the verge of the wood.

Two battalions of rifle corps immediately filed off the road, mounted the hill, and began a most severe skirmish with the enemy, who made such a desperate opposition, that the rifles were obliged to close; the French charged, but the rifles were immoveable, and, for two or three minutes, the combatants were firing in each other's faces. At last the rifles beat them back, and carried the wood.

We could also see the right of the enemy formed on some heights round a windmill two miles to our left, where the sixth division attacked them; and the cannon continued to play at this point. While the right of our army made a demonstration of crossing to the right bank of the Adour, opposite the town of Tarbes, two hundred *chasseurs a cheval* blocked up the wide road opposite to us. It had hedges on each side; our regiment formed column to the left of it, on a piece of waste ground; and a troop of the tenth hussars rode up and formed across it from hedge to hedge, opposed to the French horse. Two vedettes of the *chasseurs* instantly walked their horses within one hundred yards of the tenth, and invited them to charge; several of us stood on the flank of our dragoons, and told them to stop a minute or two, until a company crept along the hedge to take the *chasseurs* in flank when, their main body seeing this, instantly wheeled threes about and unmasked two pieces of cannon, which they fired at half range, and both balls flew close over the heads of the hussars. Owing to the attack of the sixth division taking the right of the enemy in reverse, they were thrown on two sides of a square, and obliged to retire from Tarbes, refusing their right face, while covering the retreat of their left wing!

The horse artillery now came forward at full trot, protected by the tenth hussars, who by half-squadrons, filled up the intervals between the guns, which presented a most picturesque and martial effect. Without further delay, the rest of our division followed up the hill to the left, in support of the rifles; and on reaching the summit a most interesting spectacle presented itself.

The town of Tarbes lay in the valley to the right close to the Adour; the dense red columns of our right wing were in the act of passing it with cavalry and artillery; while the glitter of the enemy's bayonets formed a brilliant spectacle, and the tail of their winding columns covered the country, as they rapidly threaded the by-roads through small woods, villages, and over hill and dale. They were also running in a dense crowd on the high road towards Tournay, (threatened by the hussars, and the horse-artillery) where a rapid interchange of cannon balls took place, and we were in momentary expectation of overtaking them, when broken ground and hedges suddenly intervened, and they eluded our grasp.

A French captain stood by the roadside imploring his life, and calling out for the English, in evident fear of the Portuguese and Spaniards; he held a commission in his hand, and both his eyes were shot out of their sockets, and hanging on his cheeks!

On our descending from the rough country into a valley, the enemy were ascending a steep ridge rising out of it, covered at its base by a rivulet. Our army were forming up in order of battle ready for the assault, but the day was too far advanced: the French then opened their cannon all along the ridge, and particularly against our right wing, opposite the high road leading to the town of Tournay. During the twilight, the bright flashes of the cannon had a very pretty effect—the sixth division had followed them up, and we could hear their firing an hour after, nightfall, while still attacking and taking in reverse the extreme right of the enemy—which obliged them to retreat during the night from this formidable range of heights.

On the following morning we crossed the heights in our front, the enemy being in full retreat towards Toulouse—by a flank march to the right. We cut in upon the high road towards St. Gaudens, on which the second division were marching. The weather was cold, with sharp cutting winds, and a succession of rains set in.

The second day we entered a small town crowded with troops; the rain descended in such torrents, that the cavalry horses were put into the lower rooms of the houses, and we were quartered in the house of a cobbler, which was divided into three compartments: the soldiers filled the loft; the horses the kitchen; and we put up in the shop, in which there were two beds in dark recesses. The little cobbler, seeing our boots soaked through, very good humouredly proposed making us some *bonne soupe,* and, without further preamble, set about the *cuisine.* His figure was unique—he wore a cocked-hat square to the front, and as old as the hills. His hair was greased to excess, and grimed with the remains of powder, ending in a *queue* of nine inches long, and about four in circumference, tightly bound with a leathern thong. His height was hardly more than five feet: he possessed a swarthy broad bony visage, small penetrating grey eyes, thick, bushy, black eye brows, a short neck, long sinewy arms, covered with hair, (the shirt sleeves being tucked up), large hands and feet, narrow shoulders, short body, broad hips, and bow-legs—and was the reputed father of a delicate daughter of about fifteen years of age, with light hair, skin as fair as alabaster, and cheeks vying with roses;—she meekly lent a willing hand in making us welcome to their abode, strewed with old shoes, *sabot-lasts*, leather, soles, heels, waxed ends, and live poultry—the latter being tolerated as guests, owing to the urgent entreaties of the little *grisette*, who was in great dread that they might be plucked, if left to roost in the loft amongst the soldiery.

A large iron kettle was slung over the wood fire, and filled with water, into which a few cabbage leaves were first immersed, and, when it simmered, half a pound of hog's lard was added (from an earthen jar hanging by a cord from a large beam), with a little pepper and salt; half a dozen brown pans were then laid out, into which our host cut with a clasp knife some slices of coarse bread, and with a wooden ladle, the contents of the cauldron were poured over it, the grease floating on the surface of the boiling liquid. *"La voilá!"* said our host. *"La voilá, messieurs, la bonne soupe!"*

To refrain from appreciating the kind intentions of the cobbler, and his fair daughter, was impossible; but we could not partake of such a mess. The times of scarcity were gone by, and as our canteens arrived at this juncture, stored with everything good, and a keg of excellent wine, we invited the civil little cobbler to partake, and he spent a glorious evening, shedding tears over his cups, and declaring that *les Anglais* were *de trés bons garçons;* while the daughter sitting, in the chimney corner, sang some pretty French songs.

At the usual hour of rest, by common consent we laid down on one bed, and the cobbler and his daughter turned into the other; but, for the sake of decorum, the father lay with his head on the bolster, and the daughter placed a pillow at the foot of the bed, and thus turning *dos-á-dos,* they avoided each others feet, and by the glimmer of the fire, we could see the little girls bright eyes under the coverlet.

Making our *adieu* on the following morning, and the weather clearing up, we continued our march, at the end of which the troops entered the various chateaux and farmhouses on each side of the way. The country being very much intersected with hedges, green fields, plantations, and gardens, we suddenly encountered an old man near some scattered cottages, who was so terrified at our unexpected appearance, that he ran up, seized the bridles of our horses, and led us to a large oven, filled with ready-baked bread, all of which he insisted upon giving to the soldiers: thence he took us to an outhouse, where there was a quantity of wine casks: "All, *messieurs*," exclaimed the peasant, "is yours."

We assured him that everything consumed would be duly paid for, which he would not hear of, in his over eagerness and civility, and, breaking from us, he rushed into the ranks of the soldiers, (who were quietly at ordered arms, waiting until the different houses should be marked off for their reception, according to usage), and bawled out, *"Camarades!* Although your officers will not sanction your having bread and wine, I insist upon supplying you." At length, to put an end to such rhapsodies, we agreed that, at the utmost, he might give to each soldier a pint of wine, of which they cheerfully and thankfully partook.

On the following morning, when the soldiers had fallen in, and the over-generous peasant found what an orderly set of people he had to do with, he boldly came forward and demanded payment, and, when expostulated with, bawled out with the greatest indecency, before the rest of the assembled villagers, that we were *des voleurs,* and with the greatest effrontery put himself at the head of the company, as if to stop its march. Such vile behaviour so disgusted us, that we ordered one of the soldiers to put him out of the way.

The rain began to pour down in torrents, and the road was of such a clayey substance, and so sticky, that it tore the gaiter-straps and the shoes from off the soldiers' feet, and they were obliged to put them on the tops of their knapsacks, while trudging along bare-footed, and hardly able to drag one leg after the other. This so much impeded our march, that it was nearly dark before we halted on the road, and the mounted officers were ordered to seek shelter for the men, right and left, but not further than a mile from the post of alarm.

Several officers started across the country, each fixing on some particular house. As I perceived a hill a short way off, I galloped up it, from whence, half a mile further, I saw a spacious farm and barns, the whole being enclosed by a high wall. Knowing the general civility and peaceable demeanour of the inhabitants, without further precaution, I rapped loudly at the large gates; but no person came forward, and all the windows were closed; however, quite satisfied of getting an entrance upon the arrival of the company, I rode round, to convince myself of the place being inhabited, when all at once a powerful and ferocious wolf dog bounded over the wall, and tore at the hind quarters of my horse with such ferocity, that the animal trembled, and although I used my spurs, was almost immoveable. I then drew my sabre, but, whichever way I turned my horse, the dog kept behind, and to add to my danger, a man opened a shutter with a gun in his hand. As I could not get my animal to stir, the only resource left was to dismount and engage the savage brute in foot, (my sabre had a sharp rough edge), trusting that the peasant might miss me the first shot. At this critical moment, the company mounted the hill, and the man called off his dog.

My horse was bleeding, and the heel was nearly torn off my boot—the women came forth from the house, and threw wide the gates for our admittance, and almost prostrated themselves at our feet, expressing the greatest solicitude, and protesting, that the dog had broken loose; and, when questioned about the gun, they vehemently assured us that the man, knowing I was in danger, as a last resource intended to shoot his own dog; this excuse was ridiculous, for the moment the animal heard the voice of its master it ceased to attack. Although we were aware that these were false assertions,

283

both from the actions and professions of the people, yet we could not do otherwise than feign to believe them.

Without doubt, on my first appearance, they thought me a straggling marauder, and they were only about to act as we might have done against foreigners in our own country, who might perchance come for the purpose of eating our provisions, levying contributions, and trampling down our fields; for although such outrages were strictly forbidden in the British army, yet people living in secluded farmhouses could not be supposed to credit such peaceable reports, until they had received ocular demonstration of the fact.

Notwithstanding the gaiety of our manner for the rest of the day, the women seemed to dread the coming night, feeling conscious of an act having been committed which they apprehended would not pass unpunished. The men did not show themselves after dark, and it was droll to witness the many little kind acts of the females, to strive to banish from our minds the occurrence. Even on the following morning, they loaded our animals with poultry, and filled our keg with fourteen pints of inestimable wine. As they seemed in affluent circumstances, we did not refuse these peace-offerings.

At the close of this day, we were quartered in a chateau, not unlike an old-fashioned gentleman's house in England. The outhouses were in a dilapidated condition, the grounds were indifferently laid out, with the trees and avenues cut into various shapes, in representation of birds, &c. An old carriage stood in an outhouse, and the horses had long tails, and were as fat as butter, and not unlike a Flanders cart horse.

The French gentleman, while showing his premises, held a rake in his hand, and was dressed in a green velvet forage cap, a frieze coat made like a dressing gown, coarse trousers, and wooden shoes; but in the evening he was well attired; in fact quite metamorphosed. The linen, napkins and plate were in plenty, but we were much surprised at the common clasp knives at table; otherwise, everything (such as massive plate and old fashioned china) was good, and well laid out. The stairs were carpeted and polished, and the rooms were without grates, the wood being burnt on hobs. The *filles de chambre* left their wooden clogs at the bottom of the stairs, walking about the rooms in their stockinged feet, and, although coarsely dressed, and of rough exterior, they executed all the necessary offices with a respectful attention and extreme good nature, and, when offered some silver in the morning, they refused it, as if to say, *"Ciel!* how can we take the money of *les étrangers, et lesjeunes officiers?"*

On the sixth day we entered a town within a short distance of Toulouse. The enemy lined the opposite bank of a small rapid river, about four hundred yards from the town; a howitzer was planted over the bridge, and a group of French officers were assembled in conversation.

Another officer and myself by degrees sauntered past our sentinels, who were not pushed beyond the houses of the town. When within a hundred yards of them, we made the usual salute, but, to our astonishment, it was not returned, and the whole of the group, left the spot, with the exception of one officer, who leaned on the breech of the gun, as much as to intimate that we were too far in their country to expect confabs and that the time was come to stand to their cannon.

We regretted having placed ourselves so completely in their power: to go back was impossible with any security, if their intentions were of a hostile nature. Trusting however to, the well-known courtesy of *les militaires Français,* we left the road, and walked up to the bank of the river, within fifteen yards of a French sentinel, who, with his musket carelessly thrown across his body, eyed us steadily, as if to examine whether our approach should be received in a hostile, or amicable manner. Appearances certainly looked as if we had come expressly to reconnoitre the nature of the ground, and as we slowly retired, we momentarily expected a round of grape shot, and were not a little relieved to find ourselves once more behind the houses; for there was not a bush or anything to screen us from their observation the whole of the way.

CHAPTER 23

The Battle of Toulouse

In the middle of the night we were aroused and ordered to pack up and accoutre, and make a flank march to the right, over execrable roads, in order to support the second division, who were to cross the river Garonne above Toulouse, at the village of Portet. The number of pontoons, however, proving inadequate to cover the width of the river, it was tried elsewhere

On the 31st of March the pontoons were laid down within a short distance of Roques, General Hill crossed, but the ground was found so swampy, that he was obliged to re-pass the river.

In this part of the country, wine abounded to such an extent, that serious alarm was experienced for the morals and sobriety of the troops. Almost every shed, and even the stables, were half filled with wine casks, (owing to the long war, and to the want of exportation), and, during the rainy weather, it was necessary to beg of the soldiers to be moderate. Publicly they were not permitted to partake of the wine; but how could they be effectually hindered from broaching casks under which they slept, after being covered with the mud of the miry roads, or soaked through and through from incessant rains? And such was the abundance of the juice of the grape, that a peasant was glad to sell a hogshead of the best wine for twenty *francs,* which was divided among our several small messes.

The people of Gascony have a particular method of feeding their cattle: the trap doors or sliding partitions communicate with the interior of the kitchens, and when thrown aside, the oxen or cows .thrust in their heads, and are fed by the hand with the stalks of maize, or Indian corn.

One evening, while in the kitchen of a small, house, round the cheerful blaze of a crackling wood-fire, partaking of our dinner, and the servant girls standing behind us feeding the cattle, we were suddenly aroused by the cackling of the poultry in a large outhouse—where the soldiers were quartered; and, on ascending the ladder, we observed some feathers scattered about the floor. The soldiers stood up and saluted, as if no depredations had been committed. One soldier alone remained sitting, and feigning to be in great pain from the effects of a sore foot. The officer with me, having shrewd suspicions of this individual, said, "Get up,—surely you can stand upon one leg."

"Oh no!" Answered this piece of innocence, possessing a muscular frame and a face as brown as a berry, "No indeed sir, I cannot; for, besides the pain in my foot, I am otherwise much indisposed."

Finding however that we were determined, he slowly and reluctantly arose from his crouching posture, by which he had concealed a half-plucked goose. This was death by martial law, and we put on a most ferocious aspect, and threatened I know not what. However, as soon as the lecture was over, and we were out of the soldier's sight, we could no longer refrain from giving way to our hilarity, at the old marauder being so fully detected. Who could kill an old soldier for plucking a goose? The bird being duly paid for, the kind-hearted woman not only gave it back to the soldiers, but, we understood, cooked it for their supper.

We now halted at St. Simon and pushed our advanced posts within two miles of Toulouse, situated on the right bank of the Garonne; but the enemy still held the Faubourg of St. Ciprien, facing us on the left of the river.

One day we passed in a handsome chateau, with all the rooms on the *parterre;* it was well furnished, and the doors and windows opened on a spacious lawn, from which descended a flight of stone steps of about thirty feet in breadth, to an extensive garden laid out *á la Anglaise,* in broad and serpentine walks, labyrinths, fish ponds, fruit trees, exotics, rose trees and flower beds, which in the summer must altogether have formed a lovely retreat. The inhabitants had fled from the chateau, and all its windows and doors were flapping and jarring in the wind; the knapsacks were suspended in the gilded ornaments of its mirrors, and the soldiers reposed on the silken covering of the chairs and couches.

On the night of the 3rd of April, our division broke up from before Toulouse, (the second division taking our station), crossed the river Touch and marched northerly down the Garonne, as a corps of communication between the right and left wings of the army—in readiness to move to either flank.

On the morning of the 4th the left wing under Lord Beresford crossed the Garonne, just above the town of Grenade, by a pontoon-bridge. In the afternoon the rain came down in torrents, and the river was so swollen and the current so strong, that the pontoon-bridge was obliged to be taken up, and Lord Beresford was cut off with his corps for four days on the right bank of the river, while the enemy had the opportunity of attacking him, or debouching by the Faubourg of St. Ciprien against him—of which they did not take advantage.

During these few days we obtained good shelter in the fine large farmhouses with which the country abounded, every one of them having a large round pigeon-house at the corner, which was entered by a regular door from the interior of the house; the swarms of pigeons were so great, that they literally covered the whole face of the country. Here we ate pigeon-pie, omelettes, and eggs in profusion. *"Diable,"* said the French, *"comme les Anglais mangent des œufs!"*

On the 8th the bridge of boats being restored, we mounted our horses to see a Spanish army cross; and a more bombastical display I never beheld. The Spaniards crossed by companies: at the head of each marched an officer with a drawn sword, accompanied by a drummer, and strutting in time to the tapping or roll of the drum; exclaiming, while looking pompously over his shoulder, *"Vamos, guerréros?"* The very bridge seemed to respond to such glorious appeals, for it rose and fell with a gentle undulating motion, to the *rub dub, rub a dub,* of Spain's martial drum.

As soon as these *guerréros* had formed column on the sod of Languedoc, a heavy brigade of artillery passed the bridge, and one of the cannon becoming stationary in the middle of it, one of the pontoons nearly went under water; and, had not the drivers whipped and spurred with all their might, in another instant, the boat would have been swamped, and the gun would have dragged the horses and drivers into the rapid and furious torrent.

The bridge was again taken up during the night, and on the following day our division formed on a rising ground near Aussonne to be in readiness to pass it; but, having waited nearly the whole day, Lord Wellington quitted the spot extremely angry, leaving Sir Colin Campbell to superintend the finishing of it.

At two o'clock on the morning of the 10th, our division crossed the pontoon-bridge, and, bringing up our left shoulder near Fenoulhiet, six miles from Toulouse, the army marched in parallel columns on that place.

The country north of the town is flat, and on every side intersected with rural cottages, enclosed by gardens, fruit trees, and small plains, or fields of corn.

When within two miles of Toulouse, we could distinguish the black columns of the enemy filing out of the town to the eastward, and forming in order of battle on the Terre de Cabade, which was crowned with redoubts, and constituted apex of their grand position nearly three miles long, and extending in a southerly direction by Calvinet, towards the road of Montauban. They also occupied with a small body of troops and two pieces of light artillery, the detached eminence of La Borde de la Pugade, for the purpose of watching the movements on the left and centre of our army. This small hill was of fallow ground, without hedges, trees, or entrenchments.

At the first view, the French army seemed to be formed from the right bank of the Garonne, and resting their right flank on the detached hill of La Borde de la Pugade, which, in reality, only formed a dislocated elbow of their position. The ancient wall of the town was lined by the enemy, being covered at a short distance by the royal canal, which communicates with the Garonne and runs in a half circle round the north and west sides of Toulouse. Over it there were six bridges, within five miles, occupied as *têtes-du-pont*; the three to the southward being marked by the before mentioned heights, which gave the enemy an exceedingly strong position, and to embrace which it was necessary to split our army into three distinct bodies, to be ready to fight independently of each other—as follows:

Lord Hill's corps was stationed on the left bank of the Garonne (to coop up the enemy in the entrenched Faubourg of St. Ciprien), but was so completely cut off from the army destined to fight the battle, owing to the river intervening, that the nearest communication with it was, at least, sixteen miles by the pontoon bridge we had crossed in the morning—although, as the bird flew, little more than two miles from the right flank of the army, composed of four divisions, and a corps of Spaniards which were destined to fight the battle. The right wing consisted of the third, and light divisions, the centre of the Spaniards, and the left wing of the fourth and sixth divisions with the great bulk of the cavalry, ready to shoot forward from the village of Montblanc, to throw the enemy on two sides of a square.

At nine o'clock in the morning the forcing began on the Paris road near a large building in front of the *tête-du-pont,* in the vicinity of Graniague, by the third division with its right on the river Garonne. The left brigade of the Light Division branched off to the right, to make a sham attack opposite the *tête-du-pont,* near Les Minimes, and to keep up the link with the third division; while the first brigade edged off to the left to support the Spaniards now moving forwards in echelon on our left. While they were crossing a small rivulet, two of the enemy's cannon fired on them from the detached eminence of La Borde de la Pugade. As soon as the Spaniards had crossed the stream or ditch, they rapidly advanced and drove the French from their advanced post, behind which they formed in columns for the grand attack. At this time a sprinkling musketry was kept up to our right by the third division and our second brigade, while driving the enemy behind their *têtes-du-pont.*

At eleven o'clock the Spaniards moved forward single-handed, to attack the heights of La Pugade, under a heavy fire of musketry and grape shot, which thinned their ranks and galled them sadly. The ground was fallow, of a gentle ascent, without hedges or trees, so that every shot told with a fatal precision. Notwithstanding this, they closed, and kept onwards.

The French position was a blaze of flashing cannon, and sparkling musketry, and the iron balls were cutting through the fallow ground, tearing up the earth and bounding wantonly through the country. The fatal moment had arrived: the Spaniards could do no more: the shouting of the French army was daggers to their hearts, and thunder to their ears, and when within fifty yards of crowning all their hopes, down went the head of their column, as if the earth had opened and swallowed them up.

A deep hollow road ran parallel with the enemy's works, into which the affrighted column crowded. Terrible shelter! For at this time the enemy sprang over their entrenchments, and stood over their victims, pouring down the bullets on their devoted heads with fatal precision, so that two thousand of them fell a prey to the adversary, without destroying hardly any of their opponents; and, as if in anticipation of such a result, the enemy had constructed a battery of heavy calibre at the bridge of Montauban, which raked the road, and ploughed up the heaps of the living and the dead—the former crawling under the latter to screen themselves for a few short moments from the merciless effects of the enemy's projectiles.

The rear of the Spaniards now closed up, and, stretching their necks over the brink of the fatal gulf, they turned about and fled like chaff before the wind, amid the volume and dense clouds of rolling smoke majestically floating in the air, as if to veil from the enemy the great extent of their triumph.

As soon as the fugitives could be scraped together in a lump, they once again moved forward to make a second attack, led on by a group of Spanish officers, on foot, and on horseback. The shot levelled them to the earth, without any chance of success: the disorganized column once more stood in a mass on the bank of the fatal hollow road, by this means bringing all the enemy's fire to a focus; but at the sight of the mangled bodies of their dying comrades, their last sparks of courage forsook them, and they fled from the field, heedless of the exhortations of many of their officers, who showed an example worthy of their ancient renown.

The French again bounded over their entrenchments, and at full run came round the left flank of the disconcerted Spaniards at a point where the road was not so deep, and plied them with more bullets, nor ceased to follow them, until they were stopped by the fire of a brigade of guns, supported by a regiment of English heavy dragoons, and attacked on their left flank by the rifle corps, supported by our brigade. This movement prevented them from cutting asunder and separating the two wings of our army.

The enemy, finding that they had totally defeated the Spaniards, immediately moved a body of troops to make head against the fourth and sixth divisions, and cavalry, which were now moving along the river Ers, parallel with the heights of Calvanet, before bringing up their left shoulders to attack that position; but, owing to the marshy state of the ground, the troops were much impeded on their march.

After the, repulse of the Spaniards, the battle almost ceased, with the exception of an irregular musketry fire amongst the detached houses bordering the canal. During this pause in the grand event, several of us fell asleep under the gentle rays of an April sun, from want of rest, having been under arms all the previous day and marching nearly the whole of the night.

How long I enjoyed this slumber I cannot say, for a round shot whizzing, close over my head; caused me hastily to start on my feet. For a few seconds, I almost fancied I was at a review, or dreaming of it, for the right wing of the British army were within less than cannon range opposite the left wing of the enemy, whose bright arms and brazen eagles glistened on the venerable towers of Toulouse.

Soon after this, we descried an officer of our regiment, who was an extra aide-de-camp to Gen. Baron Alten, riding at the base of the enemy's position, and turning and twisting his horse at full speed, which induced us to imagine that he was wounded, and no longer able to manage the animal, which appeared to be running away with him. Suddenly he fell from his saddle to the ground, and the horse made a dead stop. Of course we thought he was killed, when, to our great surprise, he re-mounted, and came towards us at a canter with a hare in his arms, that he had ridden down.

In the middle of the day, the sixth division crossed the valley opposite the heights of Calvanet; and the interchanged cannon shots, and the forked musketry, rattled without intermission. At length, amid charges of cavalry and sanguinary fighting (for the enemy marched down the hill to meet them,) this division gained the French position, and took a redoubt, which, however, they could hardly maintain, owing to the great loss they had sustained in moving up the hill; for, while struggling with the enemy's infantry in front, their second line had been charged by the French horse.*

* It will always be a matter of surprise to me how the sixth division managed to carry the front of so formidable a position almost single-handed. The following day, while passing over the range of heights, the fire-locks of one of its brigade were piled, and I counted only five hundred, out of eighteen hundred stand effective on the morning of the battle. Both brigades suffered enormously in killed and wounded.

During this part of the combat the fourth division was edging off by an oblique march to its left, to turn the enemy's right flank near the road of Montauban, which manoeuvre greatly enhanced the victory on this hard-fought day.

The French several times returned to the charge on the plateau, and made a most desperate attempt at four o'clock in the afternoon to retake the great redoubt in the centre, but without effect.

Owing to this failure the French quietly evacuated the redoubts on the left of their position on the canal, on the heights of Terre Cabade, and their whole army retired behind the *têtes-du-pont*, and the Faubourg of St. Etienne.

On the following day the Duke of Dalmatia held the town hemmed in almost on every side; but, as there was not any firing, an officer and myself rode towards the road where the Spaniards had been repulsed. Its steep banks were at least twenty-five feet in depth, with two or three narrow pathways by which the Spaniards had descended in hopes of obtaining a little shelter. This spot was strewed with heaps of the slain, piled on the top of each other in strange confusion, many having tumbled over the precipitous banks, and remaining stuck on the twisted bayonets on whose points they bad fallen.

Death here appeared in every possible shape; some were jammed in the crowd, and propped up in an erect posture against the bank; others were standing on their heads, or sprawling with legs and arms spread out to their fullest extent. Almost the whole of the cadaverous dead were without caps, which in the *mélée* had been knocked off, and were intermixed with knapsacks, breast-plates, broken arms, bayonets, and swords. A mournful silence reigned around. No voice broke on the stillness that reigned over the lacerated remains of the swarthy Spaniards!

While looking down on these inanimate objects swept off by the scythe of war, I noticed a naked man lying on his back at my feet: as there was no appearance of any wound about his person, we were lost in conjectures as to the probable cause of his death. A Spaniard who stood by was so overcome with curiosity, that he laid hold of the dead man's hair; but, to his inexpressible wonder the head was as light as a feather, for it now appeared, that a cannon ball had struck him sideways, leaving nothing of the head remaining but the scalp and face. The sight was too horrible to look upon, and we hastily remounted our horses, and returned from this melancholy spectacle.

While riding over the field of battle, the motion of a horse is the most gentle and easy to be fancied: the animals cock their ears, snort, look down, and plant their feet with a light and springing motion, as if fearful of trampling on the dead soldiers.

The heights of the Terre Cabade and Calvanet are free from trees or hedges, and have two hollow roads cutting through the middle of them, which protected the French from our cavalry. The banks of these roads are so steep, and at the same time so imperceptible, that a whole brigade of dragoons at a canter might be swallowed up without any previous warning. Many dead horses lay in this hollow way, with their lifeless riders thrown to a distance, maimed, bruised, or with broken limbs.

The ascent in front of this position is very steep, but southerly; where the fourth division attacked, it is of a gentle acclivity.

The bodies of the soldiers of the sixth division lay very thick, in front of the heights of Calvanet, and also round a fort of the *maison des Augustins.* Here the Highlanders and English soldiers were intermixed with the French. The town of Toulouse lay nearly within point blank range on the west of these heights, from, whence we could see the enemy's columns under arms at the *têtes-du-pont* which protected the various bridges across the canal. They were in a manner besieged in the town, as the only road left open to them was by a narrow strip of land south of Toulouse, between the canal and the river Garonne.

On the night of the 11th the enemy retreated towards Carcassone, taking the road by St. Aigne, Montgiscard, Baziege, and Villefranche, to Castelnaudary.

CHAPTER 24

Languedoc

April 12th, 1814—Camp of the Light Division, British army, on the north-east bank of the Canal du Midi, and one mile from the fair city of Toulouse, the spires and venerable turrets of which overhang the rapid waters of the river Garonne. The sun shone merrily, and early this day I threw my leg across the back of my right-trusty little Spanish *jennet*. My cloak was no longer rolled across the pummel of my saddle, the coiled rope or halter had disappeared from the head of my steed, and the blanket, which was usually folded under my saddle, was left behind with buoyant disdain, for I now wished to consider myself mounted only like an armed gentleman. My moustache bristling up with an extra twist from the sugar canister, off I started from humble camp, at a good round canter, for the little Pont Jumeau, and was happy to find that my faithful animal was not lamed by the effects of an accident which happened two nights before.

To accelerate the passing of the Spanish infantry at the late battle of Toulouse, a frail bridge had been constructed across a broad ditch or rivulet. It consisted of a few limbs of trees, with boughs loosely thrown athwart them. I was dashing over this at full speed, in the darkness, but I soon found that my horse was sinking at every step, and I stuck spurs to its sides. The animal plunged violently with all fours to regain its legs, one of which had now penetrated through the apertures in the branches of this treacherous bridge. At length we luckily gained the opposite bank, but the animal was down upon its nose, and the sinews of my legs were much strained from the exertions made to keep anything like a seat on so boisterous an occasion. Making a final effort, however, man and horse were once more erect, but the animal trembled so violently that I was fain to dismount to coax it before I proceeded on my way.

Reaching the Paris road, I had a good opportunity of examining the little bridge, called the Pont Jumeau, constructed with a single arch across the Canal du Midi, precisely like those thrown over canals in England, or elsewhere, and which bridge had been unsuccessfully attacked by two regiments of general Sir T. Picton's division on the day of the battle.

The broad road leading to the Jumeau bridge was a dead flat, and the earth entrenchment, thrown across it to defend the pass over the canal, looked at a short distance like a trifling embankment; but upon coming close to it the dry ditch was found to be six feet deep, and as many wide; on the opposite side, the earth bank, behind which the French soldiers were posted, rose about five feet, so that the assailants had to climb eleven feet from the bottom of the ditch.

The British troops, of the third division, who were charged with the assault of this work, had run along the flat road several hundred yards under a sharp cracking of small arms, but being without ladders they could not surmount this obstacle, and were glad to run back again, with some loss in killed and wounded; they were thus baffled by one of the most insignificant looking banks that probably ever was seen. There can be little doubt that a few short ladders might have been found in some of the houses adjacent to the ground occupied by the third division.

While this was taking place at the Pont Jumeau, the riflemen of the Light Division, who were stationed opposite a similar bridge, the Pont des Minimes, were ever and anon aiming a cool shot at their opponents, without, however, attempting to attack the position. Their orders were only to hold the enemy in check on that point. The possession of the bridge would have been of no utility, as beyond it was a space of flat exposed ground of more than a quarter of a mile in extent, immediately overlooked from the old walls and towers of Toulouse.

The repulse of this part of the third division was *la fortune de la guerre,* and history, from the earliest days, tells of the hard knocks that the bravest soldiers have sustained against stone walls or entrenchments, in Spain as well as elsewhere.

The general brilliancy of the victory of Toulouse dazzled the public sight, and somewhat screened this attack from so much notice as it might otherwise have received; yet as it was the last effort made by the gallant third division during this eventful war, it may be called an unlucky occurrence. No division more felt it to be so than the light, which always watched the motions of the third with so much pleasure, and was ever the foremost to give a meed of praise to the "fighting division" whose well-timed assistance was often of so much benefit to it. The feeling was the stronger in consequence of these two divisions having composed one and the same after the battle of Talavera de la Reyna, in Spain. If any rivalry did exist, it was only which of them should be foremost to serve its king and country. But before I drop this little failure at the *tête de pont,* I will just hint, that had such an occurrence happened in the Western or New World, more would have been said about it, whether justly or unjustly.

And now, first claiming the same privilege, of recounting ailments or pleasures, which is allowed to other travellers, I will slowly jog along at a walk or a trot, as the case may be, making my observations on the joys or the sorrows of the people with whom I may chance to associate. But, before I proceed, let me be indulged in one remark as to the close of this great European war drama.

Of the many officers and soldiers who had figured in the Peninsular conflict, it fell to the lot of few to reach the walls of Toulouse. The most of them were now away from the soul-inspiring accompaniments of martial appeals and aides-de-camp at full gallop. Then, again, other military men shouting and huzzaing—come on—go on my fine fellows—now here—now there—and oh, for God's sake keep together! Then, again, the intonation of the cannon's roar, the volumes of smoke rolling past the silent columns of reserve of horse and foot, and the lighted matches of the cannoneer.—But truce, my pen.

As we trotted, one after the other, under the gateway into the city of Toulouse, nothing could exceed the joyful transports of its good people. The authorities greeted Lord Wellington officially, and the *canaille* knocked the bust of Napoleon from the front of the capitol, and dashed it to fragments on the pavement! We may derive an excellent moral lesson from the popular frenzy which could thus treat the bust of a man who, only a brief space of time before, was the idol of these very people.

Young as I was at the time, I could not help laughing in my sleeve at the inconsistency of this brute violence. Groups of ladies promenaded the streets, and crowds of *grisettes*, in their lace caps and holiday suits, rushed from place to place, crying, *"Vive notre bon Roi!—Vive Vellington!—Vive les Anglais!—Vive les Espagnols!—Vive les Portugais!"* and familiarly approached us to feel, with their ruddy hands, *les habits rouge*.

In the height of this display of popular frenzy I was not a little shocked to see moving through the crowd a car-load of their countrymen, hussars and chasseurs, with their heads and faces wrapped in the folds of blood-stained bandages, their arms in slings or splints, and their jackets nearly glued to their backs from sabre-cuts. The poor patient inanimate creatures looked as if life were on the ebb, and that they were quite unconscious of the fiddling and the noisy mirth in the streets, which resembled a sort of unmasked carnival.

The following day I joined a long procession of British officers, on foot, to attend the funeral of Lieut.-Colonel Forbes, of the forty-fifth regiment, who was killed opposite the aforesaid little *tête de pont*. He was interred with military honours at *Le Pape la Marque,* a piece of flat ground half a mile north-north west of the city, and near the Canal du Midi.

In the evening the theatre was thrown open *gratis* to the British officers, and was filled to excess. It is moderately spacious, but indifferently painted. Between the first performance and the afterpiece an actor came forward to announce the abdication of Napoleon at Fontainebleau. This was the first intimation of that event given to the British army, and to convey an idea of our astonishment would be out of the question. Such is the want of communications in those countries, and so unlooked for was the event, that when it was first announced from the stage, I absolutely felt a sort of chill of surprise pass through my veins, and a sensation as if the hairs of my head were bristling up to keep my moustache company.

At first a few stifled acclamations escaped the citizens in the pit; but to such a surprising piece of news we could hardly give credit, and we looked doubtingly at one another. A buzz ran through the theatre, and the actor being again called for he came forward, with a theatrical air, turning his eyes on every side for admiration, as though vanity prompted him to consider himself the dispenser of great events. While settling his cravat, he awaited with the utmost *sang froid* until the ebullition of the public applause had somewhat subsided. Then, with two measured steps, he placed himself close to the stage lamps, to enable the varied group of spectators to witness the extent of his loyalty, and the orchestra struck up *Vive Henri Quatre.*

At the conclusion of the drama the whole town presented a blaze of light; the streets were thronged with people, all the cafés were thrown open, and the females who preside in them, and who may be said to sit in state, were seated behind semicircular counters, which were covered with artificial bouquets, glasses, sweetmeats, and refreshments. These females, who are usually selected for their beauty, wore caps of an extraordinary size, highly decorated, and tied under the point of the chin, which added much to the expression of their countenance.

Being so gaily bedizened they looked at a little distance not unlike wax-dolls, but presented a lively effect. Their glances are so adroitly managed that each swain, seated at a marble slab, who may be partaking of *eau de vie* from a small silver bowl or sipping *café* or *orgeat*, flatters himself that he is the object of her peculiar notice. A young man with a well-frizzed head, *qui mange les bonbons,* is generally seated or lolling near the fair one's elbow, and assists at an agreeable *tête-à-tête,* which is by no means a bad arrangement, as it prevents strangers from incommoding her by a too lengthened strain of complimentary expressions.

A truly laughable incident happened while I was lounging in this ancient city. A friend of mine who had received a classical education, and who afterwards could boast of speaking the French tongue pretty fluently, was on all occasions quizzing me for my English-French pronunciation; but at this time he was sorely puzzled to see written up in large characters at every few yards *Ici on coupe le cheveux,* "There," said he, "look! Again it is written up *Coupe le cheveux!*" Having passed a considerable number of these notices he at last exclaimed, putting on a most wonderfully grave physiognomy, "If ever I knew so many horse-cutters in a town in my life!" Need I say, certainly not to old campaigners, as an explanation, that my companion, fresh from camp, with the snorting of Spanish stallions and the other unmusical accompaniments of the entire ass and the mule still ringing in his ears, mistook *Coupe le cheveux,* hair-cutter, which he translated as horse-cutter, as if it had been written up *Ici on coupe les chevaux,* the *a* being the letter which completely changes the meaning.

A detachment of highland soldiers and also the national guard did duty at the hotel of Lord Wellington. The latter were clothed in well made blue uniforms, with red epaulets, white cross-belts, a cocked hat, and a nodding feather; this *tout-ensemble* exhibited a handsome appearance, and they seemed highly pleased with their novel occupation.

Three or four days after our entrance, Lord Wellington gave a ball, to which several of us were invited. The mansion was handsomely hung with silken drapery, the salon was well lighted, and the floor highly polished, setting off to advantage the small satin slipper of the *belles de Toulouse*, who were elegantly attired in the newest Paris fashion. Their waists were ridiculously short, and they wore their hair without curls, drawn tight up and twisted round the top of the head, interspersed with a wreath of flowers. At the first glance this style of costume appeared preposterous, but it was *à la mode,* and who can refrain from admiring *une dame charmante* in all fashions? Their manner of dancing was truly elegant, and I cannot call to mind, at any period of my life, a more highly finished quadrille party, for they glided with noiseless step to the exact measure of the silver strains of the music.

During our stay at Toulouse we had a good opportunity of noticing the costume of its inhabitants, who are considered in this part of the country *les vrais Français.* The ladies wore large bonnets and ruffs, their dresses were well trimmed and highly decorated. *Les bourgeois* were habited in a very unbecoming fashion, a small round hat was perched, *à côté,* on the top of the head; the coats, principally of a light mixed colour, with large buttons, were high collared and long waisted, with short broad skirts, and fitted their slim bodies loosely; the lower garments, or *inexpressibles*, were made tight as far down as the calf of the leg, and then so wide and long as almost to trail on the ground.

His Britannic Majesty's foot guards, the King's German legion, Lord Aylmer's brigade, and the fifth division, had not, like ourselves, dived into the interior of France, but merely skirted the sea-coast, and the banks of the Nive and the Adour, for the blockade of the fortress of Bayonne. This position likewise protected the rear of the British army, and secured a retreat should it become indispensable. For Wellington, like other generals, gave way to an approaching storm when necessity required it, to avert greater evils, and prudently floated with the military current, when it was no longer to be stemmed.

More than once had the British retreated, in the south of Europe, and might be obliged to retreat again, for Mars is a fickle god, and has sometimes given the greatest heroes the slip at the moment when his desertion of them was least expected. It cannot therefore be wondered at, that we all felt considerable surprise when the news came to us that the garrison of Bayonne had made a sortie before daylight, on the morning of the 14th of April, and had wounded and taken prisoner the British commander General Sir John Hope; and that more than 900 men on either side had fallen, without the least benefit to French or English. The sole result of this fight was a savage and vindictive carnage, for, after it both parties kept their positions, the blockaders being, as before, without the walls of the fortress, and the blockaded within them.

While we were walking in a by-street near a large house, we observed a most fascinating young lady enter the porch, whom I shall hereafter have occasion to mention, who flew up the spacious staircase, and presented herself at the window, her peculiar headdress setting off her beautiful countenance to the most exquisite advantage. It consisted of a white satin hat, *à la militaire,* with a rim about two inches broad, and rolled up at the sides, something after the fashion of the rim of a round hat, but with a lofty crown, garnished at the top with an ample rosette *à côté,* and a nodding ostrich feather. The latter, gently agitated, gave grace to the costume of one of the prettiest fairies that ever flitted past my vision.

This lovely being was often the theme of our subsequent conversation, and our after meeting with her, at a distant place, was quite a circumstance of romance. Looking at each other in wonderment, we were half inclined to doubt whether she had not descended from the ethereal regions in Cupid's car, to gladden our eyes with another sight of her animated countenance, and of her faultless proportions, robed in transparent and flowing drapery, and her feet and ankles, cast in beauty's mould, cased in tiny slippers, shaped to grace only the feet of her who wore them.

The war was considered as concluded, but still the Duke of Dalmatia declined negotiating, pleading his want of authority to do so, and it was a laughable circumstance that he had dispersed printed hand-bills over the country, accusing the English of coming amongst them with the torch of anarchy to foment discord, when, in point of fact, the political state of the nation had already reached the acme of confusion, desertions having taken place from the French army to a great extent. In truth, it was almost impossible to believe, that the small force under the Duke of Dalmatia could be the residue of that mighty phalanx of troops that so short a time before traversed Spain with martial strides.

The moveable columns of Suchet, Duke of Albufera, were talked of among the British troops, but the major part of his force was locked up in the Catalonian posts and fortresses, and his disposable troops had dwindled into insignificance in point of numbers, so that it was all a farce to talk of their acting south of the Pyrenees, against the Anglo-Portuguese and Spanish armies, which so outnumbered them. Added to this, there had been a sort of military flirtation a month before, when King Ferdinand crossed the Pyrenees into Catalonia, after his long and close captivity in France. It was the restoration of the monarch to the crown of his ancestors which brought about the flirtation in question, as part of a Spanish and French army were drawn out face to face, presenting arms one to the other. This sort of coquetting tended to neutralize the efforts of their allies and brethren south of the Pyrenees; while the Dukes of Dalmatia and Albufera were constantly sending despatches one to the other on the means of making the last stand, to extricate themselves from the labyrinth of difficulties by which they were compassed.

For some days the Duke of Dalmatia continued to decline negotiating with Wellington. We were, therefore, once again put in motion, and marched some leagues on the road to Villefranche. We had, however, hardly taken up our ground on the tented field, when a carriage was driven past at a swing trot, escorted on one side by an English heavy dragoon in red, and on the other by a French horse-chasseur, dressed in green. This equipage conveyed the Count de Gazan, for the purpose of treating with Wellington on the part of the Dukes of Dalmatia and Albufera.

The preliminaries of an armistice being in course of adjustment, we retraced our march towards Toulouse, and, as two hundred soldiers from England had joined our corps two or three days after the battle of Toulouse, there was no lack of officers. A party of us, therefore, threw off all restraint, scraped together our best uniforms, made for Toulouse at full gallop, dashed into the courtyard of the *Hotel d'Angleterre,* and ordered dinner, which was to consist of every delicacy in season. Every face was decked in smiles while quaffing the choicest wines, and the delicious *liqueur à la Dantzic.* This jovial repast being finished, we repaired to the capitol, where a ball was to be given by the inhabitants of the town.

Upwards of two thousand people attended upon this occasion, and the ballroom was so crowded that for some hours a quadrille could scarcely be formed, and the waltzers were obliged to content themselves by turning on their own circle. A clumsy *militaire,* who was a perfect novice in that art, must needs seize hold of a charming *demoiselle* round the waist to figure away in a pair of long and ragged-pronged screwed spurs. While he was making a rapid whirl with heels up in the air, one of his spurs got entangled in the folds of a young lady's rose-coloured satin slip, and rent it in twain—terrible catastrophe!

The fair one lifted up the tattered skirt, and at the doleful sight turned up her beautiful blue eyes, and fell fainting into her mamma's arms. She was the most lovely girl in the room, and it was utterly impossible to gaze on the anguish portrayed on her innocent countenance, as the burning tears rolled down her blooming cheeks, without deeply sympathizing in her misfortune, for she was forced to quit the brilliant salon, filled by youthful warriors, who were clad in the most splendid uniforms of all the colours of the rainbow, which were embroidered with a profusion of gold and silver lace—a costume ever in unison with the rich dresses, sparkling with costly ornaments, which bedeck the fair sex.

At the expiration of two or three days the rejoicings at Toulouse began to subside; we, therefore, ordered out our horses, and rode off on the Paris road, towards Montauban, in search of our regiment. The evening was freezingly cold for the season of the year, and, consequently, after a pretty long ride we found our appetites much increased. We therefore reined in and entered a small *auberge;* but, although this public-house was encircled by a plentiful country, nothing could be more miserable than its accommodation, and we were obliged to content ourselves with an *omelette* and *un petit goût d'eau-de-vie.*

Having fed our horses we again started, but, darkness coming on, we were for some hours benighted, and could obtain no tidings of our division; at last, seeing a glimmering light through the casement of a cottage, we made towards it, and were directed by the amiable country folks to Montech, a few hundred yards to the right, on the road branching off to Montauban. On entering the small town the shops were all closed, the streets were quite empty, and hardly a light was to be seen at any of the windows, and myself and companion agreed that we had got into rather a gloomy place for our cantonment.

After traversing a street or two we came on a stray soldier, who conducted us to a large rusty looking brick-built mansion, which was chalked off for our *billet de logement.* As soon as the door was opened, our hopes revived at beholding a pretty *demoiselle,* who was busily employed in hurrying and pushing forward a couple of *filles de chambre* with lights to conduct us along a spacious passage, from whence we were ushered unto a comfortable room with a blazing wood fire.

A supper table was already laid out, with an invitation to assist mamma and daughter in anatomizing a roast capon, garnished with sausages, and with keen appetites we set to work, and could not refrain from an inward smile of satisfaction at our *bon fortune,* as we curled our moustaches, and quaffed off, by half goblets, *du bon vin de Bourgogne.*

Had we been mamma's own darlings, she could not have watched over our *petit soupe* with more solicitude. Mademoiselle Clementine Adelaide asked us, with the utmost *naïveté,* whether it was really true that *les dames Anglaises* possessed feet *aussi longues que sa bras?* Although our present sentiments savoured very much of two deserters, yet we still had sufficient patriotism left to intimate that she had been misinformed as to the deficiency of charms in our fair countrywomen; assuring her that English ladies were as fair as lilies, *très bien faites* and of *joli tournure.* Now as Adelaide's complexion had a strong dash of the *brunette,* the colour instantly mantled her cheeks, her dark southern eyes emitted sparks of fire—and hanging down her head, she said, "then, *Messieurs,* I presume *vou admirez les blondes.*"

We spent a delightful evening, and, as we were provided with fine sheets and good beds, the sun had risen some hours before we awoke from our tranquil repose. As there was no longer any hasty packing of portmanteaus, nothing could exceed our happiness on descending a flight of steps which communicated with the garden, where we found Adelaide ready to receive us, with a blooming rose in each hand, which she presented with that gentle manner so peculiar to the French.

The town, which looked so uninviting the night before, now assumed quite a different aspect. It is nearly encircled by a promenade, and its inhabitants are almost entirely composed of those economical and genteel families which inhabit the plains of Languedoc. The river Garonne runs two miles west of this place, and four miles to the eastward stands the large and populous town of Montauban, which is approached from Montech by an excellent road passing through a fruitful district.

The country abounds with extensive plains of corn, vine-yards, flower-gardens, and fruit-trees, which envelope the various mansions and cottages—all articles of provision, as well as wines, are abundant in the neighbourhood, and at a very low price. Wood is the only article consumed with a sparing hand; small forests are reared in the vicinity for firewood, but the growth is unequal to the consumption; and although the Garonne is within so short a distance of the place, yet the stream flows downwards with such rapidity that it can only he used with advantage for exportation.

The inhabitants of Montech are principally royalists; therefore, during our stay at this place, our time was exclusively devoted to pleasure. During the latter end of April and the beginning of May nothing can be more charming than the face of the country; the fruit-trees are covered with variegated blossoms, and the gardens are decked with the gayest flowers; and could I do full justice to the scene, and the whirl of festivities which followed at the close of a sanguinary war, the narrative would be treated as savouring more of a romance than a story of reality. Every door was thrown open; wives and daughters were entrusted to our care; every night there was a ball, and every day a *pique nique,* or a *fete champêtre,* Madame la Maréchale de Pêrignon was the principal lady in the place, and the family consisted of the youthful Comtesse de Lanusse and Mademoiselle Caroline Perignon, a charming young lady about fifteen years of age, so ladylike, and free from affectation.

This family we escorted everywhere, and when the carriage of the Perignons chanced to be filled with ladies, another vehicle was invariably provided for us, so that we might join the cavalcade; and to give a faint idea of the manner we passed six weeks in the sunny plains of Languedoc, I must draw an outline of some of the parties. The hall-door of Madame la Maréchale was never closed, and should there he a lack of amusement elsewhere, the *soiree* was always spent there, with either music, dancing, or games of forfeits.

At this period the Duke d'Angouleme was to pass through Montauban on his way from Toulouse towards Paris; preparations were accordingly made by the garrison to receive him, festoons of evergreens interspersed with flowers were hanging across the streets, and the town was illuminated and thronged with people.

We formed part of the Perignons' escort in a *cabriolet,* and the blaze of light produced such a vivid effect that we could no longer manage the unruly horse; it began to back, rear up, kick, and plunge in such a manner as to threaten total destruction to us and the clumsy vehicle; first we got a jolt on one side, then a shrill scream from the women and children assailed us on the other; everyone cried out in alarm, but no one proffered any assistance, until at length a French grenadier, who was on duty, deliberately walked up, and led his helpless captives through the bright flaring torches, which reflected on our scarlet uniforms and confused countenances.

At every clank of the horse's hoofs on the pavement, men, women, and children, excited by curiosity, demanded, "Who are they?"—"*Oh rien*" replied the *vieux moustache, "que les Anglais, qui allez au bal avec notre bon Prince."*

On alighting we found the antechamber of the *salon* thronged with French officers, twisting their moustaches, and pacing up and down with fierce looks, and giving us a wide berth. On entering the *salon* we rejoined our party.

La Maréchale de Perignon entered the ballroom with her daughters, La Maréchale on one arm of Captain W. Freer, and Mademoiselle on the vacant sleeve, he having lost his arm at the storming of Badajos. He has often declared to me since, that while he was standing on the summit of the great breach, he several times, with his sword, put the bayonets of the French aside as they placed the muzzles of their pieces over the parapet, so as to depress them sufficiently to fire down the slope of the breach, the crest of which was guarded from ingress by *chevaux-de-frise.*

In this way the Dukes d'Angouleme, Dalmatia, and Albufera, came to pay their respects to Madame la Maréchale. Marshal Soult asked a British officer if he had served, who being, at this epoch, far from *au fait* at the French language, replied promptly and energetically, and laying the great stress upon the last word, *Oui, mon duc—k;* this was final and conclusive. And the phrase of *mon duck* was not lost as a *bon mot.*

Many of the French people would not or could not comprehend how it was possible for officers to have served so long without a mark of distinction; and the more we endeavoured to explain the thing away, the more complex and difficult were their questions to solve. They would ask, "but how is this? If the superior officers wear decorations, why not the others, if deserving them?" And when they were made to understand that there was a rule, nothing could exceed their mirth; and they would hold our buttons, and jeeringly say, that it was true we had ten buttons aside, and were well decorated.

The French generals retired soon from the ball, to enjoy a few hours' repose for the coming review, which was to take place early the following morning.

The room was crowded with ladies, but few of the French officers deigned to enter, and those few were very ill received. What a change a few weeks had brought about towards those warriors whose smiles were then so coveted, and whose exploits were the theme of every tongue, but who were now slighted and scorned by their own countrywomen. During the waltz my friend was at my elbow; but as a young lady tightly grasped his epaulette, to support herself during the exertion of the waltz, he whispered to her in the most droll manner, "take hold of my hair, ear, or anywhere else you please, but pray let go my epaulette."

The dance continued until daylight; we then walked to the promenade, where the French infantry were formed three deep under the trees, dressed in new white breeches and gaiters; they looked crestfallen and cast down, but some unsubdued spirits muttered angry expressions as we passed along their line. Being once more seated in our cabriolet, we afforded exquisite amusement to a regiment of French hussars dressed in brown, or rather it was afforded by our soldier-servant, who was in full uniform, mounted on a pony with his knees nearly touching his chin, and toes turned out, with a pair of saddle-bags thrown across the back of the saddle; and as the hussars cried *vive, vive,* we slyly looked at him through the glass behind our leather-headed vehicle, until we were so convulsed with laughter, that we nearly drove into a ditch.

The next *fête champêtre* was at a chateau some distance from Montech. All the crazy vehicles were put into requisition for the ladies, and a sort of triumphal car, handsomely painted and gilded, was drawn by six bullocks, the horns of which were tastefully decorated with wreaths of flowers; this car was given to the Comtesse de Lanusse by the Queen of Naples, wife to Murat and sister to Napoleon. The officers escorted this cortege on horseback; on arriving at the chateau, we found the garden tastefully embellished for the occasion, and a long table laid out on the lawn with a *déjeuné à la fourchette.*

Here we passed a very happy day, playing all sorts of gambols amongst the shaded walks and fragrant shrubs, and completed the festivities by dancing to the lively roll of a village drum. The resplendent orb of heaven was sinking behind the verdant and vine-clad hills of Gascony before the cavalcade was again formed for our return; and ere long the pale light of the moon reflected its rays on the peaceful cottages by the wayside, adorned with intermingled garlands of the jessamine, the rose, and the honeysuckle. The nightingale warbled his thrilling notes, and the ladies chaunted in chorus as the cavalcade slowly wended along, inhaling the odoriferous sweets from a May vegetation: the gentle air was refreshing after the heat of the day, but on this tranquil evening it was not of sufficient force to fan into motion the leaves of the shrubs in the plains of Languedoc.

On reaching the precincts of the town, the band was in waiting, and the whole of the ladies descended from their equipages, each chaperoned by an officer, and walked into the town, two and two, with the music playing a lively air; a quadrille was formed in the market-place, and ended amid the plaudits of the well-conducted inhabitants; moving thence in procession we drew up facing the house of *la* Maréchale, where a single drum beat the rub-a-dub of village festivities. A supper table was laid out for our reception; round this board we closed the midnight revelry, and a happy morn guided our footsteps to our various abodes.

Pleasure, it is truly said, is seldom without alloy; an accident occurred amidst our gaieties which seemed a bad omen, for the next evening it was intimated that an English officer had been assailed on the bridge at Montauban by twenty French officers, who had pulled a white cockade out of his cap; and we also heard that some officers of other corps had been told, that should they be inclined to visit Montauban, they had better appear in their shirtsleeves, with *l'epée à la main,* without doubt a hint sufficiently broad for those who were not in the habit of figuring away at such exhibitions, or at the *assaut d'armes.*

The officer who had been so rudely treated, informed us that, while crossing the bridge near Montauban, on his return to quarters, a string of French officers accosted him, and, before he was aware of their intentions, two of them seized the bridle of his horse, and a third snatched the forage-cap from his head and plucked from it the white cockade. Being unarmed, and beset by such disproportionate odds, he was, for the moment, under the painful necessity of submitting to the gross insult, but, as a matter of course, he was fully determined to pursue the only remedy on such occasions, by striving to find out and call to account one of the principal actors.

My messmate, who was one of the best linguists in the corps, unhesitatingly took upon himself to seek out the French officer, and without more ado he rode towards Montauban. The French officers in that city were highly and very justly exasperated at the numerous and petty insults heaped upon their heads from all quarters, and above all by a despicable *canaille,* who had not dared to share in their toils and dangers, yet had selected this opportunity of spitting their mean spite and venom on men whom fate from their cradles bad destined to live in unsettled times, without the liberty of choosing their future profession, and who were still compelled to be tools in the hands of their fallen superiors.

The *bonnet rouge* bad long ceased to be a talisman to a certain class. Doomed to meet with the exit of an old round hat, it had been consigned to the horny fingers of the *chiffonnier*, who now handled such a thing as an unworthy associate with the rest of his rags. The tree of liberty, as it was called, had been transplanted to other countries, and with great pains nurtured and pruned with the knife of monopoly by a class of gentlemen of small inheritance, who had not failed to help themselves largely of its golden fruit, but were now too happy to turn their backs upon it, and be permitted to embrace legitimacy, that they might retain those titles and revolutionary estates which, at the outset of their career, they had pretended to despise.

Although these individuals, who tenaciously clung to the walls of the Tuileries, St. Cloud, and Versailles, were fascinated by the odour of the aristocratic bouquets of the Faubourg St. Germain, and dashed aside the humble cup of *vin ordinaire,* it was not so with the *sous-officiers* of the French army; their patriotic affection for *la belle France* led them to fight duels to maintain her honour, and to uphold a martial renown which was so dearly bought.

The officer of our regiment, selected upon the occasion of the *cocarde blanc,* reached the bridge of Montauban on horseback, and was implored by the townspeople not to risk his person alone amongst the enraged French officers; but, knowing of old that a British officer, divested of any badge of insult, was always safe amongst men who had so often fought in the field of honour, he was deaf to their entreaties. For at heart, neither he nor I cared more about the *cocarde blanc* than the *chiffonnier* did about the *bonnet rouge.* The thing, however, could not possibly be passed over, as the cockade had been indiscretely worn by a British officer without any deliberate intention of insult. It is not a little singular that I said to the individual who wore the cockade, "don't go into Montauban with that badge; you will be insulted, and, as British officers, *we* have no business to make such a display." But the person in question failed to profit by my friendly caution.

A considerable group of French officers were in deep and anxious conversation in the Grand Place, having been just dismissed from parade, when the English officer rode towards them, in full scarlet uniform. On his dismounting from his steed, they all, as though they were aware of his errand, turned round to look at his comely figure. When he was within a few paces of them he saluted, and said, "*Messieurs les officiers,* an English officer was insulted yesterday on the bridge, and I am deputed by him to demand that the individual who took the white cockade from his *bonnet* shall come forward to give that satisfaction which one *militaire.* expects from another after such an outrage."

The French officers bowed assent, and, after a little delay, an officer stepped forward and invited our officer to his *billet de logement.* The parties being seated and a bottle of wine produced, and the nature of the visit fully made known, the French officer opened a small table drawer and said, "*là voila la cocarde blanc, c'est moi qui la prise,* and I will give the English officer satisfaction." It was then agreed that a meeting should take place, with pistols, at six o'clock that evening, half-way between Montauban and Montech, each of the principals to be attended by two friends.

Accordingly, everything being in readiness, and our horses saddled, I was selected as one of the friends. We were on the point of setting out when a *billet* came from the French officer to say that his general had put him under close arrest, and that he could not for the present leave his quarters, but as soon as he was released he would not fail to make his liberation known, and give the required meeting.

A few days after this event, a French gentleman gave *a, fête* in his pleasure-grounds, where the *tambour du village,* the violin, and the military music enlivened the scene, and the joyful strains were wafted by the gentle zephyrs of a beautiful evening, while the dancers were gaily footing *la colonne à l'Anglaise* on the greensward of the terrace overlooking the bright waters of the Garonne and the golden plains of Languedoc, which were fast ripening for the sickle of the husbandman.

A messenger, of a suspicious aspect, from Montauban, stalked, through this happy assemblage, and delivered a *billet* from the French officer, intimating that he was released from his arrest, and appointing eleven o'clock on the morrow to decide the quarrel of *la cocarde blanc.* Scarely had we perused its contents before the *colonne de dance* was dispersed, the music ceased to play, and a scene of wild confusion commenced; ladies were fainting, chairs and tables were, tossed over, and in a few minutes both our officers were placed under an arrest, that is to say, the principal and he who had ridden into Montauban to require satisfaction.

A young lady came running towards me with an affrighted countenance; in each hand she had a lettuce leaf, shining with oil and covered with pepper, which was held at arm's length to prevent its soiling her transparent muslin dress.

"Que voulez vous faire, messieurs," exclaimed she, *"ah, comme tu es méchant! le pauvre officier! cet méchant billet!"* They must not fight."

The senior officer took my arm, and, after several turns, assuming an air of sternness, told me that he had ordered the two officers into confinement, and demanded of me all particulars; my answer was evasive; he then loosed my arm, saying, "Remember you must stand the consequences of everything which may occur."

"Adieu," I answered, and left him.

The interest taken in this squabble by the royalists was beyond all credibility; the town was in a perfect uproar, and some of its inhabitants offered to join in the fray, while others did all in their power to put an end to it, by protesting that they would oppose our egress from the town; we were cross-questioned by everybody, and all our motions carefully watched by the townspeople. Notwithstanding, by the contrivance of various emissaries, we succeeded in eluding their vigilance, and by five o'clock in the morning our horses had left the town; the two officers broke the arrest, the principal by sliding down a steep wall; and tramping over the country by circuitous paths, we all united, without further obstruction, at the preconcerted rendezvous. There we found our servants and horses in attendance, within half a mile of the spot where we expected to find the French officers.

The tedious hours passed on leaden wings. It was within half an hour of the appointed time, when an officer went forward in search of our antagonist to make the final arrangements, while myself and the principal waited in a flower garden. We were all in full uniform, but as the principal had his white facings buttoned back, I persuaded him to button over, as so much white cloth might present too conspicuous a mark of direction for the Frenchman to fire at.

In about an hour an officer came towards us at full gallop, and informed us that five French officers, instead of three, as previously agreed upon, were waiting in the middle of a fallow field, armed with small swords, and insisted on fighting with that weapon, although it was originally arranged, by common consent, that the combat should be with pistols.

Under such evasive circumstances I offered to go to hear what they had to say, leaving the principal to ruminate alone. I was induced to act thus by the apprehension that, under an excitement, he might be tempted to fight with the small sword, with the use of which he was by no means well acquainted. We found the five French officers standing in a field, behind the hedges of which a number of French peasantry, in white night caps, were watching the result of a *rencontre* so public. On reaching them we dismounted, and, after mutual salutations had been exchanged, we asked the reason why, in two instances, they had swerved from the original arrangements.

In the first place they pleaded their want of pistols: this objection was soon done away with, by pointing to our holsters, in which there were two pairs already loaded, and a pair was offered for their use; but to that proposition they declined acceding, on the ground that they did not understand the use of them; and the principal remarked that the English officer whom he had insulted was not present.

"That is true," we replied, "but he is at that house" pointing towards the flower-garden, "ready to exchange shots at a shorter distance than usual, if the French officer does not, as he avers, consider himself a good marksman."

They then proposed that one pistol should be loaded and the other not, and covered over with a handkerchief and taken by either party at a hazard, and for the principals to stand close, face to face, and for both to pull the triggers at the same moment. To this proposition, in our turn, we objected.

At this moment a Swiss officer stepped forward, and taking each of us by the hand, remarked how extremely odd it was that the English officers should wear white cockades, as they were not subjects of nor in any way connected with the French throne, or the internal broils of the French people. This was undoubtedly very reasonable. The Swiss officer went on to state that he had for many years been the friend of the principal, who was a first-rate soldier, and had served his country every way. He suggested, that, should his friend prove successful against the English officer, it would be his ruin, as the affair had become so public that it was now more a national than a private quarrel, and he appealed to us as to the very awkward position in which they were placed.

But it was too evident that all the stumbling blocks thrown in the way about swords was from some ulterior orders they had received from a higher quarter. This interview ended by their still refusing to engage with pistols, while, on the other hand, we reminded them that pistols were everywhere used on such occasions, and withheld our consent to permit our countryman to engage with swords with their companion, who was evidently picked out to do the business effectually as a *matador,* he being, most probably, a *maître d'armes.* He was a well-made man, about thirty years of age, of sedate aspect, and his countenance bronzed with many campaigns, and stood five feet ten inches in height, English measure; he wore a broad-topped *chaco,* a blue uniform, with a gold epaulette, blue pantaloons, and hessian boots, his small sword was buckled round his waist in a plain black leather belt, and his moustache of dark colour was well trimmed, and plenty of it. The other French officers were similarly attired, save that with his blue pantaloons, one of the four friends wore boots with brown tops.

After a still further discussion they begged to postpone the affair, and leave it to the arbitration of the French officers at Montauban. In justice to these *militaires,* we could not for a moment doubt their courage; but it was evident, from the hubbub amongst the civilians at Montauban, and an official report, with an account of the whole circumstance, having been forwarded to the restored Bourbons at Paris, that these officers only wanted to withdraw from the quarrel in a plausible manner, or, under some pretext, to give satisfaction to both parties; but that was impossible, as so many clashing interests and long smothered passions had now burst forth and were kindled into a flame of discord. However, before we separated, we reminded the French officers that the English officer would always be ready for the encounter with a weapon used by gentlemen, not only throughout Europe but in all parts of the world.

When we were within half a mile of Montech we found Monsieur —— and his son waiting by the side of the road; and during the whole course of my existence never had I witnessed so much anxiety depicted in any man's countenance. Without affording us time to inform him of the result, he forced us from our horses, embraced us, and wept bitterly; but when we told him that the French officers had declined fighting with pistols, his rage knew no bounds, he threw off his hat, trampled it under foot in the dust, and then kicked it up in the air, his eyes almost starting from their sockets, as he vehemently exclaimed, "*Oh les coquins! les poltrons! Ma foi! les pistolets sont les armes de tout le monde!* They take *la cocarde blanc comme les voleurs*, and refuse to fight! *Eh bien, mes chères enfans, venez diner chez un royaliste. C'est vrai que nous sommes les Français à present.*"

Many of our officers were so angry at the conduct of the French officers, in breaking their agreement in two instances, that they sent their sabres to be ground down, ready to meet a given number of the regiment to which the Frenchman belonged; and an officer of our corps, who had lost his right arm, insisted on making one of the party. However, in the afternoon, a French officer came expressly with an invitation from the general commanding at Montauban, requesting to have our company to dinner, when it was proposed that the French officer should meet the English officer, embrace him, and make every concession in his power.

This French officer dined and spent the evening with us. He assured us that their situation was horrible in the extreme, as the *bourgeois* of Montauban insulted them publicly in the streets, and had torn an epaulette from an officer's shoulder at noonday, saluting him with the most disgusting epithets, such as *Les brigands de Maréchal Soult, ou les officiers de quatre sous par jour.* "Come to Montauban," said he, "be *nos bons camarades;* we will meet you at the bridge; then should anyone insult you the quarrel shall be ours; we respect the English officers, we wish to be good friends; but we are convinced you will not interfere with our domestic concerns."

We told him that an answer would be returned to the French general on the morrow, but, in the meanwhile, an order came out, to forbid any further meeting or association with the French officers. It was issued by General Baron

Alten, who, after the Salamanca campaign, had succeeded Sir Andrew Barnard in the command of the Light Division. Thus the affair dropped.

Our officers had once broken their arrest; we could do no more, and, under the plea of existing circumstances, a polite excuse was sent to the French general. A fresh round of gaieties was now resorted to; Madame la Maréchale de Perignon gave a dress ball, and invited the resident gentry from the various chateaux in the neighbourhood of Toulouse and Montauban. The night was remarkably fine, crowds of smilng *grisettes* clustered round the hall-door, and the wide staircase was lined on each side with small lamps and exotics, which produced a delightful effect.

On making our bow to the young countess, she presented to each of us a small *bouquet* with the grace and affability of manner so peculiar to herself. The dancing was kept up until a late hour, when the supper-rooms were thrown open, brilliantly illuminated, and the lights interspersed with fragrant plants made the place resemble a fairy bower; pretty verses and couplets, said to be written for the occasion, extolling the beauty and known accomplishments of the different ladies encircling the festive board, were recited after the supper by various gentlemen; and it was broad daylight ere this agreeable scene concluded.

We then hastened home, for the purpose of enjoying a few hours repose, before again setting out, *en cavalcade,* with the same party for a chateau, where we were to pass the day, thence to proceed to Castel-sarrasin, where the second brigade of the Light Division were about to give a ball. The *salon* was crowded to excess, a splendid supper was provided, and the whole night passed like the former. At this period we had the bricklayers at work at Montech, in knocking two houses into one, for the purpose of forming a *salon* sufficiently large to contain the whole of our intended visitors. Some Italian artists were also employed in painting and decorating it for the occasion, with gilded *fleurs-de-lis* and other appropriate devices.

The two hundred soldiers which had lately arrived from England were sent to Montauban, for the purpose of carrying on their heads the numerous soups, covered dishes, pies, pastry, and sweetmeats, for the entertainment, and as the young soldiers followed one after the other in single files, carefully picking their steps and balancing themselves, they presented a highly amusing and interesting string, extending for nearly three quarters of a mile, calculating the intervals between each dish at six paces. The dress ball went off to our satisfaction, and with much *éclat*, until the female Italian artist joined the quadrille, which so shocked some of the company that they departed in prodigious wrath at such a monstrosity mixing with the party.

Major-General Sir James Kempt, who was just going off to America, occupied a chateau in the neighbourhood, and was involved in fetes as well as ourselves. Ours was, however, the great emporium of festivities. A sham fort was erected in the handsome ground laid out *à l'Anglais*, which was to be stormed by Amazons or young ladies. Three or four of us dined with the general, and just as we were entering the *salle-à-manger* the young lady, full dressed, whose beauty had so struck us at Toulouse, glided into the room. It would be superfluous to say how exceedingly delighted we were to see one whose person had been extolled every day since we first got a glimpse of her, and I sat in silent enjoyment to see whether she again knew my friend, whose person excelled other males as much as this young lady did her own sex—but more of this at a proper moment.

Mademoiselle L—— was the fair one selected to have the honour of leading the forlorn hope. After having taken coffee and liqueur we all stationed ourselves behind some shrubs. Everything being in readiness, blue lights were thrown from the fort, and mademoiselle, accompanied by several young ladies, armed with wooden swords, and their heads crowned with paste-board helmets, led on the assault amidst a blaze of fireworks; but, when the foremost were in the act of stepping on the draw-bridge, one of the ropes broke and the bridge fell on one side into the *fosse;* a mishap, added to the hissing of the fireworks, which frightened the young ladies to such a degree, that they came running back out of breath, and were hailed by a general burst of laughter. This so incensed Mademoiselle L——, that she seized the little flag out of one of the maiden's hands, and wildly rushing forward with all her life and soul, jumped into the *fosse,* actually scrambled into the fort with her petticoats above her knees, amid the plaudits of the bystanders, hauled down the standard, and waved it over the painted battlements. The fort being nearly demolished, we re-entered the chateau, and a short French comedy was performed by a few of the visitors, which closed the diversions.

The following morning, after breakfast, we all sallied from the chateau to examine the remains of the fort, and began to throw the squib papers at each other.

Mademoiselle L——, being the leader of the sport, was full of sportiveness and joy, and in the height of her mirth rubbed the venerable and lean marquis's face all over with gunpowder. He made a hasty retreat into his chateau, but speedily returned, and took post behind a shrub, armed with an enormous syringe. Mademoiselle having collected certain projectiles, hastened to dislodge him, but her stock of ammunition being all expended, she rushed to the close, and when she was within a yard of the marquis he discharged the whole contents of his water-engine into the middle of her lap, which pierced her summer garments of thin texture through and through. She uttered an involuntary shriek, which so penetrated the heart of an aide-de-camp, who was the marquis's bottle-bolder, that, in a fit of excitement, he raised the heavy stone pitcher, and emptied its contents of cold spring water on the powdered bald pate of the marquis, who ran off as fast as his slender legs would carry him, and was soon seen waving a crimson pocket-handkerchief from one of the upper windows as a symbol of peace and harmony. On entering we found his head sorely lacerated and cut with the weight of the pitcher, a mishap which he bore with extreme good humour.

Thus closed our six weeks' gaieties at the end of a sanguinary war.

The whole British army being now setting out for Bordeaux, the dark Portuguese separated from them, for the purpose of returning through Spain to the rocks of their own country. And oh, let me string the cords of memory! Once, while at the foot of the hill on which Alfayates stands, in Portugal, sixty or seventy young lads, almost in a state of nudity, passed me; their wrists tied one to the other with ropes, or manacled with iron handcuffs; and, on asking where they were going, I was told, with a laugh, that they were "volunteers for the Portuguese army."

These troops, that had fought for so many years side by side with the British, had attained the highest state of discipline, and seemed to take as much to heart the present separation as if they were about to be torn from their own countrymen; they looked dejected and cast down, and as our troops merrily wished them adieu, they were almost speechless. These feelings were not put on, for I suppose these, our allies, had their services been required, would have followed the divisions they had fought with to any part of the globe.

In June, being the rear division, we quitted Montech and its vicinity, to the unfeigned regret of the inhabitants, who accompanied us to the banks of the Garonne, the officers being dismounted behind the regiment, and in this manner they walked arm in arm with the ladies of Languedoc, who took leave of us on the banks of the river with tears in their eyes, saying that they never should cease to think of *les habits rouge et le collet blanc*.

As the soldiers entered the boats for the passage of the river, crowds of *grisettes* were crying after their lovers—so much for female patriotism—and one, more desperate than the rest, floundered into the river to drown herself; but, fortunately, before she was exhausted, the soldiers succeeded in rescuing and hauling her into the boat, and in this way carried her across the river, and she was finally united in holy wedlock to the happy sergeant for whom she had risked so much.

Some of us went back for a day or two, and I must not fail to mention that the evening amusements of the French gentry were diversified and frolicsome.

Amongst others, Monsieur L—— at his own house would pin a twisted sheet of writing paper to that part of the trousers called the seat; then a second person, male or female, would strive to set the wriggling paper on fire with a candle, but monsieur possessed so much suppleness, that the paper, projecting like a tail from his nether end, was seldom ignited, or seen in flames, from the *fandango*-like motions of that nameless part, (which is usually kept sacred, and covered with broad cloth, save and except of light infantry officers, hussars, and the horse-artillery, for, alack-a-day, we could not then boast of the lancer,) going through such contortions as to make the ladies hide their glances with their pocket-handkerchiefs; for fans did not expand at this time in Languedoc, like those machines of gone-by antiquity.

After a further stay of two days amongst these kind people, early in the morning those who had stopped behind bade a long and last farewell; and at one house we were ushered upstairs into a bedroom, where we found a young couple in bed, lying side by side, this husband and wife both shed tears and embraced us tenderly, but, although I was now an experienced continental traveller, I could hardly contain my smiles at this strange and novel scene.

But at the conclusion of the war, there was such an abundance of kissing, as probably the like of it was never seen before, which put one in mind of the adage, "that none but the brave deserve the fair." There was kissing in the valleys, and kissing upon the hills, and in short, there was embracing, kissing, and counter-kissing, from Toulouse to Bordeaux.

Chapter 25

Gascony

At the end of two days' march we arrived at Lectoure, the birth place of Marshal Lannes, the valiant duke of Montebello, once the Orlando of the French army. The town is situated on a lofty hill, whence is a vast and extensive view over a beautifully shaped country, adorned with vast forests, and every description of vegetation to beautify the land, which is rich in almost every production for the wants of man.

Myself and friend were this day quartered at a gentleman's house, and, upon entering, we saw a very interesting young lady at the window, and were not a little gratified at the father coming towards us in the hall, with the most polite professions, saying that everything in the house was at our service. In anticipation of spending a pleasant day, we threw off our marching-dress, and, in short, were resolved to say a great many pretty things to the young lady. But to our utter chagrin, hour after hour passed without a message or invitation of any sort to join the family circle; the house was silence personified, and in utter despair we rushed forth, and consoled ourselves with the fine prospect from a summer-house on the top of this charming hill. Dinner time came, yet we saw nothing of our French gentleman and his professions, nor of his charming daughter.

Chagrined at this freezing reception, we said all sorts of ill-natured things, and at last vowed if we were to meet her in the passage that we would not bow or speak to her. This

325

was, indeed, a long day, and we over and over again cogitated whether the fault could rest with the father or the *demoiselle*; but it was finally decided to emanate from the young lady, otherwise she would at least have contrived to come out of a door in a hurry, and just give a glance towards us. For even the nieces of the *curés* would do this in spite of bolt, key, or other priestly contrivances. Notwithstanding we wandered about in such a passion, first going to the garret of the house, then to the back towards the stables, and crossing and re-crossing the passage, listening from time to time, all was as disagreeably quiet as the cloisters of any convent.

At last, oh glorious intelligence! the ladies of the town sent a deputation to request that the English officers would give them a ball, offering at the same time a small amateur theatre belonging to the private families of the place. Now, what an opportunity was here presented to show our mean spite! We vowed that we would not invite the young lady of this house, or even let her know that a dance was to take place. And this, in some measure, consoled us for the abominable slight put upon our red-coated persons, in a country, where we had been made too much of; for no two children could have been more vexed at the loss of a toy than we were by the unaccountable want of taste which we considered this piece of female marble as having displayed.

Still we hoped she would be at the ball, that we might have an opportunity of asking the young lady or ladies right and left of her to dance, without our taking any notice of her. She, however, was not there. We danced all night, and obtained permission to remain behind the regiment, and getting up at nine o'clock the next morning, we went to the stable, coiled up the halters, and putting the bridles upon our horses, which were already saddled, we mounted and left the house, by the gate of the yard. There we saw the young lady at the front window. How shall I find words to describe her? She gave a faint smile, but we turned away our indignant faces, set spurs to our horses and trotted off, without deigning to stop. But snatching a glance, I saw her put her pocket-handkerchief to her eyes— how remarkable! how unaccountable!

What must be her feelings to know that the inmates of her house were dancing all night, and that she was not allowed to participate in the darling amusement of the fair sex, and with *les étrangers aussi;* added to which, my companion M—— was one of the handsomest young officers that ever was seen; wherever he went all eyes were turned on him, in France, England, and Spain. The men admired him universally, and the fair sex loved him unanimously, aye in a body. This must demonstrate his merit past all manner of doubt; for when both sexes with one accord unite in admiration, doubt can no longer exist. No portrait could do justice to the expression of his eyes, his fine healthful cheeks, white forehead, dark locks, moustache, and commanding person.

We were now convinced that the fault did not rest with the fair object already spoken of. She was now a dear, charming, lovely girl, shut up in a cage—poor dear thing—and, as we jogged along the pleasant way, we regretted that we had not kissed our hands to her. Really our behaviour was unpardonable, cruel, barbarous. But let it be remembered, in extenuation, that the pain we had endured had made us lose for a moment the equilibrium of our politeness, nay, even our affection as general lovers.

The portraiture of my good friend M—— may seem overdrawn to all those who did not know him; but such was his influence over the fair sex, that upon one occasion a Dutch woman burst out crying because a barber had made too free with his locks. He had a brother in the rifle corps, extremely tall, and always full of genuine humour; in fact, wherever he showed himself some fun was always going on; he was exceedingly good tempered, but was most confoundedly annoyed when officers of the rifle corps were taken for Portuguese, which was very often the case. Then, again, the foreigners could not understand their not wearing epaulettes, and they were under the painful necessity of telling the people in every town they went to that they were really officers. "But," said the people, "where's the epaulette?"

And then there was another mistake, for when they wore their *pelisses* they were mistaken for hussars. Then came another long explanation to satisfy the curious French, how it was that foot riflemen wore clothes like hussars. So that whenever this rifle-officer came to me, I used to pay, "but where's the epaulette?" well knowing he would pay me off with interest the first good opportunity. For he would often bawl out a secret, to the utter dismay of worthy individuals, who really and truly wished to keep some little flirtation from publicity. But this rifle-officer was privileged and irresistible, and I have often seen a crowd of culprits disperse when he was in sight, coming on at full drive to turn gravity into monstrous ridicule.

The following day leaving Lectoure, we entered Condom, where we halted one whole day, and the young lady of the house was so struck with the appearance of my friend M—— that she brought all the young ladies in the town to see the *beau jeune Anglais,* by which title they were pleased to designate him.

We now approached Bordeaux by easy marches, having daily *billets de logement,* either in good towns or chateaux, the cellars filled with the choicest wines, and the gardens abounding in flowers and luscious strawberries. The soil round Bordeaux is sandy; here the vine is regularly planted and highly cultivated, and is generally about the size of a gooseberry bush. Bullocks or horses drag a light plough between them, which turns up the fresh sand or mould and revives their stems.

In this neighbourhood the *grisettes* are better dressed than in any other part of France that I ever visited; they wear large handsome white transparent caps, which are extremely becoming.

While we were marching in broad sections, we met many of the squalid and lean French prisoners returning from their long confinement at Norman-cross, Stapleton, Dartmoor, and

Mill prisons, and the hulks of England, who were obliged to stand by the side of the road or in the ditches, to make way for the soldiers, from whose cockades drooped roses or various other flowers, as they merrily tramped along the dusty roads under a clear sky, chuckling at the idea of getting the best *cognac* for a *franc* a bottle. This sight must have been extremely mortifying after the protracted sufferings of these unhappy Frenchmen, whose bad fortune still pursued them, in dooming them to be cast into their native country at a time when their former services and long captivity produced no sympathy for all the hardships they had endured.

As soon as we had passed through the thronged streets of Bordeaux, the clouds of dust flying up in dense volumes, we halted in a wood about three miles from it, and had hardly time to brush off the dust of the march when we were ordered to form all along the high road to be reviewed by the newly created Duke of Wellington. We were at the same time informed, that some of the other divisions, which, like ourselves, had marched from the coast of Portugal to Bordeaux under his command, had cheered his Grace, but that there was an order against any more cheering. The Portuguese riflemen, or Caçadores, clothed in brown, having left us, with another regiment, the Light Division composed little more in numbers than a strong brigade.

The Duke of Wellington passed along the line from right to left, mounted on a white charger, which was covered with a netting. His Grace was dressed in the scarlet uniform of a field-marshal, and decorated with orders and military distinctions, the blue riband being across his right shoulder.

A few hours after this review we were told that a French young lady asked to have the honour of kissing the Duke's hand, and that, instead of presenting his hand, his Grace dismounted and most gallantly imprinted a kiss upon her fair cheek; her emotions on receiving this unexpected honour so overcame her, that Mademoiselle fell into her father's arms dissolved in tears.

In the afternoon most of us rode into Bordeaux, and were highly pleased with so fine a city and its amusements. Our division then proceeded to Blanchefort camp, where still remained encamped a great many regiments of the army; from whence by degrees some of them were drawn off for England, while others were destined for the United States of America, the Court of St. James's still being at war with the Union. At this camp three of us contrived to ensconce ourselves in a chateau at the extremity of an avenue, a short way behind the great plain or tented field. The weather continued exceedingly fine.

Jack Rag was our cook, a well known soldier, who had cooked for many a departed master; he and another soldier named Robinson were the two great rivals in this exquisite art in our camps. They were fighting cooks withal. Robinson I saw wounded at the battle of Vittoria; a musket-ball entered his abdomen. This celebrated and accomplished cook had on two pairs of trousers at the time, which luckily saved his life. The bullet forced the cloth of both pairs into the body without perforating or even rupturing the cloth, and it was extracted by laying hold of each end of the waistband. The man soon recovered, and rejoined his corps, to elicit more smiles from those who did not turn up their noses at a good ragout, or his prodigal way of melting down the *mantèca de puérco de España*.

This camp was the scene of many curious extravagancies, and was converted into a sort of racecourse for equestrian courtesans a-straddle on hack-horses, and in male attire, from Bordeaux. Many of their full-moon faces, and other large proportions both before and behind, were strikingly prominent, and rolling from side to side like the hull of a ship in a gale of wind; they were, in fact, the very acme of fat women with leather saddles betwixt their legs, and of gross vulgarity in all its, most unfeminine deformity.

The hardy and swarthy-faced Spanish muleteers with fili-gree buttons had been paid the residue of their demands on the English army with treasury-bills; but hearing, that these bills, after reaching England in safety, would be discharged with other paper, these *pincaros* were taken aback, for they knew as much about the Bank of England, the Stock Exchange of London, the English monetary system, and Long Annuities, Indian Bonds, Scrip, or Consols, as they did about the inhabitants of the moon. Under these circumstances, they were willing to dispose of the said treasury-bills at such a discount as would have made an antiquated usurer bite his nails and gnaw his finger-ends at the loss of such a bargain.

Some of the followers of the army, who happened to have hard dollars and other coins under lock and key, were the thrice lucky caitiffs to buy and hoard up these treasury-bills for one half, or, more properly speaking, for one-third of their real value. The premium, in favour of these Spanish and Portuguese pastoral travellers, did rise a little when the circumstances of this extraordinary monopoly got wind; but not till it was too late to rectify the fraud executed by the moneyed followers of the army, many of whom had stored in strong box the cash, which had been carried at the public expense; some of the specie, which was thus employed, consisted of the very doubloons and dollars taken on the field of Vittoria, or purloined from other sources, in spite of the vigilance of the provost-martial with his crimson feather, his crimson sash and his red nose, with a rope's end dangling from the pummel of his saddle on one side, and a cat-o-nine tails from the other. I must observe, *en passant,* that the provosts, in general, had the look of jolly fellows who were devoted to the ardent spirit called, in Spain, Aguardiente.

I can vouch that the working officers had little to do with the treasury-bills in question; for I hardly ever knew one of these children of war, these receivers of bullets at point blank distance, who had a couple of spare dollars in his pocket, without their being soon melted down at the *café* or elsewhere.

For my part, at the end of the war I had a pair of white wash trousers. A most accomplished and lovely French *demoiselle,* after dancing all night, once took my rumpled trousers under her arm to get them washed for the coming evening dance. I can boast, and it is a proud boast, that all the time I was in Portugal, Spain, and France, I only spent seventy pounds over and above his Majesty's pay, after my first fitting out; but some others squandered very large sums of money, and their expenses were enhanced by dollars often being procurable only at a most enormous and ruinous discount. I should have crossed my pen over this statement of my own little expenditure, and have said nothing about the drawing of my purse-strings, or rather those of an old worsted stocking, had not others told, *on their legs*, in plaintive terms how little self and friends had made in his Majesty's service to keep up appearances.

At that period, the price of everything was excessively enhanced. Biscuit, hard, soft, and rotten, was masticated by us in camp, at the enormous cost to the British government of half-a-crown a pound on many occasions; it having been brought up hundreds of leagues on mules' backs for the army. This is calculating the tonnage of shipping for its first transport, and thence travelling from mountain to river, over extensive plains, according to the circles, half-circles, quarter-circles, zigzags, and other forward, retrograde, and flank movements of military strategy.

Our camp ground being traced out, we made for Bordeaux to pass a few days, where we sold all our cattle at a very low rate; and the wonder was how we disposed of them or found purchasers, for the whole army were selling off cattle almost at the same time. My Rosinante, with English saddle and bridle, brought me twenty-five dollars, having served me for upwards of three years, and never sent but once sick to the rear without its rider; this trusty animal I was forced to part with much against my inclination: my other animal, although excellent of its kind, brought me very little. The different restaurateurs and *cafés* in Bordeaux reaped a fine harvest from the pockets of the British officers, who spent vast sums of money amongst them.

La Maréchale Perignon and her family now arrived from Montech, with whom we resumed our intimacy, and daily escorted them on some delightful excursions, to a Jew's gardens and chateau, and other places in the neighbourhood. The king's box was given up for their accommodation in the theatre, which is an extremely fine piece of architecture: it was magnificently fitted up with mirrors; the drapery was of orange silk, fringed with gold bullion two inches long. The Bordelais are exquisite dancers, and get up their ballets in the first style.

Here we saw two *figurantes* dance on each aide of a gauze curtain; and so exact were their dress and all their movements that the two looked like one female dancing before a mirror. This dance was afterwards got up and represented in England. A second ballet was amazingly well managed; a group of men with short swords and broad blades, similar to those anciently used by the Romans, danced and engaged at the same instant, beating time with their feet, striking the measure while twisting and turning from one to the other, and going through the intricacies and windings of the dance with a precision truly astonishing; the clashing of the swords to the cadence of the music produced a martial clangour, like the sound of innumerable triangles in a musical band. This was the best executed dance I ever beheld, with the exception of, I may say, the noble Spanish *bolero,* for in that dance all that is wild and graceful is combined; and the rattling of the *castanets,* marking the time, produces a thrilling sensation too deeply felt to be described.

Before the British army was all embarked, the discontented French officers poured into Bordeaux in full uniform, and took lodgings for the express purpose of seeking personal quarrels and revenge, and they selected the *cafés*, the restaurateurs, and the theatre, to begin their brawls.

At the latter place, one night, swords were drawn, and knock-down blows were given and taken. One French officer was struck in the face by Lieut. the Hon. Francis Russell, and knocked out of the first tier of boxes into the pit. This officer had also knocked one or two French grenadiers down at the battle of Pampeluna with the colour-pole of the 7th fusiliers, to which he belonged. An Englishman received a bloody nose, and called out the Frenchman the next morning. Lamps and mirrors were smashed, and black bottles and decanters flew in all directions in the lobby. The hubbub was at its height; all the refreshment tables and counters were broken or overturned in the saloon; oranges and sweetmeats were squeezed and crushed under foot; and the finest Champagne, Burgundy, and Chateau Margeaux were streaming on the floor. This scene of confusion ended in various duels fought between the English and Germans and the French.

The British officers, by an order from their own superiors, were now forbidden to enter the theatre, to prevent a further contest, as the French were daily flocking into the city, and these quarrels would at last have ended by a general battle. It is singular enough that many of the British officers purchased round hats, and groups of them, walking arm in arm with the utmost gravity, wore them with their scarlet uniforms in Bordeaux, so much disgusted and ashamed were they of their unsightly and ill-shaped military caps. Their disgust was quite natural, for, distorted by the alternate rain and sunshine, as well as by having served as pillows and night-caps, the caps had assumed the most monstrous and grotesque shapes, and many of the tattered oilskins flirted about like a bundle of rags upon their heads, so that the covering had a most unsightly appearance and excited peals of laughter and the oddest remarks from the witty little French boys and girls in the streets, who wondered whether these queer castors could possibly belong to or be the proper head-pieces to men who had fought in such sweeping and desperate battles. But what made the thing still more ridiculous was, these round hats worn in *self defence* to avoid the sneers of the people, were construed by many of the Napoleonist officers into a mark of insult towards them; they were considered as an allusion to their being themselves doomed so soon to cast their uniforms aside, and to wear round hats.

At the end of June we marched for Pouillac, and while halting at a village, some ladies at a chateau invited us to breakfast. I fastened my borrowed horse, as I thought, securely to a tree out of sight, but during the repast one of the young ladies jumped up with horror at seeing a raw-boned animal on the lawn, adorned with a green velvet saddle, embroidered with silver, with only one rusty stirrup suspended from it by a piece of rope. There was no time for explanation; I felt my face colour up, and being quite ashamed to own the animal, I took my leave at full speed, on the plea that I could no longer remain from my corps, and leaving the house I sent a soldier to say that the beast belonged to a suttler. The horse was of English breed, and had done so much work, and passed through so many hands, that it was quite knocked up and beyond selling. It was lent to me by another officer, with its housings fitted up as described.

At the end of this day's march, I and my friend were quartered on a very handsome chateau. Just as I entered the grounds my bridle broke, and the provoking animal actually, for the first time, went up the avenue at a rough trot, and as the green velvet saddle was made in the hussar fashion, I could not throw myself off. When opposite the house, it turned off the beaten path, and its hoofs were buried up to the fetlocks in a flowerbed, in the presence of two antiquated old maids who stood at the hall-door to receive us.

Nothing could exceed the civility of these two females, but they were so excessively ill-favoured in point of appearance, and so like each other, that we were glad when the hour of repose arrived. They had sallow complexions, pale watery blue eyes, white eye-lashes, flaxen hair, thin lips, wide mouths, and yellow teeth; their stiff and starched figures were so flounced, that it was impossible to know positively whether they were well or ill made; while one of them held my hand with an iron grasp in her long tapering cold fingers, a thrill of the most painful sensation run through my veins. To get rid of their excessive civility, and in part payment for the excellent fare they had spread before us, with the utmost magnanimity we presented to their arms a little English terrier dog, which was not our own, having gone astray, and followed us to the house. The poor little animal had, however, as little relish for the spinsters as ourselves, and soon after we got to bed it came crying to our door. In the morning this living present was packed in a hamper, and in this way we stole our over-night's present out of the house.

The two pieces of flounced antiquity had just finished the labours of the toilette, and were descending the polished stairs, as we were quitting the place. This added speed to our footsteps, for in truth all our compliments were exhausted, and we feared to be cross-questioned about the dog. On our reaching, the road, the little animal licked our hands, and scampered off in search of his real owner.

At this chateau part of the three provisional regiments of militia had been quartered, but did not enter Bordeaux, some twenty-three miles up the river or more. The militias had volunteered to serve abroad towards the winding up of the war, but were too late, which does not at all derogate from their merit in so handsomely offering to take the field. The officers were reduced after this short service, with the same half-pay as those who were of the line, which was extremely bountiful to them on the part of the government.

On reaching the town of Pouiilac, on the left bank of the river Garonne, which here resembles an arm of the sea, and is many miles in breadth, we embarked in boats to go on board the *Queen Charlotte* and the *Dublin*. As I was hastily dismounting from my iron-grey palfrey, I offered it a free gift to some of the French bystanders; but the poor beast cut such a doleful figure, that nobody would accept it, and they turned their heads away as if in fear of such a bargain being palmed off upon them; or more probably they nourished some suspicions that I had come unfairly by it, its *tout-ensemble* being so thoroughly un-English. I could not divest myself of a smile, as my parting glance fell upon the worn-out animal, quietly pacing up the street by itself, the rein of the rotten bridle trailing in the dust, and the old rusty stirrup hanging by a cord from the left side of the hussar saddle, of faded green velvet, and its once gay but now tarnished silver embroidery.

This was the last of the Light Division. The separation now came. Though amongst the regiments which composed it there existed an unanimity which was almost without a parallel in war, yet there was a shade of difference between them, a something peculiar to each corps, distinguishing it from all the others; which was the more remarkable as amongst them there was a sort of fraternal compact, and it has occurred that three brothers held commissions at the same time in the forty-third, fifty-second, and rifle corps.

The forty-third were a gay set—the dandies of the army; the great encouragers of dramatic performances, dinner parties, and balls, of which their head-quarters was the pivot.

The fifty-second were highly gentlemanly men, of a steady aspect; they mixed little with other corps, but attended the theatricals of the forty-third with circumspect good humour, and now and then relaxed, but were soon again the fifty-second.

The rifle-corps were skirmishers in every sense of the word, a sort of wild sportsmen, and up to every description of fun and good humour; nought came amiss; the very trees responded to their merriment, and scraps of their sarcastic rhymes past current through all the camps and bivouacs.

In this way the brothers of the three regiments met together, each being the very type of the corps to which he belonged. Amongst them are to be enumerated the Napiers, the Maddens, the Booths, the Rowans, the Whichcotes, the Maynes, the Dobbs, the Patricksons, the Harvests, and others. And before we take our farewell, I may affirm, that, although these troops were bound together by an iron code of discipline, no Roman tribune could ever boast of more camp orators, nor was there any fraternity that ever lived in happier independence when off duty.

Some of the officers of the Light Division were such young men, that it was not uncommon to see one of them of eighteen or nineteen years of age or younger, going along the road to seek for wood and water, or on some important mission, with the most unconscious gravity.

CHAPTER 26

To England

The rays of the sun shone brilliantly on the bright waters of the Garonne; the greater portion of our corps were now rowed on board the *Queen Charlotte*, commanded by Viscount Keith, Admiral of the Channel Fleet; the remainder went on board the *Dublin*. Lord Keith had a milch-cow on board, and made his own butter, which was floating in pretty little pats in bowls, and hung in the state cabin, which was well fitted up.

This man-of-war, crammed with the red and blue jackets, represented a beehive. Its officers were exceedingly kind and attentive, and we messed together in the ward-room, and also dined by turns with the admiral. Some of us took post in the gun-room, and as my mattress was opposite one of the stern-ports, one morning the ship for an instant backed sail, and into the port rushed the salt-water, sousing and wetting my nest, and soaking my sheets and blankets.

Although I was rather sea-sick, I had sunk into a gentle nap; but now, without more ado, I started on my feet, and gasping for breath, with my mouth wide open, half drowned, and fancying, as the water flew over me, that I was at the bottom of the ocean.

My companion in sea-sickness, who, by the bye, seldom lost his appetite, said to a young middy, who good-naturedly brought him down the devilled wing of a turkey, "Now, my dear boy, how could you think of coming to sea? Pray tell me where your parents live?"

" In Dublin," answered the open-hearted middy.

"Ah!" responded the reclining soldier; "then I would never go to see them."

An expression which somewhat startled him of the seafaring life, who smilingly asked, "Why not?"

"Why, because I never mean to go to sea any more. Now, for example, the master of the fleet is thought a very clever man; notwithstanding his cleverness, here we have been for four long days, without being able to weather Cape Ushant."

"But the wind is foul," said the highly-amused middy.

"Well! Well!" responded he of the land service; "and that now is the very thing I dislike. Believe me, that I would not be admiral of the channel fleet tomorrow, but would rather live upon *vingt sous par jour.*"

This last effusion from the sick man being finished, the middy laughed outright, and ran off to tell the youngsters in the cock-pit, that a soldier-officer had said that he would not change places with the *commander of a fleet.*

****

After nine days' voyage, in the beginning of July, the *Queen Charlotte* dropped her ponderous anchor in Plymouth-Sound. The bay on three sides is skirted by highlands, and on looking towards Old Plymouth town, a great many fine objects crowd on the eye; to the left is the little town of Cawsand, situated at the water's edge, and above are the Maker heights, and their forts rising in the background; adjoining to this is the wood-covered hill of Mount Edgecumbe, its variegated foliage tinted with beautiful lights and shades, out of which peep the pinnacles of mock-ruined towers and temples, while from some of the fissures of the rock the trunks of the trees recline their stems and lateral branches, overshadowing the rocks as if to dip their boughs into the briny element which foams at its base.

Directly in front is the rocky and fortified island of St. Nicholas; and a little further inland appear the rocks, from the summit of which slopes downwards the greensward of the Hoe and its landmarks; adjoining is the bastioned citadel on the same hill, overlooking the bay; this hill screens the greater part of the old town of Plymouth, the quays of which jut into the water.

On the right-hand side of the bay are shingled, ragged, and dangerous rocks, here and there scattered in the surf, and over these rocks rise the steep acclivities, the ascent of which is entangled with brushwood difficult to penetrate; above all are the bare hills stretching out in bold headlands; and beneath this promontory a solitary lighter is seen lowering with a crane a shapeless block of granite of many tons weight for the contemplated Herculean task of forming the breakwater. This barrier of sunken rocks is designed to extend for a mile across the entrance of the harbour, in order to break the mighty swell which rolls in towards Plymouth from the channel, to the great danger of shipping at anchor or even coming into port.

The sparkling sunbeams now dance upon the waters of this spacious bay, in which the countless fishing-smacks, with their tar-bedaubed canvass, skim the surface, or ply coastwise, while in the offing the white sails of other ships or craft, as it were in specks on the line of the horizon, are making way from distant hemispheres. Constructed on a dangerous rock, twelve or fourteen miles from land, is the Eddystone lighthouse, to which pleasure-parties take excursions, and often come back more sea-sick than otherwise, vowing within themselves for the future to confine their joys and pastimes to their native hills.

On every side flit the light and gaily painted men-of-war's gigs, which are swiftly pulled to and fro by sailors picked for the occasion; the naval officers are seated astern in their characteristic blue uniforms, with gold epaulettes and gold-laced cocked hats, worn, to use the nautical phrase, "fore and aft," and their white hilted sabres, or the more handy dirk, suspended in a blue silken waist-belt.

Many bum-boats, the paint quite worn off them, with patched sails and spliced oars, came alongside sculled by women, who were the pictures of sound health and as brown as gipsies. These boats, or rather tubs, are stored with pipes, the weed of Virginia, pipe-clay for the marines, bread, butter, vegetables, and other fresh commodities, to gratify the appetite of the home-bound mariner.

Viscount Keith and the officers of his majesty's ship *Queen Charlotte* dined with us at the Fountain Hotel, in Fore-street, Devonport, where we spent a carousing evening. Many little farcical incidents happened on landing; amongst others was that of an officer who perambulated the streets with a beard of many days' growth, as if time had not been given him to use the razor before or since quitting the fine city of Bordeaux, and we agreed that this was being rather martial, considering the war was closed, and that there was no want of time or apparatus to make his face look a little smooth.

An interchange of county militias had taken place between Great Britain and Ireland, the Irish militias coming to this country, and on the other hand those from England doing duty in Ireland. The soldiers from Spain were incorporated with the Cork and Devon militias at the guard mounting in front pf the government-house; the former were so tanned by a southern sun that they resembled Creoles, and here and there patches of dark faces in the line, according to the different detached guards, were in brown contrast with those of the militia, and were conspicuous at a considerable distance.

Although the militia had been for so long a period a nursery for the line, and had been so often drained by large drafts made from it into the regular army as volunteers, still this domestic force maintained a fine aspect, both on duty as well as by exemplary and general good conduct in quarters; the uniforms were beautifully clean and the martial music excellent From these ranks the regulars could boast of having drawn some of their best soldiers; there was not a forlorn hope, a storming or an escalade party, or any other desperate enterprise in this eventful war, in which men originally from the militia did not largely partake.

The European struggle being ended, these militias were ordered to their several counties, there to be disbanded; a small staff was, however, kept together, on which constitutional stem, in times of dangerous and sudden exigencies, a proper force can, without delay, be raised by order of the government, under their several colonels or lords-lieutenant of respective counties.

Almost within a stone's throw of the lines of Devonport, by which it is overlooked, is Stonehouse-bridge; it is thrown over a creek, and was constructed at the cost of a private individual. The troops on duty, passing and re-passing this bridge, were obliged to pay a halfpenny each, or make a circuit of a mile by the Naval Hospital, near the head of the creek, although the highway leading over the bridge was a direct line, and a necessary link between the citadel, old Plymouth town, and the entrenchments which enclose the government house, the dockyard, and the town of Devonport.

There was a singular circumstance connected with this toll-bar. When a body of troops were coming from Stonehouse, and were within a few hundred yards of Devonport, they were necessitated to pay, or go by the head of the creek; a debate took place as to whether the men would pay or make a circuitous march. Upon these occasions the question was put to the vote, to ascertain whether the soldiers were unanimous or not—for a majority or a casting voice was not sufficient to carry the measure—and one or two dissentient votes obliged the rest of the detachment to go the round. In every instance, at the foot of this bridge, the soldiers were not unanimous, which, from the novelty of such an occurrence, is worthy of notice. Whether it was put to the vote before quitting their private parade, or at the point specified, came to one and the same thing, and more than once I have known not only an individual but a whole detachment respectfully decline paying in this way while employed on public duties, and declare that, whether they went the round or not, it was all in the day's work.

Orderlies with their books going to the government house for daily orders, musicians attending daily guard-mounting, and many other classes were under the necessity of paying this toll, otherwise, from the time at which they were marched from their private parades, the military arrangements of one of the largest garrisons in England would have been totally disorganized. This toll proved a heavy tax upon the orderly and well-disposed soldiers throughout the year; for, however trifling the sum may appear to men with pockets better lined, still these little surcharges often deprived the soldier of his ball of pipe-clay, soap, and an extra whiff of tobacco. After this injudicious obstacle had existed several years, it was altered for the benefit of the soldier, and the better communication between the different parts of the garrison of Plymouth.

One fine day, while strolling near the verge of the sea, on the green slope leading down to the government stores, I saw a male and female sculler seated in a bum-boat about a hundred yards from the beach, basking in the sultry rays of the sun. Their arms were coiled round each other's necks, and they were billing and cooing like a pair of turtle-doves. The water was transparent, and its surface as resplendent as a looking-glass. Near the circular stairs, a landing place, there was also a gaily painted man-of-war's gig, with a party of sailors gambolling about in playful mood. The tars wore white canvass shoes without stockings, and ever and anon one of them would hitch up the unbraced canvass trousers with one hand, while he turned a large quid with the other. The elastic Guernsey frock fitted skin-tight upon their brawny arms and backs. Their tails were of great length and of considerable compass, hanging down their broad backs like a small hawser; long corkscrew ringlets waved on either side of their sunburnt cheeks, and their heads were surmounted by a polished gold-lettered black round hat, to denote to what ship they belonged.

At this moment the ferryman and his female companion all of a sudden rose from the middle seat, and moved to take post at opposite ends of the boat; but from their staggering motions it was evident that they were labouring under the stupefying effects of those potent liquors, which the commonalty too often swill to excess. The groggy pair having thus scrambled to either end of the boat, and apparently being excited to a more dignified mode than the ordinary style of "mutton-cove" caresses, they at once made an attempt to fly towards each other with extended arms, intending, no doubt, to lock together in hugging embrace; but, unluckily, the woman forgot the seat in the middle of the boat, and the lubberly sculler at the same time lost his equilibrium, and fell back in the bottom of the boat, in the most ludicrous posture, and looking mighty wise; the woman's knees coming in contact with the seat, she at once threw a half Somerset over the starboard side of the boat into the water, and for a few moments sunk from view.

Missing his wench, the sculler, after more than one fruitless attempt, at length righted, and regained his legs, but he was quite bewildered on seeing at the same time four objects floating round the boat; they consisted of his hat, which had fallen overboard, the woman's bonnet, and one of the oars that had slipped out of the boat pegs, and, moreover, of a large globular bundle, around were coiled sundry nameless garments, of coarse texture, compassing that part of the female proportions which the goddess of beauty and the graces are represented as exposing to view for the benefit of the chisel, the pencil, and the optics of the curious literati.

The latter was, in truth, the rotundity of the female, which was buoyant, for by an unaccountable entanglement of habiliments, her head and heels were under the surface of the water. The muzzy sculler rubbed his eyes, and amongst so many floating objects could not at first make up his mind which of the four he ought first to pick up, and, in point of fact, which was the real object of his search. His capacity, however, had not altogether left him, for he mechanically grasped hold of an oar, no doubt with the laudable intention of affording succour to his unfortunate partner. He pushed out his oar to one object, and then to the other, and at last imagining that the buoyant bundle was the head instead of the tail of his last partner, he began to poke away at the globular protuberance of the woman, still the only part of her person which was above water-mark. But the moment he touched the bundle with his rod, down it bobbed like a floating ball, he calling out lustily, with husky voice, "take hold! why don't you take hold!"

So quickly had the woman tumbled overboard, and after the first splash was over, assumed a quiet position, presenting the floating bundle as already described, that the Jack-tars on the beach were not aware of what had occurred, until my voice and that of the drunken boatman made known to them the mishap. But the instant they were made aware of the misfortune of a sinking frigate with its hull only above water, they bounded and scrambled into their boat, and with lightning strokes pulled towards the woman. The boat flew through the water with such velocity, that in a minute or two they had reached the place; and half a dozen brawny arms were stretched forth with nervous grasp, the garments of the woman were laid hold of, and she was at once lifted out of the water, and replaced in her own boat.

So short a space of time had elapsed before the poor woman was rescued from a watery grave, that, after cascading up some salt water, grog, and other contents of her stomach, she speedily recovered from the effects of her submersion, and in a few minutes, though dripping at all parts, was charming well again, and restored to the loving hug of her partner, with whom she was again seated in the boat, closely embraced, apparently as happy as before she met with her capsize.

The description of the above immersion may seem to savour somewhat of levity, or a want of compassion, a proper feeling towards the softer sex, and, undoubtedly, it would be liable to such a charge, had the woman's ablution lasted much longer. But the combination of ludicrous circumstances, and Cupid's torch being so quickly extinguished and all his flames put out, without any serious injury being inflicted, will, I trust, suffice for my exculpation.

Taking up our quarters in the long room, technically called the Lancashire hut barracks, from the militia of that county having so long occupied them, I now obtained a short respite; and, soon after, the rapid wheels of the usual conveyance whirled me to the banks of the Thames, in the fair county of Middlesex.

The crowned heads from the north of Europe and other illustrious princes and generals had departed, leaving in their wake the wreck of the great *fêtes* in honour of their visit to this country. The most strange and unaccountable stories were afloat of the jeopardy Prince Blucher had more than once been placed in by our fair countrywomen of inverted refinement; from which it would appear that the kissing and making it up again in honour of Napoleon's captivity, lacked not on either side of the channel, and that the *vieux* moustaches were in no way formidable to those bright eyes which were then unaccustomed to such grisly sights. Indeed, it would appear as if the ladies in general had been taking advantage of circumstances and giving loose to Greenwich hill gambols, and that the sex, whether of France or England, liked best the boys who were rocked in a foreign cradle, so that the very Cossack himself, while leering at the contents of the street lamps, was lifted into astonishment at his own importance.

I saw the last of the grand illuminations. It was strange enough, that, having arrived in London only the night before, and going to see the sham attack made on the American fleet got up in miniature for the occasion, on the Serpentine river in Hyde Park, I buttoned an olive *pelisse* coat over the very uniform which I afterwards wore at New Orleans.

This sham fighting did not savour of good taste, because at that time peace was anxiously looked for in that quarter of the globe; and many of these scenes, acted during the delirium of the moment, fell to a great discount when the senses of Englishmen recovered their equilibrium, and they found that they did not possess Aladdin's lamp.

In addition to which it may be remarked, that a sham fight is as unlike a real one as the two most opposite things in nature. In this instance the show was exceedingly *mal-à-propos*, and anything but prophetic; for, although the wild *bonnet rouge* had been laid low, yet the broad brim retained its steadiness. These last remarks may uncork the bottle of Eau de Cologne to those who travel with fixed principles, and only deign to cast a glance at certain pictures.

A dash of the pen now whirls me four times to and from Plymouth to the metropolis. I am about to nestle upon two months leave of absence, when a large letter (official) comes to hand to prepare for embarkation. I am again at Plymouth, and once more about to proceed to a foreign land.

LEONAUR

ALSO FROM LEONAUR

AVAILABLE IN SOFTCOVER OR HARDCOVER WITH DUST JACKET

SEPOYS, SIEGE & STORM *by Charles John Griffiths*—The Experiences of a young officer of H.M.'s 61st Regiment at Ferozepore, Delhi ridge and at the fall of Delhi during the Indian mutiny 1857.

CAMPAIGNING IN ZULULAND *by W. E. Montague*—Experiences on campaign during the Zulu war of 1879 with the 94th Regiment.

THE STORY OF THE GUIDES *by G. J. Younghusband*—The Exploits of the Soldiers of the famous Indian Army Regiment from the northwest frontier 1847 - 1900..

ZULU: 1879 *by D.C.F. Moodie & the Leonaur Editors*—The Anglo-Zulu War of 1879 from contemporary sources: First Hand Accounts, Interviews, Dispatches, Official Documents & Newspaper Reports.

THE RECOLLECTIONS OF SKINNER OF SKINNER'S HORSE *by James Skinner*—James Skinner and his 'Yellow Boys' Irregular cavalry in the wars of India between the British, Mahratta, Rajput, Mogul, Sikh & Pindarree Forces.

TOMMY ATKINS' WAR STORIES 14 FIRST HAND ACCOUNTS—Fourteen first hand accounts from the ranks of the British Army during Queen Victoria's Empire Original & True Battle Stories Recollections of the Indian Mutiny With the 49th in the Crimea With the Guards in Egypt The Charge of the Six Hundred With Wolseley in Ashanti Alma, Inkermann and Magdala With the Gunners at Tel-el-Kebir Russian Guns and Indian Rebels Rough Work in the Crimea In the Maori Rising Facing the Zulus From Sebastopol to Lucknow Sent to Save Gordon On the March to Chitral Tommy by Rudyard Kipling

CHASSEUR OF 1914 *by Marcel Dupont*—Experiences of the twilight of the French Light Cavalry by a young officer during the early battles of the great war in Europe.

TROOP HORSE & TRENCH *by R. A. Lloyd*—The experiences of a British Lifeguardsman of the household cavalry fighting on the western front during the First World War 1914-18.

THE EAST AFRICAN MOUNTED RIFLES *by C. J. Wilson*—Experiences of the campaign in the East African bush during the First World War.

THE FIGHTING CAMELIERS *by Frank Reid*—The exploits of the Imperial Camel Corps in the desert and Palestine campaigns of the First World War.

9 781846 773228